TOWARD A HUMANIST POLITICAL ECONOMY

TOWARD A HUMANIST POLITICAL ECONOMY

*Harold Chorney
and Phillip Hansen*

Montréal/New York

Copyright © 1992. BLACK ROSE BOOKS LTD.

No part of this book may be reproduced or transmitted in any form, by any means — electronic or mechanical, including photocopying and recording, or by any information storage or retrieval system— without written permission from the publisher or, in the case of photocopying or other reprographic copying, a licence from the Canadian Reprography Collective, except for brief passages quoted by a reviewer in a newspaper or magazine.

BLACK ROSE BOOKS No. V176
Hardcover ISBN: 1-895431-23-9
Paperback ISBN: 1-895431-22-0
Library of Congress Catalog No. 92-70623

Canadian Cataloguing in Publication Data

Chorney, Harold, 1946-
Toward a humanist political economy

ISBN: 1-895431-23-9 (bound) — ISBN: 1-895431-22-0 (pbk.)

1. Liberalism. 2. Socialism. 3. Social change. I. Hansen, Phillip Birger, 1949- II. Title.

JA71.C48 1992   320.5'13   C92-090135-2

Cover Illustration: *The Lady of Côte-Ste-Catherine,* by Harold Chorney

Mailing Address

BLACK ROSE BOOKS
C.P. 1258
Succ. Place du Parc
Montréal, Québec
H2W 2R3 Canada

BLACK ROSE BOOKS
340 Nagel Drive
Cheektowaga, New York
14225 USA

A publication of the Institute of Policy Alternatives of Montréal (IPAM)

Printed in Canada

TABLE OF CONTENTS

Preface and Acknowledgements	1
Introduction *Harold Chorney and Phillip Hansen*	3

PART ONE   Political Culture and Political Economy

Chapter 1	Amnesia, Integration and Repression: The Roots of Canadian Urban Political Culture *Harold Chorney*	10
Chapter 2	Neo-Conservatism, Social Democracy and Province Building: The Experience of Manitoba *Harold Chorney and Phillip Hansen*	40
Chapter 3	The Falling Rate of Legitimation *Harold Chorney and Phillip Hansen*	72

PART TWO   Economics and Political Economy

Chapter 4	The Power of Reason and the Legacy of Keynes *Harold Chorney*	102
Chapter 5	The Deficit: Hysteria and the Current Crisis *Harold Chorney*	112

PART THREE   Public Life and Political Economy

Chapter 6	Hannah Arendt: Speech and the Public Space of Appearance *Phillip Hansen*	136
Chapter 7	Orwell and Arendt on Total Control and Ontology *Phillip Hansen*	161
Chapter 8	Ideology and Beyond: Adorno Lynd and Some Implications for Critical Education *Phillip Hansen*	185
Chapter 9	Beyond All Reason: Max Weber, Walter Benjamin and Modernity *Harold Chorney*	200

Preface and Acknowledgements

These essays were written over the past decade For the most part we have chosen to publish them here in their original form. In all cases we have tried to correct errors and stylistic problems. In some cases we have added new material where we thought it was important to do so. Where this occurs the new material is indicated by brackets.

A number of these essays were published in *The Canadian Review of Sociology and Anthropology, The Canadian Journal of Political and Social Theory, Studies in Political Economy, Urbanization and Urban Planning in Capitalist Society*, A. Scott and M. Dear, eds., and in monograph form by the Canadian Centre for Policy Alternatives. We thank the editors for permission to republish.

We would like to acknowledge the help and support of many friends and colleagues who over the years have encouraged us in our work.

Specifically we would like to single out Alvin Finkel, Stephen Block, Andrew Molloy, Alkis Kontos, the late C.B. Macpherson, Ken Reshaur, Joe Roberts, Meyer Brownstone, Mel Watkins and Ron Manzer. In preparing this book for publication Ana Gomez, Carol Acoose and Nat Klym have been indispensable. Joel Segal has been very helpful in offering design advice about the cover. Finally, we would also like to acknowledge the support of our respective universities, Concordia University and the University of Regina and in the case of some of the essays, the S.S.H.R.C.

* * *

Dedication in friendship and love: For Susannah and Sam, H.C.
and for Alicja, P.H.
and to the memory of
Miriam Tessler Chorney and Sheva Cohen Zipursky, H.C

Introduction

by Harold Chorney and Phillip Hansen

These essays were written both jointly and individually over a period of close to two decades. They represent an attempt to confront the problems of modern society and the inability of the traditional explanations offered by the left to account for the predicaments of modernity. Much left wing analysis from a democratic socialist and social democratic perspective has been seriously undermined by historical events and recent developments. In these essays we have attempted to indicate the barriers that have blocked the road to social progress in twentieth century society. Some of the essays suffer from a youthful utopianism that, although understandable given our age and the era in which these pieces were written, we have now abandoned. But the hope for a better society which was at the heart of the earlier essays remains central to all of them.

At the beginning of this century, Marxist, anarchist, syndicalist and socialist philosophies had a real following among both intellectuals and working people. These radical currents faithfully reflected widespread popular aspirations for a more decent and democratic society. There was a sense of optimism that the world could be reformed in fundamental ways. The enlightenment belief in progress was still a powerful force in the culture of everyday life.

The twentieth century has not been kind to these hopes and aspirations. Modernity remains an unfinished project — a project which perhaps is condemned by its very nature to be unrealizable. In particular, the end of the century has brought with it a major shift away from traditional radical approaches to the problems of industrial society. Pessimism rather than optimism, post-modernism rather than modernism, fear rather than hope, irony rather than certainty now dominate the cultural landscape. While ecologist, feminist and communitarian approaches command a certain following among activists and some intellectuals, the rapid growth of right wing movements, tendencies and ideologies has largely filled the gap brought about by the collapse of traditional socialism and the retreat from liberalism.

This growth of the right wing has been all the more powerful because the right has succeeded in appropriating much of the language, and even the moral fervour, that was once associated with the left. By contrast, the left itself, or what remains of it, has ironically become much more fearful of the present and the future. Too many people on the left have been willing to accept as gospel neo-conservative nostrums masquerading as sensible public policy. They have also far too willingly accepted conservative assumptions about the limits of democracy, the constraints of the private market and the futility of social change.

Of course traditional left analysis has not been without blame for this predicament. Many who identified with the left for too long embraced a conception of social change and radical reform that denied the very impulses they supposedly championed. There was a largely uncritical acceptance of the eschatological character of the Marxian model and the resulting glorification of the historic task of the working class. While this model had great appeal for intellectuals, it failed adequately to reflect the real world of working people and the nature of actual existing societies. As well, as social theory is inevitably wont to do, its artistic character as radical aesthetic made it unlikely to have practical relevance.

To be sure, many people on the left in Western democracies always rejected the Stalinist perversions of the socialist ideal that were paraded as actually existing socialism. But the obsession with actually existing Stalinist States and orthodox Marxist theory hampered the quest for a humanistic, democratic and realistic response to the very real injustices and problems of capitalist society and the prospects for fundamental social reform. Coupled with the ideological deep freeze of the cold war, these tendencies immobilized the forces for popular progressive change and strengthened the stranglehold of the right on culture, politics and economics.

Of course, Stalinism was by no means the only perspective evident on the organized or intellectual left. Other critical perspectives included the critical theory of the Frankfurt school, the iconoclastic writings of various interpreters on the margins of intellectual and political life such as Thorstein Veblen, Walter Benjamin, George Orwell, Hannah Arendt, C.W. Mills, George Steiner and Michael Harrington, and even the work of some thought to be more closely attached to the establishment, such as John Maynard Keynes and J.K. Galbraith.As well there was a long tradition of libertarian thought. More recently feminist and ecologist writing has had enormous influence. The long and rich traditions of political liberalism and populism that had provided powerful alternative perspectives on modern industrial society were also important currents. But the chilling impact of the cold war has prevented these from developing and flourishing as completely successful theoretical approaches and mass political movements. In the case of certain analysts the pressure of the cold war even turned their original critical perspective into a defensive posture that first swore allegiance to the defense of militarized democracy and then directed its attention to social and political reform. Of course, this meant that the real benefits of their humanistic tradition were largely lost.

Our own intellectual development has been shaped by these forces. Our writings reflect a long struggle to escape the confines of dominant ideas and ideologies, including that of youthful romanticism and to stake out what we hope is a more satisfactory account of the prospects for progressive change. While we haven't always agreed about the specifics of practical politics and the relevance of specific social theories we have agreed about the broad objectives involved.

For us, the challenge has been to work out a new method for analysing modern society that remains in touch with the great humanist strivings of the past, and that at the same time avoids the narcissistic and inward tradition of Nietzsche that is today associated with certain more extreme tendencies in post modernism. In this context, we have attempted to avoid two equally unpalatable alternatives. On the one hand, we have tried to shed the excesses and illusions of traditional eschatological analysis. On the other hand, we have sought to resist succumbing to the false imperatives of the neo-conservative age.

Our attempt to steer this course has involved three broad areas of concern: culture and its impact on political consciousness; the nature of economic life which includes not only public policy models and debates like Keynesianism versus monetarism or sound finance versus deficit spending but also social, cultural and philosophical issues; and public life, that is, a politics not restricted to formal institutions and practices alone, but one which also involves those values, needs and purposes which sustain solidarity and community.

CULTURE

It was of course the critical theorists of the Frankfurt School who made culture the central focus of a critical analysis of advanced industrial society. Max Horkheimer, T.W. Adorno, Walter Benjamin and Herbert Marcuse, among others, were generally faithful to a Marxist economic analysis and committed to some form of socialism. Their Marxist economics was and is of little use. However, unlike more orthodox Marxists they never accepted that economics determined everything. They made clear that ideas and cultural values were not merely reflexes of "objective" economic processes. Mass culture was vital in forming the conceptions that people had of themselves as social and political actors. Films, music, art and the everyday life of the metropolitan urban dweller shaped the consciousness of individuals. As well, the critical theorists drew upon Freud to develop a psychological theory of mass behaviour. Among other things, their approach made clear that religious, ethnic and nationalist notions played a powerful role in the process of individual and group development, frequently in ways unrelated to and even at odds with people's economic class location.

In sum the members of the Frankfurt School repudiated the simplistic and anti-hedonistic psychology of mainstream Marxism. They argued that people were creatures of pleasure and desire, fantasy and imagination, whose longings played a vital role in everything from patterns of authority in the family and society, to the character of sexuality and the understandings they developed of themselves as embodied individuals.

Critical theorists were concerned to show how culture had during the course of capitalist development become commodified, a source of private profit and cultural conditioning, and thus had been transformed into an affirmation of the existing society rather than a critical challenge to it. But the members of the Frankfurt School had another motive for their efforts. They sought to demonstrate that culture was the connecting link between individual consciousness and social structure, past and present, thought and action, subject and object. They were concerned to show how Marxism in particular could not account for how ideas might become living forces in people's lives, how people acquired and experienced motives for their actions in the world. In short they attempted to discover the actual basis of human behaviour in modern society. Their work taught us how to understand better the twentieth century and the great and tragic failures of those who had sought to reform it in fundamental ways.

In many of the essays included in this book the influence of the Frankfurt school is clear. This is particularly so in our essays in parts one and three. Some of these pieces attempt to deepen our understanding of the cultural roots of modern society, and role of culture in contemporary political and social life.

ECONOMIC LIFE

In the realm of economic policy and political economy, part two, our guide has been the work of John Maynard Keynes. Keynes, unlike Marx, was a twentieth century student of capitalism. It has become altogether too fashionable to dismiss Keynes as passe or appropriate only to a national capitalism that did not involve the kind of globalized economy we face today. In fact, there is much in his methodology and analysis that speaks powerfully to the current predicament of the world economy. In the essay on Keynes and the essay on the deficit the influence of his approach is apparent. The essay on the deficit, which was written by Chorney in 1984 and was the first of a series of essays he has written on this subject, exposes the ideological and illogical basis of conventional wisdom on this issue. Both neo-conservatives and neo-Marxists have shared a common distrust of public sector deficits. In the case of the neo-conservatives it has been for obvious ideological reasons. As for the neo-Marxists, in their zeal to predict the collapse of capitalism, they have forgotten how to reform it, and by default have embraced a monetarist version of how it works. In short they have accepted the supposed inner logic of the system and by so doing have excluded viable options for managing it in the interests of everyone as opposed to a dominant elite.

It is because of this that we discuss not just the economy but more broadly, economic life and specifically the role of both reason and morality in social and political and economic thought. In this sense these essays share a perspective with Keynes that is premodern - a concern that what is immoral must be irrational and mediocre in logic. What Keynes found objectionable in neo-classical economic theory was precisely this fact. Any theory which justified such an immoral policy outcome as unemployment must be false in logic. His entire work set out to demonstrate this. We have followed a similar line of thought in our work.

PUBLIC LIFE

In much of the contemporary writing on the State and politics far too little attention has been paid to what we regard as the more central issues: those of solidarity, citizenship and public life. These concerns involves a realm of understandings, norms and practices through which people come to see themselves as sharing a way of life. The collapse of community in modern society has posed serious difficulties for the healthy functioning of public life and politics. It is for this reason that the problem of community has been of concern to theorists of both conservative and radical persuasion. The most damaging consequence of neo-conservatism has been precisely its disavowal of both social solidarity and community. Communing with one's bank account is no substitute for the web of human affiliations that constitute us as responsible and caring human beings. The past decade has seen the social landscape littered with the wreckage from policies that place no priority on the objectives of solidarity and community. The victims of these policies haunt our city streets. Their anguished faces and exhausted stares force us to confront the immorality of our current public policies.

Unfortunately, the dominant currents of left or radical thought and social reform broadly understood have focused on the structures of the State. This emphasis has missed the moral and ethical significance of politics as community. Since human beings are moral beings, this focus on the State has been unable to account for changes in society, nor has it been successful in appealing to people's deepest urges for a moral society that stresses the social bonds among people. This failure on the part of the left has permitted the neo-conservative right to penetrate the consciousness of people, albeit perversely, because the right has been able to speak to concerns that the left has addressed inadequately.

This failure is not only a moral failure but also a strategic error. For above all the left requires that people come to take politics as more personal and morally compelling if there is to be any hope for fundamental change or reform.

In light of the fact that dominant left ideas have been both unconcerned with community in the sense in which we mean it, and also overly scholastic in nature, we have been drawn to thinkers and writers who were for a long time ignored by the academic left.

The key figure for Hansen in his essays in Part Three which deal with the problems of public life is Hannah Arendt. Arendt has a unique and powerful conception of citizenship and politics that is of immense value for those seeking a more vibrant public life. That she has been badly misinterpreted by both right and left is itself a measure of how indifferent dominant ideologies have been to questions of citizenship and community.

The final essay by Chorney on Max Weber, Walter Benjamin and modernity seeks to answer the question: What is the relationship between social theory and the world of practical politics? The answer offered is that social theory, if it is to be aesthetically successful, must lean to the utopian, while practical politics, by necessity, draws upon pragmatic reason.

The crisis of socialism in Western society is in large measure an intellectual crisis. This in part reflects the original influence of both Marxist and social democratic economism. This is not to say that economic reform ought not to be the centrepiece of a strategy for social change. But the success of such a strategy will depend upon the degree to which cultural questions are integrated into the analysis and public life, participation and citizenship are made as central as economic concerns.

We hope that these essays, despite their youthful lapses, point the way to a reconsideration of political economy as a humanist enterprise that could contribute to fundamental social reform.

PART ONE

Political Culture and Political Economy

1

AMNESIA, INTEGRATION AND REPRESSION: THE ROOTS OF CANADIAN URBAN POLITICAL CULTURE [1]

Harold Chorney

This essay was written in Toronto in 1980. It attempted to incorporate certain features of Canadian labour history with a social and theoretical treatment of the historic fate of working class socialism in Canada in its major urban centres in the early twentieth century. Many of the defeats of that epoch cemented in place the political economic system as we have come to know it over the last 80 years. But because of the pressure of working class socialism and the demands for social justice that the movement raised, considerable reforms were gradually implemented. So the failures eventually bore useful fruit.

The essay is also an exploration of the problem of the survival of community in a world which is hostile to these values. It thus contains themes that are later treated in my book *City of Dreams: Social Theory and the Urban Experience*. All of the Marxist inclined language and analysis now strikes me as romantically utopian. It no longer represents how I think. But given the kind of rapacious capitalism that prevailed in that epoch it is perhaps less inappropriate in describing those times than it is today. Although capitalism continues to display rapacious tendencies in this neo-conservative epoch I would not write the essay in this way today. But its basic thrust still has an explanatory appeal because of its emphasis upon the collective historical memory, the role of repression and the presence of amnesia in North American urban society.

* * *

INTRODUCTION

Canada's existence as a nation is highly artificial. Because of its immense size, but geographically concentrated population, it better resembles a chain of city-States than one nation State.[2] Each link dominates its own vast hinterland and is focus for both political culture and daily life. But though they are extended linearly across the country, these major cities are themselves organized within a hierarchy of dominance. Consequently, the rivalry among these city-states is considerable and contributes to intense regionalism.

The relative underdevelopment of class politics and class consciousness which characterizes Canadian society cannot be separated from the nature of her urban and regional structure. Despite all the prognoses that a modern industrialized, urbanized working class would result in class consciousness and class conflict, Canada and her urban culture continues to be largely devoid of class-consciousness politics. What urban politics do exist have hardly moved beyond interest-group politics — sometimes militant interest-group politics to be sure, but interest-group politics, nonetheless. This has been far more apparent in English Canada than in Québec, where in recent years an emergent nationalist movement contains within it significant fragments of class-conscious politics.[3]

The nature of politics in Canada, then, is genuinely contradictory. Fractionalism is a direct outgrowth of the frictions between the French and English language groups, the influence of an ethnically diverse and substantial immigrant population, and the intense rivalries among the distinct regions. But the successful repression of class politics by the dominant class has integrated all political expression into established and controllable forms. This combination of fragmentation and integration has promoted widespread passivity.

Despite the current crisis of accumulation in Canada, a crisis of legitimation and cultural reproduction has yet to appear. In fact, the current economic crisis has been accompanied by a significant swing to the right in Canadian politics and the entrenchment of a "welfare backlash" among substantial portions of the Canadian working class.[4]

In order to understand how class consciousness and the urban political culture have been moulded in Canada, and the roots of the current situation, it is necessary to delve at some length into the early history of urban settlement and economic development. I should stress that most of what I discuss is not original, but is drawn from the considerable scholarship that has been accomplished on Canadian economic, labour and urban history. But, unless one understands the historic basis of regionalism, ethnic division, economic dependence, repression and integration, it is impossible to understand the underdeveloped nature of Canadian urban political culture.

I shall begin the survey with a short recapitulation of the history of the Canadian political economy. This is essential if we are to situate Canadian urban culture within the process of capital accumulation in a metropolitan-hinterland economy. The process of capital accumulation in Canada has imposed an inescapable commercial nexus of relationships upon the culture of Canadian cities. In many respects the cultural parameters of daily life in urban Canada revolve solely around earning a living. Work, achievement and material success define the limits of daily life. In this sense, urbanism in Canada carries with it little of the precapitalist urban tradition that Canadians recognize in European cities. The longing for a "European holiday" reflects the deep seated yearning for a daily life which transcends the narrow instrumentality of Canadian cities.

I then turn to an examination of the role of immigration. This has played a very special role in the formation and deformation of urban class consciousness in Canada. I explore this problem at some length because I feel that it holds the key to unlocking part of the mystery of the state of urban class consciousness in Canada.

I then examine in some detail the process of the establishment of a routinized system of labour relations and the repression of radical labourism, because I believe that this process of State intervention is crucial to understanding the process of integration. Indeed, one is tempted to argue that the integration of the working class through collective bargaining resembled, in certain respects, the process of urbanization itself.

Urbanization can be regarded as the transcendence of the communal intimacy of the Gemeinschaft of precapitalist society. The transcendence implies the weakening of the common conscience and the capacity for collective behaviour, the substitution of instrumental reason and calculation for the emotional and natural will, and the overwhelming of the cultural traditions central to the formation of class consciousness by the philosophy of money.[5] Communal and collective institutions give way to impersonal intermediary ones.

This reduction of interpersonal relationships to instrumental means within the emerging metropolis, and the mediation of the money economy and all that it entails between workers of the same class, is the paradoxical outcome of the collection and concentration of workers in space according to the principles of capital accumulation.[6]

In a similar fashion, trade-union integration has also involved the mediation of the State and the union, and the reduction of class conflict between workers and capitalists to routinized instrumental wage bargaining. The notion of interest has come to replace that of the need of a universal class for a revolutionary transformation of society. Working-class interest, however, is no substitute for working-class consciousness.[7]

Finally I explore in considerable detail, as a kind of case study, the Winnipeg General Strike. I do so, not only because of my interest in Canadian labour history and my roots in Winnipeg, but also because I believe that the strike and its aftermath illustrates my argument.

My goal in this essay is to explore the problem of urban class consciousness which is central to any analysis of the urban question and the role of radical politics. Urbanism in its modern metropolitan manifestations can be seen to be the spatial-cultural expression of modern capitalist society. As the locus for capital accumulation and the social reproduction of labour, it had usually been regarded by Marxists and other reformers as the arena in which class consciousness and political activism would develop.[8] Yet, as we shall argue, despite this mysterious faith about the city and social life, urbanization in the metropolitan sense has had a much different impact. It has historically and dialectically facilitated both the accumulation of capital and the cultural reproduction of capitalism. At the same time, it has changed the very nature of capitalism itself. (Space and time, the two most powerful impulses of modern capitalism are produced in a very special way by the metropolis.)

My argument, the rudiments of which I can only sketch in this essay, is that urbanization as a mode of social control, as well as an engine of capital accumulation, has thus far successfully facilitated the synthesis of amnesia, integration and repression as a powerful bulwark against the development of class consciousness and community based politics.

THE ORIGINS OF CANADA'S URBAN SYSTEM

The principal urban centres in Canada were developed as part of a pattern of trade and settlement directed by economic forces centred in England and France, when the foundations of mercantile capitalism were being laid.[9] The earliest Canadian cities were founded either as fishing settlements, fur trading posts, military outposts or entrepot centres designed to facilitate the trade in staple goods from the colony to the motherland.

From the very beginning of the European invasion, the rationale for urban settlement had been imposed from the outside by a dominant external culture for purely commercial reasons. This pattern of settlement clearly has similarities to the historical origins of European cities. But, whereas most European cities were founded either during the classical period of the Roman empire or during the precapitalist medieval period, even the oldest of Canadian cities were founded at the birth of capitalism. This fact has certain important implications which cannot be ignored if we wish to understand the nature of urban culture in Canada. It has meant, in particular, that urban social relations have occurred in an environment wholly shaped by capitalist requirements.

By the middle of the nineteenth century a string of cities and towns had been established. As we can see from Table 1, the population of these towns and cities was small in comparison with comparable American cities.

By the 1850s, the Canadian urban economy had begun to break the shackles of unequal colonial trade with the mother country. The economy passed through a brief period of "active capitalist involution."[10] The benefits of this growing domestic economy were allocated upon strict class lines. The local merchants and manufacturers were the principal beneficiaries. The tradesmen and unskilled labourers were the principal victims. For many impoverished tradesmen and most labourers, urban life was highly transient and harsh.[11]

Class tended to be structured along ethnic as well as socio-economic lines. In Upper Canada, for example, the Irish Catholics were largely con-

Table 1
Population of selected Canadian and American cities,
1850 and 1851 (a)

Canada, 1850		USA, 1850	
Atlantic region			
St. John's	25,000	New York	523,000
Charlottetown(b)	5,000	Philadelphia	409,000
Halifax	21,000	Baltimore	168,000
Saint John	23,000	Boston	137,000
Fredricton	4,500	Cincinnati	117,000
Lower Canada			
Quebec	42,000		
Montreal	58,000		
Trois Rivieres	5,000		
Upper Canada			
Toronto	31,000		
Hamilton	14,000		
Kingston	11,000		
London	7,000		
Ottawa	7,000		

Source: *Canada: Census* 1851, Vol. 2, pp. xvii-xix. *USA: Census* 1850, Vol.1 G. Stelter and A. Artibise (1977). *Cities in the Wilderness*, in G. Stelter and A. Artibise *The Canadian City*. Toronto: McClelland and Stewart.
a. The population of Atlantic Canada in 1851 was about 640,000, Lower Canada 890,000 and Upper Canada 952,000. The population of the United States was 23,000,000. The six largest American cities constituted 6.3% of the population. The six largest Canadian cities constituted 7.7% of the population. All numbers are rounded off.
b. 1848

centrated in lower paying occupations. Indeed, H.C. Pentland has argued that the Irish Catholics were an essential ingredient in the development of a capitalist labour market in Canada.[12] Labour unrest, in particular, among labourers involved in the construction of canals and railways was quite common. Strike leaders were usually subject to arrest and employers relied upon the use of troops to break strikes. As Pentland puts it so well, "labour relations meant troops and mounted police to overawe the labourers, government spies to learn the intentions and priests to teach them meekness." Civic officials in Montréal, Hamilton and London, most of whom were either merchants of manufacturers, availed themselves of troops to quell labour unrest on a number of occasions during this period.[13]

By the turn of the century, Canada's urban structure was firmly established. Born out of colonial development and the unequal exchange of imperial trade in staple commodities, its twentieth-century form was to be clearly rooted in commercial notions of capital accumulation. In the nineteenth century it had largely been a creature of British imperial domination. In the twentieth century it was rapidly to become an object of American imperial control.

This pattern of American penetration and control of the Canadian economy was rooted into place during the first decades following Confederation in 1867. The initial wheat and land settlement boom in the West came to an end just prior to the start of the first World War. Canada was left with a retarded domestically-controlled industrial base; a vastly overbuilt and scandalously over-subsidized railway network; a heavy financial indebtedness to British finance; a highly concentrated financial sector; and an increasingly American-controlled manufacturing sector concentrated in Southern Ontario and Montréal.[14] The basis of regional underdevelopment and metropolitan-hinterland dominance, which was to be reinforced by the process of American multinational corporation intervention into Canada, had been laid.[15]

Thus, the chronic problems of high unemployment and unstable economic development which today plague Canada more than any other leading capitalist country of comparable economic maturity, can be traced back to this period. While the marginalization of the Canadian economy has played a role in radicalizing certain strata of the working class in hinterland regions, it has also played a conservatizing role. The fragile nature of economic prosperity in Canada, seen in the light of the promise of the American "high intensity" consumption society, has made many Canadian workers highly security conscious and reluctant to experiment with radical politics at the risk of their economic livelihood. In many ways, Canada is an excellent illustration of the argument made by Michael Kalecki about the political economy of full employment policy.[16] Persistingly high unemployment in the midst of a mass-consumption, achievement-principle society, has thus far been largely successful in keeping Canadians strongly attached to job security and political caution. The nature of Canadian urban political culture, thus, cannot be separated from the chronic underdevelopment of the Canadian economy.

THE IMPACT OF IMMIGRATION

The absorption and settlement of western Canada, a region over ten times the size of France, had been central to the economic strategy that Canadian capitalists had adopted in their push for Confederation. The West had become a captive hinterland of central Canada, whose merchants and manufacturers would carry on an unequal exchange in staple commodities with the waves of settlers which they would attract to the region. The trade was to be a mirror image of the motherland-colony relationship which had governed the settlement and development of central Canada itself. Only this time the imperial capital was to be Montréal or Toronto and not London or Paris.

The key to this strategy was a massive influx of immigrants, brought not only from Britain and northern Europe, but from the "foreign" countries of central, southern and eastern Europe as well. Although this strategy had been adopted in 1867, it was not fully realized until the first decades of the twentieth century, when frontier opportunities in Canada had been thoroughly demonstrated. The world price of wheat had risen sufficiently and a boom in British capital accumulation had made possible the massive inflow of capital that was required.[17] The peak of immigration to Canada thus occurred in the years 1909 to 1914. In order to understand the impact of this wave of immigration upon the cultural life of Canadian cities, we must consider this immigration process in some detail.

Up until the last decade of the nineteenth century, the proportion of the population which was born outside of Canada, France or the British Isles was quite small. The 1851 Census of Upper and Lower Canada listed less than 1 percent of the total population of the two Canadas as "foreigners." By 1881 the "foreign" born population was 2.9 percent, 1891 3.2 percent, 1901 5.0 percent and by 1911 10.4 percent.[18]

The enormous impact which immigration had upon Canada at the turn of the century and the two decades following is made clear by Table 2.

The population of Canada in 1901 was 5.4 million people. By 1921 it was 8.8 million people.[19] Since a large proportion of those immigrants who arrived from the United States were also of non-British and non-American origin, the non-Anglo-Saxon influx into Canada during this period was substantial. The impact of this wave of "foreign" immigration was heightened by the fact that many of the new immigrants settled in the rapidly growing cities and towns of Western Canada. Tables 3 and 4 illustrate this point very well.

During the first decade of the twentieth century, Canada ranked ahead of all other Western countries in terms of population increase.[20] The most significant factor in this increase was the massive wave of immigration. It

Table 2
Origin and number of immigrant arrivals in Canada

1897-1920, in thousands
Origin

Period	UK	US	Other	Total
1867-1902	67	76	95	238
1903-1908	420	289	271	981
1909-1914	541	569	476	1,586
1915-1920	133	320	70	523
Total	1,161	1,254	913	3,328

Source: *Canada Statistical Yearbook* 1921, p. 126. Calculated from Table 20.

Table 3
Birthplace by province, 1921, in percentage terms

Province	total population	Place of birth Canada,British Isles British possessions %	"Foreign" US %	Other(a) %
PEI	88,615	98.5	1.4	.1
Nova Scotia	523,837	97.4	1.3	1.3
New Brunswick	387,876	97.2	2.2	.6
Québec	2,361,199	95.8	1.8	2.4
Ontario	2,933,662	93.8	2.4	3.8
Manitoba	610,118	82.0	3.6	14.4
Saskatchewan	757,510	73.7	11.6	14.7
Alberta	588,454	70.4	17.0	12.6
British Columbia	524,582	81.0	6.6	12.4
Yukon & NWT	12,145	91.0	5.0	4.0
Canada	8,788,483	89.9	4.3	5.9(a)

Source: *Canada Census* 1921, Vol. 11, Table 52.
(a) As a result of rounding, the Canada figures total more than 100 %

Table 4
Birthplace of population by urban areas, 1921 in percentage terms

City	Population	Canada %	British Isles and possessions %	Foreign %
Saint John NB	47,166	89.9	6.4	3.8
Moncton NB	17,488	93.2	4.1	2.7
Halifax NS	58,372	84.5	12.1	3.4
Glace Bay NS	17,007	81.1	14.0	5.0
Sydney NS	22,545	75.5	16.5	8.0
Quebec Qué	95,193	97.0	1.3	1.7
Trois Riviere Qué	22,545	94.8	1.4	3.8
Montreal Qué	618,506	81.3	8.9	9.8
Ottawa Ont	107,843	83.2	11.4	5.4
Kingston Ont	21,753	79.7	16.2	4.1
London Ont	60,959	72.6	22.5	4.9
Kitchener Ont	21,753	80.9	6.8	12.3
Peterborough Ont	20,994	78.1	18.4	3.5
St. Catherine Ont	19,881	67.5	24.0	8.5
Sault Saint Marie	21,092	66.6	12.4	21.0
Toronto Ont	521,893	62.2	28.6	9.2
Fort William Ont	20,541	62.2	28.6	20.0
Winnipeg Man	179,087	52.4	28.3	19.3
Regina Sask	34,432	56.3	26.3	17.4
Saskatoon Sask	25,739	56.6	28.7	14.7
Edmonton Alta	58,821	55.5	27.4	17.1
Calgary Alta	63,305	52.2	33.2	14.6
Vancouver BC	117,217	48.9	33.0	18.1
Victoria BC	38,727	46.4	39.7	13.9

Source: *Canada Census* 1921, Vol. 11, p. 372, Table 59.

is interesting to note that immigrant arrivals were nearly double the increase in the foreign-born proportion of the population. In fact, during the period 1901 to 1911, almost 900,000 immigrants left the country after having spent a period of time in it as largely unskilled labourers. This, as well as the fact that single males or males unaccompanied by families were a substantial proportion of the immigrants, suggests that the wave of immigration was an important source for a migrant workforce. This workforce was not very different from the migrant "guest workers" that are an important phenomenon in contemporary Western European capitalist cities.[21]

As Table 3 indicates, the Western region attracted the bulk of the "foreign" immigrants. The four Western provinces in 1921 had a total of 338,000 "foreign born," as compared to 178,000 in the older eastern provinces. Alberta and Saskatchewan, and to a lesser extent British Columbia, also attracted a large number of Americans. These were mainly farmers attracted by the homesteading opportunities in the "last best West." But they also included miners, loggers, and industrial workers, many of whom brought with them radical syndicalist ideas, and who were to play an important role in the labour movement of the West.[22]

The influx of immigrants in this period had a permanent impact upon the ethnic composition of Canadian cities. In 1971, the most ethnically diverse cities in Canada were located in Western Canada.[23]

The ethnic diversity of Canadian immigration has played a complex role in the development of urban class politics. On the one hand, the immigrants constituted a large body of exploited workers. Many had had contact with socialist and radical politics in their country of origin. They were also socially ostracized and marginalized by the mainstream Anglo-Saxon ruling class. As such, they were a fertile source for class-conscious politics. On the other hand, the very diversity of the urban workforce, the multiplicity of languages and cultures, and the role of immigrants as a cheap source of surplus labour, worked in an opposite direction. The transient attachment of many of the workers to the new country, as well as the fear of some of them that they would be rejected and sent back, without the opportunity to have saved enough to make the ordeal worthwhile, also worked against the development of consciousness. The racism of some British workers, and the fairly general racism of the elite, often deflected attention away from class issues and retarded class-conscious politics.[24] The pressure for assimilation, depending upon the culture into which the immigrants assimilated, could reinforce either tendency. This dual nature of the role of immigration in Canadian urban politics persists to this day. There can be little doubt, however, that despite the general racism of the Canadian elite, there was recognition by them of the crucial role which an immigrant workforce was to play in the accumulation process in Canada.[25] On the whole, notwithstanding the distaste which the upper class expressed for the "foreign," and sometimes "repulsive" and "primitive" nature of the immigrants' culture and customs,[26] the dividends which immigration paid to Canadian capitalism were substantial indeed. Yet the process of exploitation was not without its periods of crisis. The flood of immigration generated not only booms in real estate, but outbursts of class consciousness and militancy as well.

LABOUR RADICALISM AND URBAN DEVELOPMENT

The conservative business-union practices which dominate the majority of contemporary labour unions in Canada, are the outcome of a process of repression and State-sponsored integration which originated in the first two decades of the twentieth century. While Canadian labour radicalism was by no means a strictly urban phenomenon, there is a critical link between the urbanization process and the rise and fall of labour radicalism in Canada.

The heartland of the Canadian radical labour movement at the turn of the century was located in the West. It was centred in the coal and metal mines of British Columbia, in the growing towns which had sprung up along the lines of the Canadian Pacific Railway, and in the immigrant ghettos and working class quarters of Winnipeg and Vancouver, and the other booming Prairie cities. It was here that radical labour, socialist, syndicalist, Marxist and anarcho-syndicalist ideas freely circulated among the miners, railway workers and newly created urban proletariat.

Business-union labourism was not absent. It had, however, to complete with radical ideas which were vigorously held by an increasing number of workers. In the older urban centres in Ontario and Québec, this kind of competition had occurred in the 1880s and the battle largely had been won by the turn of the century.[27]

In addition to the European immigrants who had contact with radical working-class and peasant movements before coming to Canada, many of the recent British working-class immigrants to Western Canada were also imbued with more militant conceptions of the workers' cause than their predecessors who had immigrated to Central Canada decades earlier.[28] Finally, the influence of radical syndicalist, anarchist and Marxist ideas which American workers brought with them as they migrated up and down the Pacific coast in search of work, were an important ingredient in Western radicalism.[29] In a very real sense, the West in Canada at the turn of the century was as much a frontier of ideas and political philosophies, as it was one of economic development and settlement.

Both of the radical industrial unions which played a critical role in Canadian industrial relations at the turn of the century were affiliated to the American Labour Union (ALU). The ALU was a socialist labour federation founded to organize industrial unions in direct opposition to the narrow craft-union business philosophy which dominated the American Federation of Labour headed by Samuel Gompers.[30] The Western Federation of Miners (WFM) and the United Brotherhood of Railway Employees

(U.B.R.E.) successfully organized and mobilized large numbers of workers in British Columbia and along the route of the Canadian Pacific Railway from 1900-3. These two organizations and the workers who belonged to them were responsible for most of the class-conscious rebellion against industrial capitalism which occurred in Canada during this period.

It is a point of some significance that a large proportion of the workers who belonged to these two unions were not urban workers. While many of them did work in the new and rapidly growing cities of Western Canada, the impetus of their radicalism and rebellion originated in the isolated mining towns and resource settlements of British Columbia. This fact is not surprising. For in such company towns, the naked power of capital, symbolized by a rapacious resource company, and the exploitative nature of the wage relationship, was crystal clear.[31] It was this very clarity and the contrast which it made with the opaque and increasingly complex social and class relations in urban settlements, that was important.

Urbanization as the spatial expression of modern capital accumulation and concentration has greatly increased the heterogeneity and fragmentation of social life. This phenomenon, although sometimes falsely attributed to ecological factors, was first identified by the sociologists Durkheim, Tonnies and Simmel.[32] To the extent that class consciousness is rooted in a homogeneity of experience in the workplace, and reinforced or attenuated by the daily experience of life outside of the workplace, urbanization has played an acute role in the process of the formation of class-consciousness. For, as Marx pointed out in his work *The Eighteenth Brumaire of Louis Bonaparte*, the absence of a sense of community prevented the French peasantry from developing a sense of class solidarity. They remained, as he put is, "homologous magnitudes, much as potatoes in a sack form a sack of potatoes."

Yet Marx clearly identified urbanization in its nineteenth century form as a force enhancing the possibilities for revolutionary class consciousness. In the *Communist Manifesto, The Civil War in France* and elsewhere, Marx celebrated the city as a revolutionary hothouse.[33]

However, perhaps in the twentieth-century form, the city, at least in North America, has changed and the link between urbanization and the formation of class consciousness has been rendered more tenuous. To the extent that urbanization has weakened the sense of community and the capacity for collective action, and thereby the subjectivity of the working class, it can be seen to have made the formation of class consciousness more problematic.

While there were a number of important and violent urban labour struggles which occurred in eastern Canadian cities in the first two decades of the twentieth century, none could match the upheavals which occurred in the West, and in Cape Breton in 1909 and in the early 1920s, for the militancy of the struggle or the degree of class-conscious politics involved. Among the more important of these eastern urban conflicts were the street railway strikes which occurred in London in 1899, Toronto in

1902, Montréal in 1903 and Hamilton in 1906.[34] In all of these strikes, armed troops were to used to defeat attempts by strikers to prevent the railways from operating. A similar strike occurred in Winnipeg in 1906, where troops armed with machine guns patrolled the streets to ensure the operation of the street railway.

On the whole, most of the labour disputes which took place in the older eastern cities revolved around disputes over wages, employment of non-union labour and working conditions. In the main, they were fought by craft unions in a fairly orthodox manner.[35] The fact that craft business-unionism came to dominate the eastern Canadian urban labour movement raises some interesting questions. To what extent was this phenomenon simply a function of the age of the cities and their more diversified workforce in which skilled labour played a greater role? To what extent was it a manifestation of the power of North American urbanism, in its more mature stages, to deflect class-conscious struggles onto the safer paths of business unionism? If the process of urbanization, indeed, effectively weakened community relationships and the capacity for collective action, while at the same time increasingly reducing daily life to the making of a living and passive participation in the spectacular world of modernity, then business unionism was certainly far better suited to this world than radical labourism.

TRADE UNION INTEGRATION

The integration of workers into "safe" business-oriented trade unions was the outcome of a process of State integration and craft-oriented labour struggle. State integration policies in Canada were developed during the first decade of the century as a means of countering the threat of radical unionism which flourished in the West. A Royal Commission which investigated a series of general strikes among miners and railway workers in British Columbia (BC) in 1903 found the unions involved, the WFM and the UBRE, to be "secret political organizations with revolutionary objectives." It recommended that "legitimate trade unionism...be encouraged and protected but that [radical] organizations be prohibited and declared illegal."[36]

W.L. Mackenzie King, then Canada's Deputy Minister of Labour, served as Secretary to the Commission and undoubtedly had a major hand in the writing of the final report. King and the Commission were quick to recognize the importance of channelling labour unrest onto the safer paths of business unionism, where legitimate rights could be granted in return for predictable and controlled behaviour within the limits of capitalist enterprise.

At the same time that it condemned radical unionism, the Royal Commission recognized the importance of working-class progress. It even, in the abstract, acknowledged the desirability of reducing working hours, provided it was done gradually and only if international competitive conditions permitted.[37] This liberal approach, which stressed the benefits to be won if radicalism were eschewed, was typical of Mackenzie King.

Mackenzie King served as Canada's first Deputy Minister of labour, the Labour Minister, and then Prime Minister on three separate occasions for a period of over twenty years. His influence in Canadian political life spanned half a century. Among his many achievements was Canada's system of industrial relations, of which he was the principal architect.[38] His influence on labour relations was not restricted to Canada. He also served as special labour-relations consultant to John D. Rockefeller, beginning with the violent Colorado coal strike in 1915, and later advising such companies as General Electric, Standard Oil and International Harvester.[39]

King helped to perfect the policy of integrating the trade union movement into business-union contract bargaining under State supervision, while at the same time weaning workers from any inclination they might have toward radicalism. He was also a strong supporter and advocate of the town planning and urban reform movement in Canada.[40]

King drew upon his extensive experience in engineering the defeat of radical labour organizations, and conciliating and arbitrating labour disputes in drafting his vision of labour relations. King as early as 1915 had proposed a system of labour relations which incorporated business welfare, formal grievance procedures, an employees' bill of rights, and joint councils representing workers and management to consult on subjects ranging from health and safety to recreation and education. He reserved the right to hire and fire, however, in management hands. In *Industry and Humanity* published in 1918, King urged that the system of industrial relations be routinized, so that "guerilla warfare" could be replaced by "rules and regulations." He argued that "under collective agreements a sense of equality...between the parties" would become the basis of industrial discipline. For, "in dealing with human nature of inferior qualities," justice needed "to be tempered with mercy." The right for workers to have their own trade unions recognized was of fundamental psychological importance, provided of course, such unions were to be responsible bodies.[41]

Clearly King's contribution to labour relations theory is a significant one. This is particularly evident when we consider that he was writing in 1918, considerably before such conceptions of integration and social control were widely understood or accepted. He was an important influence in moving Canadian capitalism, albeit very gradually, beyond naked accumulation to a more sophisticated, rationalized, and therefore more powerful pattern of accumulation and legitimation, more in tune with the needs of an emerging mass consumption and increasingly urbanized society.

THE WINNIPEG GENERAL STRIKE

The culmination of the radical movement in Canada during the first decades of the twentieth century, if not for the whole of Canadian labour history up to the present, took place in Winnipeg during May and June, 1919. In order to advance our argument that urbanization in Canada has had a significant impact upon the formation of class consciousness, it is important that we examine this event in some detail. For the Winnipeg General Strike was in many ways the last sustained mass collective action of class-conscious labour at the urban level in Canada in the twentieth century. The strike is particularly revealing because it occurred at a key transitional point in North American economic and cultural development. As such, it embodied aspects of the old order of direct class-conscious confrontation. The very fact that the strike was fought by workers whose emotional commitment was class conscious in nature, in order to win the right to bargain collectively against employers who were vehemently hostile to unions, is indicative of this coexistence of two orders. While the outcome did not result in the immediate legitimacy of union recognition and collective bargaining, the focus of the confrontation was irrevocably shifted from questions of social transformation to questions of reform. The threat which the strike posed to Canadian capitalism played no small role in promoting the cause of reformers like Mackenzie King.[42] Paradoxically, one of the most radical and class-conscious struggles in Canadian labour history signalled the end of an era of radicalism, and the beginning of another era, more fundamentally linked to economic and social integration.

In many ways, Winnipeg was an appropriate venue for such an event, for its history typified so much of the Canadian urban historical tradition.[43] At the time of the Winnipeg General Strike, Winnipeg was the third largest city in Canada with a population, including its suburbs, of 227,000. It was the centre of the grain trade for Canada and the metropolitan centre of Western Canada, with major transportation, wholesale, retail, and manufacturing facilities. The local merchants and finance capitalists called the city the "bull's eye of the Dominion" and the "Chicago of the North."[44]

The Winnipeg business and upper class, not unlike their counterparts in English Eastern Canada, were rather uniformly Anglo-Saxon, staunch British loyalists, and often racist in their attitudes toward immigrants from the "foreign" countries of Europe. They were also extremely laissez-faire whenever there was any question of interference in their private business interests.[45] They never failed to lobby for substantial State intervention on their behalf, however, whenever the need arose. For example, the monopoly of the Winnipeg Street Railway Company over the supply of electricity was broken in 1909 by the establishment of a municipally owned electric power company.[46]

Power was supplied to the city at half the cost by the municipal company, and municipalization received overwhelming support by the business community. The Manitoba Free Press clearly established the rationale for this support. "Public power is the force which has carried real estate values upwards in phenomenal bounds..."[47]

Table 5
Population growth of Winnipeg and Manitoba, 1871-1921

	Winnipeg (a)	Winnipeg City	Manitoba
1871	—	241	25,228
1881	—	7,985	62,260
1891	—	25,639	152,506
1901	47,969	42,340	255,211
1911	155,563	136,035	461,394
1912	227,200	179,087	610,118

Source: A. Artibise (1977) *Winnipeg: An Illustrated History*, Table III, p. 200. See n. 48.
(a) Winnipeg (a) includes suburbs

Table 6
Population growth in principal western cities 1901-21 (excluding suburbs)

	Winnipeg	Regina	Saskatoon	Calgary	Edmonton	Vancouver
1901	42,340	2,249	113	4,392	4,176	27,010
1911	136,035	30,213	12,004	43,704	24,900	100,401
1921	79,087	34,432	25,739	63,305	58,821	163,200

Source: A. Artibise (1977) *Winnipeg: An Illustrated History*, Table IV, p.201, See n. 48.

The ethnic composition of Winnipeg by the time of the General Strike reflected the flood of immigrants which has entered Canada since the turn of the century. There was a very large Eastern European population which was residentially segregated, largely in the city's "North End." This pattern, in which ethnic origin overlapped with class, made for a strong sense of injustice among the city's immigrant population which has persisted to this day. Eighty-three percent of the Slavic population of the city in 1916 lived in the North End, where they were joined by 87 percent of the Jewish population, but less than 20 percent of the British population of the city.[48] The North End was isolated in more than just sociological terms. The vast railway yards of the CPR separated it from the rest of the city. The district was characterized by widespread poverty, illiteracy, poor-quality and overcrowded housing, poor sanitation and relatively radical politics. The south part of the city, on the other hand, separated from the central part of the Assiniboine River and well endowed with natural beauty and good drainage, was the district of the city's wealthy ruling class. It was characterized by broad boulevards, spacious lots, restrictive zoning, impressive homes, a plenitude of parks, and a largely Anglo-Saxon ethnic composition.

The wealthiest grain merchants and trading magnates reserved the attractive wooded areas bordering the Assiniboine River for their exclusive residential pleasure. One of these residential enclaves was depicted in lavish terms in a newspaper advertisement for it in 1903.

> This most desirable portion of the city is now controlled by a syndicate who have authorized us to offer a limited number of Lots for Sale, with building restrictions, ensuring the construction of handsome residences. The improvements now being made by the city and those contemplated by the syndicate with the serpentine drive…will make the Point not only the finest locality for artistic and stately homes, but it will become…the "Faubourg St. Germaine" of Winnipeg, the most fashionable drive in the city.[49]

The cultural impact which the residential segregation of immigrants imposed on the daily lives of the working class is well captured in the following excerpt from a novel about life in Winnipeg during the 1920s by John Marlyn. The excerpt describes the experience of a young Hungarian immigrant boy crossing the river into the South End for the first time.

> Freshly washed and scrubbed, dressed in a clean blouse and his Sunday pants, Sandor sat impatiently dangling his legs in the Academy Road Streetcar. Soon, he thought, and looked imploringly across at the conductor. He had been doing so ever since they had crossed the bridge, and at every glance the conductor had winked and motioned to him to remain seated.
> But this time he nodded and pressed the buzzer. Sandor sprang to his feet. The car grounded to a stop. He got off, walked a short distance up the street, and suddenly he stood still.
> It was though he had walked into a picture in one of his childhood books, past the painted margin to a land that lay smiling under a friendly spell where the sun always shone, and the clean-washed tint of sky and child and garden would never fade; where one could walk, but on tip-toe, and look and look but never touch and never speak to break the enchantment hush.
> It grew real. There was the faint murmur of the city far in the background and overhead the whisper of the wind in the trees.
> The green here was not as he had ever seen it on a leaf or weed but with the blue of the sky in it, and the air so clear that even the sky looked different here.

> In a daze he moved down the street. The boulevards ran wide and spacious to the very doors of the houses. And these houses were like palaces, great and stately surrounded by their own private parks and gardens.[50]

The hero of this novel, Sandor Hunyadi, grows up aspiring to escape from the stigma of his North End immigrant background. He later seeks assimilation through business success and the changing of his name to Alex Hunter. His ultimate failure, due to the depression, is perhaps less important than his drive for assimilation. For it movingly illustrates the haunting dilemma which confronted all immigrants to the new world from "foreign" lands, to succeed and assimilate rather than rebel. And yet the decision was not without tension, for the very social class which by its exploitation fostered rebellion, was no less anxious to avoid contagion by "foreign" elements. The fact that this novel *Under the Ribs of Death* was written in the 1950s, the nadir of North American class politics, and is set in the 1920s after the defeat of the radical labour movement, is not without significance. For, just as the end of the preceding decade was one of profound energy and class struggle, the 1920s was a decade marked by passivity, defeat and integration.

The ethnic immigrant dimension played an important role in the Winnipeg General Strike. From the perspective of the Anglo-Saxon ruling class, the strike was an alien Bolshevik plot which directly threatened not only the authority to accumulate capital and manage the work process at will, but the very foundations of their society. While most of the leadership of the strike was composed of British working-class immigrants, "foreign" immigrants were represented among the leadership, and, more significantly, among the thousands of workers and their families who supported the strike.[51]

The anti-strike campaign which was orchestrated by the establishment "Committee of 1000," devoted considerable attention to whipping up hysteria over "alien subversion" in their efforts to defeat the strike. Advertisements in Winnipeg's three daily newspapers sponsored by the Committee called on the federal government to deport "the undesirable alien and land him back in the bilge waters of European Civilization from whence he sprung and to which he properly belongs."[52]

This anti-alien campaign struck a mixed chord of response among the strikers. During the course of the strike and later in the strikers' own history of the event the alien issue was debated in ambivalent terms.

> The bosses love the alien when they can use him to break strikes. In fact, in many cases he was brought here for that purpose. Who brought the aliens to Canada? It was not the workers. They opposed it by might and main. We will support all efforts on the part of the authorities to deport all the undesirable aliens.[53] (Western Labour News, 7 June 1919)

> The bosses have no quarrel with the rich alien, no quarrel with the unorganized alien. The only aliens they complain about are those who have had sense enough of join the ranks of organized labour and therefore cannot be used to scale down wages...Employers, large and small, sent deputations to beg of the alien to come back to work. But the alien declined the tempting offers made them and they stuck tight as a postage stamp. For the workers of Winnipeg, the barriers of color, race and creed had been torn down and are now beyond hope of being rebuilt, which is as it should be.[54]

Thus we can see that the issue of "foreign" immigration to Canada played an important, but highly ambivalent, role in the formation of class consciousness.

The First World War contributed to heightening the sense of grievance felt by Canadian workers. Widespread profiteering, rapid inflation in food prices, poor living conditions, increased working hours and reduced wages, coupled with a bloody toll on the battlefield, generated considerable militancy. This working-class militancy and unrest was parallel in other Western countries. France, Germany, Italy, Hungary, Britain, Australia, the United States and, of course, Russia were all the scenes of strikes, widespread unrest, attempted and successful revolutions of varying degrees of importance.[55]

The radical leadership of the Western Canadian labour movement had been strongly opposed to the war effort. The socialists among them viewed the war as "a dispute of the international capitalist class for markets (and therefore, of no real interest to the international working class.)[56] Workers in general, of course, were much more ambivalent, depending upon their degree of political consciousness. While many did enlist voluntarily for reasons of patriotism or simply because employers pressured them, a significant minority refused to enlist and resisted conscription when it was imposed.[57]

The disillusionment which the war had brought, and the expectations of a different kind of post-war world which it created among working people, were critical factors in setting the stage for the radical unrest which occurred.[58]

The Russian Revolution was also an event of enormous psychological importance. The hopes of many workers, in Western Canada, in particular, were raised by the overthrow of the Czar and the later succession to power of the Bolsheviks. Among a number of immigrant labour groups from Eastern Europe, sympathy and political appreciation for the Russian revolution was widespread. Many of these immigrants were located in Winnipeg.

The optimism inspired by the Revolution, the growth of the One Big Union movement in Australia, and the growing socialist orientation of the British labour movement, contributed toward an increasing interest in socialist, direct action and syndicalist solutions.⁵⁹ A series of successful strikes occurred in the West, including two short general strikes in Winnipeg and Vancouver.

During the one-day Vancouver strike, held in August 1918 to protest the shooting of a prominent BC draft evader by the police, a mob of soldiers wrecked the Vancouver labour temple. Similar vigilante actions took place in Winnipeg where both immigrant "aliens" and known socialists were attacked and beaten in the streets. The government and their officials did not discourage these sorts of actions, The argument was made that it was essential that "the real sensible people of the country take into their own hands the active combating of Bolshevik propaganda."⁶⁰ The press, on the other hand, was somewhat more legalistic. The Toronto Telegram, for example, editorialized about socialists counselling workers to resist conscription.

> Socialism in Winnipeg has disgraced organized labour as socialism everywhere disgraces labour...The Canadian Government should fill the jails so full of these people that their feet should stick out of the windows.⁶¹

An official secret investigation of radicalism in 1918 concluded that a "Bolshevik conspiracy" existed in which "aliens of enemy nationality" including Russians, Ukrainians, and Finns affiliated to the IWW were conspiring to foment revolution in Western Canada.⁶² On the basis of this report, a Department of Public Safety was created and a series of repressive measures undertaken. These included severe curtailment of civil liberties, a restriction on the freedom of the press and the outlawing of a number of radical organizations. The use of "foreign" languages at public meetings was also prohibited. All strikes and lockouts which would interfere with the war effort were banned.⁶³

The Western labour movement responded with a campaign of meetings and publicity against the measures. Labour councils in Victoria, Vancouver, Calgary, Edmonton, Regina and Winnipeg called for general strikes, if necessary, to force the government to rescind the measure. The government was also denounced for its participation in the armed intervention in the Russian civil war on the side of the Whites.⁶⁴

Political radicalism was gaining momentum. At a series of large meetings in Victoria, Vancouver, Calgary and Winnipeg, the federal government's actions, as well as war-time corruption and profiteering, were attacked. Resolutions were passed calling for the repeal of the repressive legislation, the release of political prisoners and the withdrawal of Canadian forces from Russia. At the Winnipeg and Calgary meetings, fraternal messages of greeting were sent to the Bolsheviks and the German Spartacists.⁶⁵

In March 1919, 250 delegates met at the Western Canadian Labour Conference in Calgary. They endorsed the creation of a new labour body, the One Big Union, which was to reorganize workers along industrial lines and to advance the workers' cause through the use of the general strike. The Conference agreed to a set of proposals by which the new organization was to be created through a referendum in the four western provinces. The referendum asked workers if they wished to leave their respective American-affiliated craft unions and the new body. The by-now familiar calls for the repeal of the repressive orders-in-council, the release of political prisoners, withdrawals of troops from Russia, and expressions of support for the Bolsheviks and Spartacists were all adopted, as well as a resolution endorsing the "principle of proletariat dictatorship." The Conference also called for a six-hour day and the five-day week.[66]

Not all of the delegates, and certainly not the majority of workers in Western Canada, endorsed such revolutionary postures. It must be remembered that organized labour was a very small proportion of the workforce. The radicals were an even smaller fraction. Nevertheless, for the time being, the radicals had considerable influence. In the heady atmosphere which prevailed at the end of the war, with revolutionary currents swirling about, and the climate of generally rising expectations for the promise of a new society, workers in Western Canada were prepared to allow the radicals to take the lead.

This militancy and radicalism was definitely not shared by the eastern labour movement. The Trade and Labour Congress of Canada viewed western radicalism as a direct threat to their control over the Canadian labour movement, at a time when their influence, and moreover, respectability was growing. The leadership, particularly those with close links to the American Federation of Labour, therefore conspired with the federal government to crush the radical labour movement and the Winnipeg General Strike, using every means at their disposal.

The general strike in Winnipeg began with a strike over union recognition and wage increases by the building and metal trade unions. This occurred in a general climate of labour unrest and employer intransigence. Because of the refusal of the employers to bargain with the unions, the Winnipeg Trades and Labour Council called for and received overwhelming support for a general strike. The general strike began on 15 May 1919, and within hours received the support of ninety-four out of a total of ninety-six unions, including police and firemen, some 12,000 organized workers and at least as many unorganized workers. During the height of the strike the economic life of the city was paralysed, with some 35,000 workers on strike out of a total work force of about 60,000. If we include the families of the strikers, close to one half of the city's population was on strike. Only essential services, such as milk and other food deliveries were operational, and these only because of the co-operation of the strike committee.

The strike was supported by many, though not all of the returned soldiers. There were marches by returned soldiers for and against the strike.

One month after the strike had begun, the Royal Northwest Mounted Police, acting on federal orders, arrested strike leaders at their homes in the middle of the night, raided other homes and labour temples, and seized documents and radical literature. A silent parade by veterans to protest the arrest of the strike leaders, the federal government's legislation to deport "undesirable aliens," including Canadian citizens, and the city's resumption of streetcar service, was scheduled for the downtown area in the vicinity of the city hall. The city banned the parade. When the crowds who had gathered to watch it, blocked the passage of a streetcar, they were attacked by mounted police armed with clubs and small arms, and by special armed police recruited by the Citizen's Committee to replace the regular police who had gone on strike. Some of the equipment which the "specials" used, including their clubs, were supplied courtesy of local department stores. At least one demonstrator was killed and more than thirty injured. The use of armed troops and armoured cars (machine guns had been secretly sent to Winnipeg by the federal government), as well as the occupation of the city by heavily armed militia, brought the strike to its knees. On 26 June 1919 the strike officially ended.[67]

The defeat of the Winnipeg General Strike marked an important watershed in Canadian labour and urban history. The strike was the last mass battle fought by urban workers affiliated to, or influenced by, the radical labour and socialist movement in Canada. In many respects, it was the high point of working-class political consciousness at the urban level. Even during the bitter class conflict endangered by the depression of the 1930s, the degree of class consciousness displayed during the strike was never equalled.

Although only three members of the official strike leadership belonged to the committee organizing the One Big Union, many of the workers on strike in Winnipeg supported the OBU idea. The One Big Union, despite the defeat of the strike, managed to recruit close to 50,000 workers from across Western Canada. These included coal and metal miners, carpenters, railwaymen, textile workers, teamsters and lumber workers. The Vancouver, Victoria, and Winnipeg Trades and Labour Councils affiliated with it. Yet by the end of 1921, the OBU had been largely defeated. Because of its radicalism, the State and the conservative national Trades and Labour Congress had marked it for destruction. The federal government intervened in labour disputes wherever the OBU was involved, declaring it to be an illegitimate organization and pressuring workers to desert it for government-sanctioned TLC affiliates. In the face of this organized hostility, with a raising unemployment rate, and strategically weakened by its association with the now-discredited notion of the general strike, the OBU was doomed to fail.[68]

Many interpreters of the Winnipeg General Strike argue that it was essentially a confrontation with employers over the question of union recognition, collective bargaining rights and wages. However, in the light of the times in which it took place, and the scope and intensity of the strike itself, clearly it involved, at the very minimum, a widespread aspiration for a radically different kind of social order. To be sure, this aspiration and the class consciousness of which it was an expression, were ambivalent, already influenced by integrative tendencies. Nevertheless, the contrast which the militancy and consciousness of these urban workers makes with their contemporary counterparts and the nature of urban labour struggles today, is a dramatic one. For we have moved from class-based struggles, with definite (if somewhat ambivalent) class consciousness, to narrowly-based interest group struggles. These current struggles, on the whole, lack significant political content, let alone a sense of social transformation. They occur in an environment in which the majority of urbanized workers view strikers as competitive with their own interests. Solidarity, as such, is largely absent. Not only has the object of labour struggles been reduced to purely job-related demands, but these struggles are thoroughly integrated into an achievement-oriented competitive treadmill. The transcendence of universal need by interest, of conscious solidarity by instrumental calculation, and of working-class culture and public space by capitalist hegemony and privatization has been thorough.

The defeat of the radical labour movement in 1919 coincided with the rise of an increasingly urban-based, mass consumption society. The newly created mass advertising industry, much like the mass production economy it was designed to support, created a new product — the mass consumer. This era also coincided with the growing depoliticization of the working class. The substitution of shopping and soap opera, the cinema and radio, for politics and social interaction, reinforced the passivity that resulted from the repression and defeat.[69] The public space in which radical politics had been possible increasingly fell victim to a conception of social life in which private achievement and personal consumption became primary goals.

> By the 1920s, the development of American consciousness industries, particularly advertising had begun to materialize as a result of the same social decisions by which mass industrialism was being developed. The priorities by which a population was being mobilized and privatized as wage earners, gave rise of necessity to a new capitalist cosmos.
> The pleasures of the marketplace, like the labour process from which they emanated [were] individuated, couched in a vision of a social world made up of anonymous and/or hostile strangers.[70]

It is not surprising that the reduction of work to abstract labour, which was the essence of the deskilling process involved in the decline of the crafts, paralleled the depoliticization of the urban worker and his conversion to a member of the mass society of emerging metropolitan life. For those two tendencies were central to the emergence of the urban way of life as a mode of social control, in which mass consumption of goods and cultural services ensured the decline of politics and therefore of radicalism.[71] This estrangement and atomization which is bound up in the social reproduction of labour as members of a mass consumer society has come to be the most powerful influence in modern urban life in Canada. The kind of militancy and political activity which characterized the Winnipeg General Strike seems difficult to imagine in contemporary urban Canada.

In fact, even in Winnipeg, where the events took place, they seem only a fading memory, largely unknown among the population at large, and of interest only to urban and labour historians. Except for occasional rhetorical allusions by labour politicians, the mythological memory of the events among some of the descendents of the strike, and the persistence of strains of radical politics in the North End of the city, "social amnesia," the forcible repression of the collective memory, has been remarkably successful. It is this power of social amnesia and the cultural homogenization of capitalist society at the urban level in North America which must be understood, if we are to make sense of the nature of urban political culture in Canada and the social reproduction of capitalism which it entails.[72]

The decline of the radical labour movement was followed by the decline of the labour movement, in general. In 1919, the high point of radicalism, there were 387,000 workers affiliated to trade unions in Canada. After the destruction of the OBU, membership in unions declined below the 300,000 level and, except for 1928 and 1929, did not surpass 300,000 until after 1935. The 1919 high-point was not surpassed until 1937 when the unions affiliated to the CIO were organized.[73]

During the 1920s, a number of factors contributed to the stagnation of the labour movement. The continuing importance of immigration and out-migration of labour, as well as the movement from rural to urban areas, increased the transient character of labour which made union organizing difficult. The rise of a managerial bureaucracy, and the larger scale of firms which accompanied the growing Americanization of Canadian business brought corporatist managerial industrial relations into vogue. On the whole, during this period, economic growth was centred around new high-technology industries making organizing difficult. With urban-based radicalism firmly defeated, and the mass production/mass consumption phase of North American capitalism under way, attention was turned toward integrating workers without the mediation of unions.[74]

The 1920s were thus the heyday of scientific management ideology which emphasized management technique and employee manipulation as the solution to labour problems. Trade unions were conformably regarded as anachronisms. For Canadian workers the 1920s were a decade of retrenchment and defeat.

CONCLUSION

This survey of some aspects of the economic, labour and social history of Canada's cities was undertaken to increase our understanding of the nature of contemporary urban politics and culture. For the roots of these contemporary phenomena, like all social phenomena, lie embedded in the past. Many of the characteristic features of Canadian urbanization were established by the 1920s. These features include: uneven regional economic development in which Canadian urban hierarchy is situated, with both regional underdevelopment and hierarchy mutually reinforcing each other; the orientation of the city as a locus for capital accumulation and commercial expansion with dominant external linkages; the critical role of immigration and migration in the process of urban development and capital accumulation; the impact of immigration and migration upon political culture; the marginalization of certain ethnic groups and the privileged positions of Anglo-Saxons and northern Europeans; the repression of radical politics and the elevation of reform; the depoliticization of urban culture; and finally the relative absence of working-class political content in urban reform movements with the possible exception of Montréal.

The "social amnesia" which, on the whole, prevails among the urban working class in Canada has its roots in the first two decades of the twentieth century.

People make their own history, it is true. But they do so subject to the struggles, victories, defeats and repressions of the past. If, as a result of these events, they come to lack consciousness then history makes them. And it does so under the dominant influence of that class which does possess consciousness. That is not to say that the present is rigidly fixed or the past forever impressed upon the present or the future.

Manuel Castells has written critically of the notion of urban culture, which he argues is used as an ideological smokescreen, a "myth" behind which the true nature of the city in capitalist society is obscured.[75] While his approach has the merit of redirecting attention away from the classless ecological models of American urban sociology towards the concrete articulations of capital formation and collective consumption within the spatial relations of the city, from our perspective he has narrowed the focus too much. If we are to make sense of the formation and deformation of class consciousness in urban North America, we must seek the answer to our questions at the level of the culture of everyday life. The fact that a police station and a parking garage stand on the site of the Old Market Square in Winnipeg, where the mass meetings of thousands of politicized workers once took place, is symbolic of what has transpired in urban political life in Canada.

The process of transformation cannot be solely rooted in concrete economic factors. Canadian capitalism, like North American capitalism of which it is an integral part, has been largely able at the spatial/environmental level to shape the city to meet its needs. It has been able to do so without being forced to incorporate or to destroy precapitalist spatial forms. As such, the numbering impact of the placelessness of much of contemporary urban design and its functioning as a mode of social control has operated without dilution or resistance.[76]

Despite the presence of an earlier urban working class, with significant strains of radicalism and class consciousness, the contemporary Canadian city has largely been cleansed of such influences. Once the actual repression of radicalism was accomplished, the stage was set for the construction of the city and the establishment of a rhythm of city life as a celebration devoted to accumulation and consumption.

The city and its streets were converted from a place where politics and public life were central to life, to a place where consumption and spectacle became central.[77] Politics was pushed aside, indoors, where it has come ultimately to be reconstituted as spectacle itself, and consumed passively as television. Public space is less and less available to facilitate the social interaction, beyond the confines of the workplace itself, which is necessary for the formulation of class consciousness.

The repression of radicalism was followed by amnesia — an amnesia which was made more powerful by an urbanism dedicated to forgetting its past. The street has become in Lefebvre's words "a sequence of showcases, an exposition of objects for sale. Thus we can speak of the colonization of urban space brought about in the street through the image, the publicity, the spectacle of objects…"[78]

It is the contrast which this image of contemporary city life makes with the pictures and discourses of the past to which I wish to draw attention. For the contrast raises quite fundamental questions about how the city and city life in Canada have changed. A sea of faces in a crowd of thousands on a street, in a park or on a square, men and women upon platforms speaking to the crowd about politics, about good and evil, about the future of humanity. The romantic and utopian unreality of these scenes seem clear when we try to imagine them in the contemporary Canadian city, not simply as special events, but as an ongoing part of political life.

The roar of automobile traffic, the crowds of shoppers, the streams of neon, and glass plastic, the McDonalds and the gas stations — can this be the same urban world?

In his final address to the jury at his trial following the Winnipeg General Strike, William Pritchard, one of the leaders of the Western radical movement, spoke of a new order which he saw on the horizon.

> Reason, wisdom, intelligence, forces of the mind and heart, whom I have always devoutly invoked, come to me, aid me, sustain my feeble voice, carry it, if that may be, to all the peoples of the world and diffuse it everywhere where there are men of goodwill to hear the beneficent truth. A new

order of things is born, the powers of evil die poisoned by their crime. The greedy and the cruel, the devourers of people are bursting with an indigestion of blood. However, sorely stricken by the sins of their blind or corrupt masters, mutilated, decimated, the proletarians remain erect; they will unite to form one universal proletariat and we shall see fulfilled the great Socialist prophecy, "the union of the workers will be the peace of the world.[79]

These words, spoken then, and even if romantic and utopian, had the ring of hopeful authenticity for many urban workers. Spoken now, they have a naive and hopelessly idealistic quality. Their present inauthenticity is a measure of how much the Canadian urban political culture has declined.

NOTES

1. I originally dedicated this article to the memory of my teacher and friend, Rubin Simkin a wonderful humanist intellectual. I renew the dedication and add to it the memory of my friend and outstanding urbanist the late Kent Gerecke who in many ways was responsible for me writing the original version. Both Simkin and Gerecke understood the importance of the collective memory and they helped shape my own sensibility.
2. Canada as of 1992 is a continental land mass, which is the largest country in the world. Its population of twenty-seven million is over 76 percent urban. Its population is less than one-half that of France which is one-eighteenth the area of Canada. In 1971, 47 percent of the Canadian population resided in twelve metropolitan areas of over 220,000 each. In 1981 56 percent of Canadians lived in 24 census metropolitan areas of more than 100,000 people each. Over seven million people lived in three metropolises, Toronto, Montréal and Vancouver. Source: Donald Higgins, *Local and Urban Politics in Canada* Toronto: Gage, 1986; *1981 Census of Canada*. D.M. Ray (ed.) (1976), *Canadian Urban Trends: National Perspective*, Vol. 1. Toronto: Copp Clark, Table 1.7:19.
3. (The Québec nationalist movement in the 1990s has lost most, if not all, of its working class orientation. Instead, it is better understood as a movement of technocratic and business class nationalism with some considerable working class support because of the support of some of the PQ's leadership and activists for social democratic goals) For a discussion of the radical urban movement and its relationship to the Québec nationalist movement, see S. Shecter (1978), *The Politics of Urban Liberation Montréal*. Black Rose Press. S. Shecter (1975) *Urban politics in Capitalist Society. Our Generation* (Fall) 11, 1: 28-41. H. Milner (1975) *City Politics—some possibilities. Our Generation* (Winter) 10, 4: 47-60. A. Limonchik (1977) *The colonization of the urban economy, Our Generation* (Fall) 12, 2:5-24. The editors (1974) *The Montréal Citizens Movement*. Our Generation (Fall) 10, 3: 3-22. M. Raboy (1978) *The Future of Montréal and the MCM*. Our Generation (Fall) 12, 4:5-18. M. Castells (1972), *The Urban Question*. London: Edward Arnold, pp. 348-60. *Reflections and a retrospective: an interview with Yvon Charbonneau. This Magazine* (July-August 1979), 13,3.
4. See G. Janosik and R. Voline (1978) *Bloodbath in the Red River Valley. This Magazine* (July-August) 12, 3. H. Chorney and P. Hansen (1980) *The falling rate of legitimation; problems of legitimation of the capitalist State in Canada*. See the next essay.

5. For the critical role of cultural institutions in the formation of class consciousness see E.P. Thompson (1968), *The Making of the English Working Class*. Harmondsworth: Penguin Books, p. 178 ff.
6. The process of urbanization and its impact upon class consciousness is the subject of a somewhat forgotten debate in urban social theory. On the one hand, the works of F. Toennies, *Gemeinschaft and Gesellschaft*; G. Simmel, "The Metropolis and Mental Life" and *The Philosophy of Money*; and to a lesser extent E. Durkheim, *The Division of Labour in Society* all focus on alienated social relations in the metropolis which are linked, to a greater or lesser extent, to the rise of capitalism itself. In social theory these insights, and particularly the work of Simmel, led directly to the work of G. Lukacs — (1971), *History and Class Consciousness*. London: Merlin Press — in which the notion of reification is introduced as a means of explaining the failure of class consciousness to emerge. Lukacs however cast his argument in terms quite different from Simmel's concern with metropolitan life, and in Marxists subsequent to Lukacs the critical connection of reification and metropolitan life was largely forgotten. Instead, these ideas have surfaced in a badly deformed way stripped of their original radicalism and connection to class and consciousness in the urban sociology of the Chicago school. (I discuss these themes and writers in my book *City of Dreams: Social Theory and the Urban Experience*. Toronto:Nelson Canada, 1990.)
7. See A. Heller (1974), *The Theory of Need in Marx*. London: Allison and Busby.
8. See for example K. Marx and F. Engels (1973) *The Communist Manifesto* in *Revolutions of 1848*. Harmondsworth: Penguin Books, pp. 71-2.
9. Mandel refers to this period as one of primitive accumulation of commercial capital. E. Mandel (1962), *Marxist Economic Theory*. London: Merlin Press, pp. 106-9.
10. For a discussion of this concept see A.G. Frank (1969), *Capitalism and Underdevelopment in Latin America*. Harmondsworth: Penguin Books.
11. See, for example, M. Katz (1976), *The People of Hamilton, Canada West: Family and Class in a Mid-Nineteenth Century City*. Cambridge, Mass.: Harvard University Press.
12. H.C. Pentland (1960) *Labour and the development of industrial capitalism in Canada* PhD. thesis, University of Toronto.
13. H.C. Pentland 1960: 400-22, 408.
14. See R.T. Naylor (1975), *The History of Canadian Business: 1867-1914*. Toronto: James Lorimer, Vols. 1 and 2. See also I. Lumsden (ed.) (1970), *Close the 49th Parallel Etc.The Americanization of Canada*. Toronto: University of Toronto Press; G. Temple (ed.) (1972), *Capitalism and the National Question in Canada*. Toronto: University of Toronto Press; R. Laxer (ed.) (1973), *Canada Ltd. The Political Economy of Dependency*. Toronto: McClelland and Stewart Ltd; C. Heron (ed.) (1977), *Imperialism, Nationalism and Canada*. Toronto and Kitchener: New Hogtown Press-Between the Lines; K. Levitt (1967), *Silent Surrender*. Toronto: Macmillan.
15. For a discussion of the impact of American investment upon regional underdevelopment in Canada see H. Chorney *Regional underdevelopment and cultural decay* in C. Heron ed. Imperialism, Nationalism and Canada.
16. See M. Kalecki (1972) *Political aspects of full employment*, in M. Kalecki, *The Last Phase in the Transformation of Capitalism*. New York: Monthly Review Press. The phrase "high intensity" is Bill Leiss's; see W. Leiss (1976), *The Limits to Satisfaction*. Toronto: University of Toronto Press.
17. K. Buckley (1974), *Capital Formation in Canada 1896-1930*. Toronto: McClelland and Stewart Ltd., pp. 4-6.
18. Canada, *Census 1851*, Vol.1, pp. 36-7. Canada, Census 1921, Vol. 1, p. xv.
19. Canada, *Census* 1901, 1921, Vol.1.
20. J. Weaver (1977), *Shaping the Canadian City: Essays on Urban Politics and Policy 1890-1920* Toronto: The Institute of Public Administration of Canada, p. 6.
21. J. Weaver 1977: 7-8. See also D. Avery (1972) *Continental European immigration in Canada, 1890-1919: from stalwart peasant to radical proletarian*, Canadian Historical Association, Historical Papers, R. Harney and H. Troper (1975), *Immigrants: A Portrait of the Urban Experience, 1890-1930*. Toronto: Van Nostrand Rheinhold; D. Avery (1979), *Dangerous Foreigners*. Toronto: McClelland and Stewart.

22. P. Phillips (1967), *No Power Greater: A Century of Labour on British Columbia.* Vancouver: BC Federation of Labour. A.R. McCormack (1977), *Reformers, Rebels and Revolutionaries: The Western Canadian Radical Movement 1899-1919.* Toronto: University of Toronto Press.
23. The only exception in Thunder Bay located in North Western Ontario and as closely connected to Western Canada as it is to Central Canada. See D.M. Ray (ed.) (1976), *Canadian Urban Trends: National Perspectives*, Vol.2. Toronto: Copp Clark, Table 5.13, p.115.
24. See for example, T. Peterson (1978) Ethnic and class politics in Manitoba, in M. Robin (ed.), *Provincial Politics.* Toronto: Prentice-Hall.
25. For an analysis of the role of immigration in shaping American class consciousness, see S. Aronowitz (1973), *False Promises, the Shaping of American Working Class Consciousness.* New York: McGraw-Hill.
26. See A. Artibise (1977) Divided city: the immigrant in Winnipeg society, 1874-1921, in A. Artibise and G. Stelter (eds.), *The Canadian City.* Toronto: McClelland and Stewart. R. Harney and H. Troper, Immigrants (1975).
27. In the main, this competition had occurred between "all-in" industrial unions like the Knights of Labour and the craft unions. See R. Hann (1976) *Brain-workers and the Knight of Labour: E.E. Sheppard, Phillips Thompson and the Toronto News, 1883-1887*, in G. Kealey and P. Warrian (eds.), *Essays in Canadian Working Class History*, Toronto: McClelland and Stewart Ltd. C. Lipton (1968), *The Trade Union Movement of Canada 1827-1959.* Montréal: Canadian Social Publications Ltd. See also M. Piva (1979), *The Condition of the Working Class in Toronto 1900-1921.* Ottawa: University of Ottawa Press. Piva argues that the decline in the labour movement in terms of effectiveness, relative size, if not militancy, began at the turn of the century and continued through the first two decades with the brief exception of 1919-20.
28. A.R. McCormack 1977: 13-14; H. Pelling (1963), *A History of British Trade Unionism.* Harmondsworth: Penguin Books, Chapter 6, pp. 93-122.
29. A.R. McCormack 1977: 98-117; P. Phillips (1968) *No Power Greater*, in M. Robin, *Radical Politics and Canadian Labour 1880-1930.* Kingston: Queen's University Press, Chapter IV.
30. A.R. McCormack 1977: 41-4.
31. This relative clarity and the radical unionism which it engenders persists. Most of the major one-company towns in Canada are noted for their more militant unions.
32. G. Simmel (1958) *Metropolis and Mental Life*, in *The Sociology of George Simmel.* Glencoe, Ill.: Free Press; F. Toennies (1957), *Community and Society.* East Lansing: Michigan State University Press; E. Durkheim (1955), *The Division of Labour in Society.* Glencoe: Free Press.
33. K. Marx (1972), *The 18th Brumaire of Louis Bonaparte.* Moscow: Progress Publishers, p. 106; Marx and Engels 1973: 71-2; K. Marx (1968), *The Class Struggles in France 1848-1850.* Moscow: Progress Publishers, pp. 37-8; K. Marx (1974) "The Civil War in France," in *The First International and After.* New York: Random House, pp. 206-21.
34. S. Jaimeson (1965), *Times of Trouble: Labour Unrest and Industrial Conflict in Canada 1900-1966.* Task Force on Labour Relations, Study Number 22, Ottawa: Information Canada. See also *Canada Labour Gazette 1900-20.*
35. *Canada Labour Gazette 1900-20.*
36. *Canada Labour Gazette 1903*, Vol. 3, pp. 133-6.
37. *Canada Labour Gazette 1903*, Vol. 3, pp. 33-6.
38. B. Rudin (n.d.) *Mackenzie King and the writing of Canada's Labour Relations Act. Canadian Dimension* mimeo. V. Levant (1977) *Capital and Labour: Partners? Two classes Two Views.* Toronto: Steel Rail Publishing.
39. W.L.M. King (1973), *Industry and Humanity.* Toronto: University of Toronto Press, introduction by D.J. Bercuson, pp.x-xi.
40. W.L.Mackenzie King 1973: 227-32.
41. W.L. Mackenzie King 1973: 133-6.
42. N. Penner (ed.) (1973), *Winnipeg 1919: The Strikers' Own History of the Winnipeg General Strike.* Toronto: James, Lewis and Samuel, p. xxi.

43. Winnipeg had originated as a fur-trading post founded by La Verendyre in 1738. The first settlers, as opposed to fur traders, arrived in 1812 as part of a colony founded by the Scottish Earl of Selkirk, who acquired a land grant by buying into Hudson's Bay Company who, in turn had received the lands by a grant of Charles II of England in 1670. An uneasy cohabitation of the area by European settlers and native Metis fur traders persisted until Manitoba was annexed by Canada in 1870. An unsuccessful rebellion led by the Metis leader Louis Riel in 1870 briefly established a Metis provincial government. At the time of the rebellion the population of the settlements in the Red River Valley, including Winnipeg, was about 12,000, including about 5,700 Metis of French-native descent, 4,000 of Anglo-Scotish-native descent and 1,600 Europeans, Canadians and Americans. See J. Howard (1973) *Strange Empire: Louis Riel and the Metis People*. Toronto: James, Lewis and Samuel; A. Artibise (1975), *Winnipeg: A Social History*. Montréal: McGill-Queens University Press.
44. A. Artibise (1975), *Winnipeg: A Social History*. Montréal: McGill-Queens University Press.
45. Artibise 1975. See also H.C. Pentland (1968) *The socio-economic background to Canadian industrial relations*, background study for *Canadian Industrial Relations: Task Force on Labour Relations*. Ottawa: Privy Council.
46. Artibise 1975: 101.
47. Artibise 1975. See also H.V. Nelles (1974) *The Politics of Development*. Toronto: Macmillan of Canada.
48. Artibise 1975: 163.
49. A. Artibise (1977), *Winnipeg: An Illustrated History*. Toronto: James Lorimer and Company, p. 66.
50. J. Marlyn (1957), *Under the Ribs of Death*. Toronto: McClelland and Stewart, p. 64.
51. See N. Penner (ed) (1973), *Winnipeg 1919: The Strikers' Own History of the General Strike*. Toronto: James, Lewis and Samuel.
52. From an advertisement in the *Winnipeg Telegram*, 6 June 1919, quoted in N. Penner (1973), "Introduction," p. xviii.
53. Quoted in T. Peterson (1978) *Ethnic and class politics in Manitoba*, in M. Robin (ed) (1978), p. 74.
54. N. Penner (ed.) 1973: 78.
55. A. Wolfe (1977), *The Limits of Legitimacy*. New York: Free Press, Collier Macmillan, pp. 117-19. See also G. Williams (1975) *Proletarian Order, Antonio Gramsci, Factory Councils and the Origins of Communism in Italy 1911-1921* London: Pluto Press.
56. *British Columbia Federationist*, 7 August 1914, quoted in A.R. MacCormack 1977: 119.
57. Robin 1968: 131-9.
58. For a literary statement of this disillusionment see J.Dos Passos (1961), *1919*. New York: Washington Square. See also D. Reed (ed) (1978), *The Great War and Canadian Society: An Oral History*. Toronto: New Hogtown Press.
59. The importance of the Russian Revolution, its perversion, and the anti-communist hysteria it aroused, cannot be underestimated in its contribution to the defeat of radicalism in North America. For the importance of British radicalism see N. Penner (1977) *The Canadian Left: A Critical Analysis*. Scarborough: Prentice-Hall. See also R.K. Murray (1955), *Red Scare: A Study in National Hysteria, 1919-1920*. New York: McGraw-Hill.
60. Letter from the chief Canadian censor to a publisher. Quoted in McCormack 1977: 162.
61. Quoted in Penner 1977: 70.
62. Robin 1968: 16-19; McCormack 1977: 150-1. The security services had attributed labour unrest to the activities of the Industrial Workers of the World (IWW). The IWW had been active in Western Canada since its founding in 1905 among transient workers who were employed as railway labourers, loggers, miners and longshoremen. By 1912 they had a membership of about 5,000. They openly and vigorously espoused revolutionary syndicalist ideas and they were an important force among the marginal unskilled and largely urbanized workers. Their propaganda played an important role in spreading the notion of direct action and the general strike. But their actual direct influence upon Western radicalism and working-class discontent was

undoubtedly exaggerated by the security service. See also J. Scott (1975), *Plunderbund and Proletariat: A History of the IWW*, in BC. Vancouver: New Star Books.
63. McCormack 1977.
64. McCormack 1977.
65. McCormack 1977: 158; see also D.C. Masters (1973) *The Winnipeg General Strike*. Toronto: University of Toronto Press, pp. 29-39.
66. Masters 1973.
67. For extensive treatment of the Winnipeg General Strike on which this account is based, see N. Penner (1973); Masters (1973); Bercuson (1974), *Confrontation at Winnipeg*. Montréal: McGill-Queens University Press; H.C. Pentland (1969) *The Winnipeg General Strike fifty years after, Canadian Dimension* (July).
68. D.J. Bercuson (1978), *Fools and Wise Men: The Rise and Fall of the One Big Union*. Toronto: McGraw-Hill Ryerson. McCormack 1977: 167-8.
69. See H. Innis (1951), *The Bias of Communication*. Toronto: University of Toronto Press, pp. 81-2, on the cultural and political importance of radio and other mass media.
70. S. and E. Ewen (1978) *Americanization and Consumption, Telos* 37 (Fall): 49.
71. For the social significance of the mediation of abstract categories in the construction of metropolitan life see Simmel (1958).
72. For the notion of social amnesia in the psychoanalytic sense, see R. Jacoby (1975), *Social Amnesia*. Boston: Deacon Press.
73. *Canada Statistical Yearbook*, 1921, 1931, 1941.
74. R. Bendix (1956), *Work and Authority in Industry*. Berkeley: University of California Press, Chapter 5. See also Pentland (1968).
75. M. Castells (1977) *The Urban Question*. London: Edward Arnold.
76. For a discussion of the phenomenological importance of placelessness see E. Relph (1977) *Place and Placelessness*. London: Pion.
77. G. Debord (1970), *Society of the Spectacle*. Detroit: Black and Red.
78. H. Lefebvre (1970), *La Révolution Urbaine*. Paris: Editions Gallimard, p. 32.
79. W. Pritchard *Address to the jury (24 March 1920)*, in N. Penner (ed.) (1973), p. 283.

2

NEO-CONSERVATISM, SOCIAL DEMOCRACY AND "PROVINCE BUILDING": THE EXPERIENCE OF MANITOBA

Harold Chorney and Phillip Hansen

We wrote this paper originally for the annual meeting of the Canadian Political Science Association in Ottawa in 1982. It was based on our experience and study of the first neo-conservative government in the English speaking world, the Conservative regime of Sterling Lyon which held power in Manitoba from 1977 until its defeat in 1981. Many of the political slogans and programmes that have flooded North American and Western European political culture since were first tested in Manitoba. Manitoba thus became a laboratory for the shape of things to come in the 1980s. What made the Manitoba situation particularly ripe for study was the nature of Manitoba politics, divided as it was between social democrats on the left and neo-conservatives on the right. At the time the Liberal party of Manitoba was not a factor, electing one member in 1977 and no members in 1981.

This polarization of politics around the challenges of neo-conservatism to the post-war conventional wisdom of liberal-social democracy was sharply drawn in Manitoba. The ideological ferocity of Sterling Lyon's attack on the social democratic government of Ed Schreyer and its ultimate defeat at the hands of a briefly resurgent NDP under the leadership of Howard Pawley, seemed to offer important lessons about the viability of social democracy in Canada. We concluded that no social democratic party could sustain itself in power on the basis of a claim to superior administrative abilities alone. If it sought to govern from too conservative a posture it would lose power to forces on the right who could always exploit social democracy's cultural illegitimacy on the one hand and the inevitable disillusionment of its supporters on the other.

This lesson would seem to still have relevance for social democrats in Canada and in Europe. The current NDP governments in Ontario, B.C. and Saskatchewan as well as the socialist party Government in France would do well to pay attention to this finding. Indeed, liberals might well pay attention as well.

Neo-conservatism, because it is a radical ideology that rejects the previous consensus about the parameters of politics, forces progressive political parties to take sides in a way they were not required to before. Simple pragmatism will not do, for neo-conservatives have the capacity to smear pragmatic liberalism as barely legitimate. This may change with political change in the 1990s, but for the decade of the 1980s when neo-conservatism held sway this kind of polarized politics had become the norm.

It is an error on the part of social democrats and liberals to accept the logic of neo-conservatism in their own formulation of policy alternatives. By doing so they permit neo-conservatives to alter fundamentally the political culture and the range of conventional wisdom. Instead it is essential to seize the high ground and expose the flaws in neo-conservative logic and policies. Politics ought to be about public education as much as power. If one only achieves power but makes no progress in educating the public about the nature of society and the tasks ahead the accomplishments will be fleeting indeed. This is the bitter lesson of the social democratic experience in Manitoba. It is lesson worth learning.

* * *

The current economic crisis (1981-1982) has had a major impact upon the ideological climate under which political debate in Canada normally occurs. The emergence of neo-conservatism which enjoys considerable media attention and widespread respectability in both intellectual and government circles is the most viable evidence of this fact.

The economic crisis has also triggered a crisis in Canadian social democracy. Because of the nature of liberal democratic societies the success of social democracy depends upon its ability to make class issues silent precisely when they are most likely to be repressed. This constraint is complicated by the role of province-building strategies as a response to marginal economic status in provinces in which social democracy has established itself as one of the competing political options. The province of Manitoba has in recent years provided an instructive forum for the expression of these forces at work in Canadian society.

The current economic crisis in Canada has had a major impact on the ideological climate in which political debate normally takes place. The most viable development has been the emergence of neo-conservatism. This dubious revival of classical free market beliefs claims to be both a diagnosis of the current state of economic ill health and a prescription of what must be done to cure it. Neo-conservative doctrines have recently enjoyed considerable publicity and even intellectual respectability, while governments at all levels have rushed to embrace neo-conservative policies.

Less visibly, but by no means less significantly, the economic decline has also triggered a crisis, both ideological and organizational, in Canadian social democracy. While unemployment mounts and social programmes are reduced, the NDP and, to some extent, the Canadian Labour Congress, seem unwilling and unable to provide an alternative programme that could mobilize working people in defence of their standard of living and, indeed, democracy itself. Since this failure goes right to the heart of Canadian capitalism and its political culture, it is worth exploring in greater detail.

The position of social democracy in a liberal democratic polity is always precarious. This state of affairs exists because of the inherent weakness of social democratic consciousness in all capitalist societies. While a social democratic party such as the NDP in Canada has potentially a numerical superiority in the electorate, conservative parties have a cultural superiority in the society. This is because the vast majority of ordinary people accept more or less uncritically capitalist principles of social and economic organization. Yet, paradoxically, a successful social democratic strategy must sensitize the population to issues of wealth and power, and therefore to issues of social and economic class. However much social democrats may obscure them, questions of class are decisive in shaping the political fortunes of social democracy: a social democratic party is more likely to be successful when class issues are salient than when they are de-emphasized.

This problem is particularly acute when social democratic parties gain office. Contrary to the impression held by many social democrats, and especially the leadership of the Canadian NDP — that political moderation is the key to electoral success — it may be that such moderation is self-defeating. Its pursuit appears to foster the decline of class as a primary political issue. In such a circumstance, where a social democratic party is in power and de-emphasizes class in favour of a strategy of technocratic management, it risks losing office to a conservative party, which by its nature benefits from the suppression of class questions. A social democratic party must constantly "show cause" why class issues should dominate in a culture in which class antagonisms are either suppressed or dismissed as spurious. In other words, a party such as the NDP must continuously seek to overcome the cultural hegemony of capitalism. The very plausibility of neo-conservatism, and not just the success of parties wedded to neo-conservative views, demonstrates the cultural barriers that confront social democracy.

Such cultural constraints define the situation of social democratic parties and movements in all democratic capitalist States. In Canada, however, these constraints are especially acute for two important reasons: 1) the pattern of highly uneven economic development that has produced regional cleavages and distinctive regional (and provincial) identities tending to complicate class issues; and 2) the existence of a fragmented, authoritarian political culture that has to a great extent succeeded in expelling explicit class questions from the realm of acceptable politics. The two factors are, of course, closely interrelated.[1] Regional underdevelopment has decisively shaped the setting in which provincial governments and movements, including social democratic ones, have operated. Irresistible pressures to facilitate higher levels of economic activity and greater opportunities have sharply limited their freedom of action. Regional political cultures have thus combined the values of the metropolitan centre, especially with respect to privatistic life-styles and consumption patterns, with those arising out of an historic legacy of regional grievances — and all framed by the limits of economies chronically prone to recession. (Chorney, 1977)

Manitoba has in recent years provided an instructive forum for expressing these forces of Canadian society. Yet it shares features of a more "advanced" formation, notably a substantial manufacturing sector and a significant, if subordinate, business class. The history of the province, and particularly the city of Winnipeg, has also exhibited an important strain of class and ethnic conflict and a significant, if lesser degree of self-conscious working-class political action. As a result of these conditions, there has emerged a relatively large and politically successful social democratic party, the Manitoba NDP, which has, since 1969, held office in the province for all but four years.

But the very circumstances that have created a strong social democratic presence have also worked to undermine its basis in Manitoba society. The ideological climate has historically reflected the bitter heritage of class tension in a marginal economy. In opposition to the norms of social democracy, the dominant class in Manitoba society has always stressed free enterprise, displaying an implacable hostility to "socialism" in any form. This class was thus particularly amenable to the growing influence of neo-conservatism in the late 1970s. Neo-conservative ideas therefore easily became dominant in the provincial Progressive Conservative party. This dominance was evident during the years of a Conservative government between 1977 and 1981.

In light of these circumstances, this essay attempts to analyze recent Manitoba political experience, including the 1981 provincial election, in order to explore the future prospects of neo-conservatism and social democracy in the province. It suggests that while neo-conservatism, *at least as it has emerged in the electoral arena*, may be limited by the currently accepted values of a liberal democracy, its ultimate fate, along with that of social democracy, remains in doubt.

And the political outcome of this contest has implications that extend beyond the borders of the province. The current political environment in Manitoba is the product of the interplay of two sets of factors. While one set is relatively more specific to Manitoba, both have significance for other liberal democratic polities. The first set of factors involves Manitoba's ongoing struggle to obtain stable economic development. In this respect, the Manitoba experience parallels that of other provinces with marginal economies, and it has provided the basis for strategies of *province-building*: the attempt, through the use of State power at the provincial level, to create and maintain locally regulated and relatively autonomous political economies. The second set of factors, which has all the more impact in

Manitoba because of the first set, involves the future size and importance of the welfare State, and the chronic, but currently very intense, opposition to it in the context of general economic decline. *This* set has wider implications for other liberal democratic polities because neo-conservative governments have made welfare State policies and institutions prime targets of attack.

The Manitoba case thus brings to light important questions that currently confront a marginal economy in a liberal democratic society during a period of general economic decline. At stake are the limits facing governments committed to province-building, the future of both social democratic and neo-conservative politics and, ultimately, the status of the welfare State itself.

This essay focuses on the relation of a system of political parties, on the one hand, to social structure and ideological climate, on the other. Political parties in a liberal democracy are the major instruments for organizing social forces in the domain of institutional politics. Given the crucial role played by the political system in maintaining the social order, parties are thus fundamental, although obviously not exclusively so, for the reproduction of social relations. Far from being merely "superstructural," they provide important clues about the quality of public life in a society and hence the possibilities for fundamental change, change that ultimately depends upon the presence — or absence — of a communal will for it.

A MARGINAL ECONOMY AND ITS POLITICAL CULTURE

The contemporary significance in Manitoba of social democratic and neo-conservative ideologies is no accident. The political culture of the province — the constellation of norms and values that orient people toward capitalism, democracy and government — has been the product of a series of traumatic historical developments. These developments shattered the original dream of the Winnipeg-based business community for imperial status in the Canadian political economy (Artibise, 1975: Part II). They also witnessed the growth of serious working-class opposition to the dominant position of private capital, an opposition culminating in the 1919 Winnipeg General Strike. The political history of Manitoba for a 50-year period following the suppression of the Strike involved a more or less successful attempt by the business community, allied with the affluent and highly conservative Anglo-Saxon agrarian community of southwestern Manitoba, to thwart the re-emergence of a class-based challenge to its dominance (Peterson, 1978).

The political culture forged under these circumstances has therefore exhibited important contradictory qualities. On the one hand the presence of working class — and ethnic class — consciousness has provided the foundations for a continuing social democratic tradition. On the other hand, that very presence has generated in the dominant class of Manitoba society a firm resolve to resist by all means necessary any challenge to their hegemony. Given the capacity of dominant classes to foster the diffusion of their norms and values throughout all areas of social life,[2] ideas that challenge the distribution of wealth and power in Manitoba society have, despite their strength, enjoyed only marginal legitimacy in the province. A "state of siege" outlook, fluctuating in visibility, has been the hallmark of Manitoba's dominant classes and the political culture as a whole.

This outlook and the class tension it has expressed have historically been reinforced by the province's position in the Canadian political economy. The failure of the Manitoba business community to achieve the pre-eminence it sought as a beneficiary of the original national policy[3] was both a basis and outcome of the provincial development as a subordinate hinterland of a maturing capitalist political economy. This process was to a considerable extent masked by the rapid growth of the provincial economy, and especially the city of Winnipeg, during the period 1880 and 1910. Such growth was the product of the exploitation of wheat as a staple and the attendant level of investment in the agricultural frontier. Its pace slackened dramatically as the "wheat economy" began to yield its dominant position as the prime engine of growth in the national economy as a whole.[4] To deal successfully with an increasingly inadequate level of capital accumulation, while at the same time maintaining social control over a restless population, became the prime political task facing the Manitoba elite.

This task and the circumstances under which it emerged decisively shaped the character and scope of the provincial State. The pressure of underdevelopment in other jurisdictions had led, or was to lead, to the increased use of the provincial State by dominant classes to foster economic activity (Armstrong and Nelles, 1973; Nelles, 1975). Such "defensive expansionism"[5] tended to develop most fully where pressures for growth coincided with the presence of the federal-provincial conflict. Ontario in the early twentieth century, and Québec and Alberta more recently, provide the clearest examples of this process in action.[6]

In Manitoba, however, the role played by the business class in the original National Policy tied that class closely to the federal government. Thus federal-provincial conflict has never been the factor in Manitoba politics that it has been elsewhere. Moreover, the very legacy of class conflict which the provincial elite sought to suppress made the expansion of the State a potentially contentious, and therefore dangerous, matter, to be avoided if possible. At the same time, the business community was able, in spite of the decline of the National Policy, to secure for itself a lucrative, if limited, position in the Canadian economy. Thus, as long as the economic surplus that still could be derived from that policy leaked in sufficient quantities to ensure that the elite could maintain its position — and there was no substantial, articulate and effective opposition from the subordinate classes in Manitoba society — the role of the provincial State could be restricted to provide a basic level of services.

The period of the limited State in Manitoba lasted almost forty years. For much of that time the province had the lowest per capita levels of both public expenditures and public debt (Chorney, 1970a: 370-378). And this restricted role for the State was matched by a withering of the political process as a whole. Between roughly 1920 and 1960, there were steady declines in the levels of electoral turnout, party competition, and political debate. From 1932 until 1953, a conservative coalition, operating under various labels, overwhelmingly dominated the provincial government and legislature; indeed from 1940 until 1942, the coalition embraced all parties, including the CCF! (Wiseman, 1973). Such political debate as did occur stressed almost exclusively the need for government to be conducted on principles of sound and frugal administration untainted by the contaminating influence of "politics." In short, the most important consequence of untrammelled conservative dominance in the political arena was a serious damage it inflicted on provincial structures of political democracy.

By the late 1950s, however, the pressures of economic stagnation finally threatened to become politically overwhelming and a different variant of the provincial State was envisaged as acceptable by a more progressive fraction of the business community.[7] In the political arena, this development culminated in the election of the "reformist" Progressive Conservative government of Duff Roblin in 1958.[8]

Of course an expanded State sector was never intended to retard class privilege, although the more reactionary members of the elite saw it in such terms.[9] The growth of the State was geared relatively more toward economic rationalization and less to an expansion of social programmes in response to the pressures of the subordinate classes.[10] This path of State activity was clearly evident in the emphasis accorded to provision of basic infrastructure, especially roads, schools, and hydro-electric installations. But it was perhaps even more clearly visible in the 1960s. Faced with chronic economic decline, the Conservatives embraced a strategy common to other marginal jurisdictions, in Canada and elsewhere: the promotion of economic growth through large-scale, government-subsidized, resource-based capital investments (Chorney, 1970a; Mathias, 1971; Glenday et al., 1978: chs. 7,9). The current flurry of interests, displayed by both federal and certain provincial governments, in so-called "mega-projects" on Canada's resource frontiers is only the most recent example of the allure this strategy holds for jurisdictions eager for growth (Doern (ed), 1982: ch. 1,4,5). In Manitoba, the Roblin government sought to entice foreign controlled capital to the resource-rich, but highly underdeveloped, northern part of the province in the hope that the ensuing development would boost the entire provincial economy.

Given Manitoba's political culture and the consequently ambiguous character of State intervention, this strategy had not simply "economic" but also ideological significance. "Mega-project" development, as pursued by the Roblin government (and, as will be seen, rediscovered years later by another Conservative ministry), represented an attempt to foster economic growth, while at the same time defusing, or at least masking, pressures for a more equal distribution of wealth and income in Manitoba society. The provision of new resource-based jobs and associated development would obviate the need to face directly the issue of inequality and its structural roots.[11]

But precisely because, in terms of both the internal distribution of income and the relation of the Manitoba economy to external forces, this strategy ignores the structural realities of a dependent capitalist economy, it is fundamentally irrational as a vehicle for economic planning. It has thus been of dubious benefit. The clearest and most notorious example was the Churchill Forest Industries debacle: the scandalous misappropriation of forty million dollars of public money committed to the construction of a one hundred million dollar pulp and paper complex in the northern Manitoba community of The Pas in the late 1960s (Chorney, 1970b; Mathias, 1971: 124-79).

In spite of its evident flaws, however, the "mega-project" strategy persisted, in the new era of State intervention, as the prime political response of the dominant business class to the pressures of underdevelopment. Hence it remained a cornerstone of government policy in the province. Its significance is thus intimately related to the emergence of recent years of what has come to be called "province-building." Manitoba has developed its own variant of province-building. The variant reveals some crucial limitations of the province-building process wherever it occurs.

The concept of "province-building" was given its most explicit formulation in a well-known and important essay by Edwin Black and Alan Cairns (1966: 27-45). The essay attempted to account for the increasing importance of provincial governments in Canadian federalism — the "defensive expansionism" noted earlier. Black and Cairns argued that business, political and bureaucratic elites, particularly those outside of Central Canada, looked to those governments as the primary vehicles for enhancing their power and influence. Decisive for this process was the failure of nationally integrated political and social structures to take root. The increasing social and economic significance of provincial legislative authority also played a key role. Both developments served to bind important provincially based interests to an expanding apparatus. The growth of provincial governments was at once the product of elite pressures and, in turn, an important influence on the growth and behaviour of the elites themselves.

The position developed by Black and Cairns is useful, in a way that more traditional legal and institutional analyses of Canadian federalism are not, in explaining the recent growth of provincial power. Especially important for the purposes of this paper is the implication that chronic economic underdevelopment is a driving force behind the growth of the provincial State. To be sure, the authors did not write from an explicitly political economy perspective.[12] Nevertheless, the argument assumed that what was actually occurring was the emergence of a new, multi-centred national policy that would compensate for the uneven development fostered by the old one. In the circumstances in which it was argued, this position was, potentially, an optimistic reading of Canadian federalism which presupposed continuous economic expansion directed from the provincial level.[13]

Needless to say, the argument of Black and Cairns was not intended to apply indiscriminately to all provinces. Nor was it meant to account for all dimensions of federal-provincial or inter-regional conflict. Thus it is a reflection of a real paradox, and not a logical contradiction, to claim that "province-building" is both a useful and, at the same time, a limited tool in exploring the dynamics of current Manitoba politics. It is precisely this paradox that highlights analyses of the problems of regional and provincial growth in a political economy characterized by structurally determined uneven development.

The notion of "province-building" can insightfully pinpoint important aspects of the role of the provincial States, and the motivations and behaviour of key economic, political, and bureaucratic actors. However it can also obscure the class nature of provincial societies and the limits to State action that this imposes. It is of course crucial to avoid reductionist explanations of the State. Yet, depending upon the array of social forces and the quality of the political culture, the meaning and character, and thus the political and ideological significance, of State activity will vary.[14] Putting it another way, province "builders" cannot create *ex nihilo* but must use the materials at hand. To the extent that province-building strategies accept as given the existing foundations of the economy and society, they suffer from a "blind spot" at their core. This blind spot relates to the fact that it is very difficult for a provincial government, relying upon an elitist strategy such as province-building, to transcend the position assigned to it by the structural division of labour in the Canadian political economy. This was precisely the problem with the Roblin government's programme in Manitoba. It is no less a problem for social democratic versions of the strategy.

Thus in a fundamental sense, the "mega-project" strategy is province-building, or at least a central element to it. That strategy will be more desperate, more delusory, more irrational to the extent that 1) the provincial economy and resource base are weak in relation to outside forces; and 2) the possibility of class questions moving to the centre of the political debate is strong. As dubious as it is, the "mega-project" strategy continued — and indeed continues — to play a significant role in Manitoba politics because it is fuelled, in the face of chronic underdevelopment, by a certain fear on the part of the dominant elite. The fear is that long suppressed class issues will return with a vengeance and, as a result, the excluded classes will ride to political power on a wave of resentment.[15]

The possibility of overtly class-based politics has of course always been close to the surface of Manitoba society. But it has become greater in the last twenty years. The fears of the reactionary elements of the provincial business community about the implications of the Roblin government's progressivism were, in a manner of speaking, wholly justified. Whatever its other limitations, the Roblin Conservatives politicized, or re-politicized, areas of social life long held to be either totally unpolitical or merely matters of simple administration. As both a correlate and a cause of this politicization the Roblin government succeeded, perhaps unwittingly, in awakening long dormant elements of the provincial electorate. Although its political vision obviously did not include the desire for fundamental social reform — and in fact it became quite conservative toward the end of its term of office — the Roblin government inaugurated a process of political "modernization" that could not be reversed.

In the electoral terms the forces set loose during the Roblin years crystallized in the 1969 election, which saw the defeat of the Conservatives (led now by Walter Weir) and the ascension to power of a minority NDP government under Ed Schreyer. This is not the place to undertake an account of the NDP or its subsequent eight years in office.[16] It is important, however, to note that the 1969 result justifies the use of the term "critical election": an election that features a fundamental alteration in the pattern of party support.[17] The Conservatives and the NDP emerged from the vote as the main contenders for office, while the liberal party, long the dominant party in the province, began its swift descent into oblivion.

It is also important to note that whatever its limitations, the NDP government in a sense completed the process of modernization launched during the Roblin years, both by explaining further the role of the State and by mobilizing the electorate along those lines. The subordinate classes decisively supported the NDP both in 1969 and again 1973, when the Schreyer government won re-election.[18]

Throughout this period, the majority of the membership of the Manitoba business community, and the entire business elite, remained utterly opposed to the new government. In its eyes, the success of the NDP was an illegitimate political aberration, the product of a peculiar configuration of political forces that in time would (hopefully) disappear.[19] The Schreyer government did lose power in 1977, but the forces that brought the NDP to prominence did note evaporate. Perhaps in recognition of the enduring social base of the NDP, the business class reached back into its historical past and, in the form of neo-conservatism, revived its traditional commitment to laissez-faire and the elimination to "politics" from government. This revival had taken root as early as 1975. It was symbolized by the replacement in that year of the moderate conservative Sterling Lyon. The stage was set for the emergence of neo-conservatism and social democracy as the key themes of party competition and political debate.

THE 1981 MANITOBA ELECTION: SOCIAL DEMOCRACY VERSUS NEO-CONSERVATISM

The 1981 provincial election saw the return of the NDP to power with 34 of the 57 seats in the Manitoba Legislative Assembly; the Conservatives captured the remaining 23 [20] (see Tables I and II). The election took place in a political and ideological climate shaped by two developments. One such development, discussed in the previous section, was the long-term transformation in the character of political debate effected by the changing balance of social and political forces in the province. The second, more immediate influence was the impact of four years in office of an avowedly neo-conservative government: the Progressive Conservative ministry of Sterling Rufus Lyon.

The conservatives had come to power in 1977 in the wake of eight years of NDP government and the consequent hostility the NDP had engendered in the business community. As a result, the party's election platform had stressed the need to reduce the size and role of the State in Manitoba society. The Conservatives believed that only private enterprise could play the leading role in generating economic growth — a "truth" that had been obscured by years of "socialist" State intervention under the

Table I
Overall Party Standings — Seats *

	1977	1981
NDP	23	34
P.C.	33	23
Progressives	—	—

*At dissolution the NDP held 20 seats, the Progressives 3 — composed of three former NDP MLAs, — the P.C. 32, with one vacant.

Table II
Overall Party Standings — Popular Vote (%)

	1977	1981
NDP	38.5 (188,124)	47.2 (228,784)
P.C.	48.6 (237,496)	43.7 (211,602)
Liberal	12.3 (59,865)	6.7 (32,373)
Progressives	—	1.8 (8,731)
Other	0.3 (1,669)	0.3 (1,402)

previous NDP government. Their main slogan during the 1977 campaign, which stressed the need to "free" Manitoba, captured perfectly their commitment to a rejuvenated private sector.

In making this appeal the conservatives could, of course, fall back on values deeply rooted in Manitoba's political culture. These values, strongly hostile to State intervention in the economy, had been the mainstay of previous conservative governments, whatever the label of the party in power. Thus with the return of the Conservative party to power in 1977, there was a general sense that the "normal" state of affairs in provincial politics had been restored.

Once in power, the Conservatives did indeed act as if they had returned Manitoba to its "proper" political path. Beginning with a highly publicized and influential task force on government reorganization, in which leading members of the business community exerted a decisive influence (Government of Manitoba, 1978), the new administration inaugurated a policy of large-scale fiscal restraint and reduction in the size and role of the government. In other words, the Lyon government provided the major testing ground for what has come to be defined as *neo-conservatism*: the "conviction that the people of Canada are better served by a greater reliance on markets rather than on politicians to solve economic and social problems" (Grubel, 1982: 58).[21] actions attempted to redeem the neo-conservative promise, as "reliance on markets" became the order of the day.

However, the performance of the Manitoba economy, and in particular its private sector, largely failed to justify the government's belief in the ability of market forces to guarantee economic prosperity for all strata of Manitoba society. This is clear from a consideration of numerous economic indicators. For example, during the Lyon government's tenure in office from 1977 to 1981, the province suffered a net inter-provincial migration population loss of 2,000 people. In per capita terms, this represented the largest population loss of any province in the country. The city of Winnipeg, for decades the fourth or fifth largest metropolitan centre in the country, dropped to seventh in the 1981 Census. The overall rate of population growth in Manitoba was the smallest in Canada during the period between 1976 and 1981. While the provincial population grew by just 0.5 percent, the population of Saskatchewan and Alberta, by contrast, grew by 5.1 percent and 21.8 percent respectively (Government of Canada, 1981). The rate of economic growth in the province also lagged significantly behind the rates of the other Prairie Provinces.[22]

To be sure, the poor performance of the Manitoba economy was clearly influenced by the decline of the Canadian economy as a whole. Nevertheless, given the commitment of the Conservatives to private economic growth, and their penchant for blaming the NDP for past economic failures, the economic record made the government substantially increase public spending during its final year in office. This increase produced the largest budgetary deficit in provincial history to that time — an irony given the government's dogmatic opposition to deficit finance.

It was with this record of performance that the Conservatives sought a renewed electoral mandate in the fall of 1981. It was this same record that induced the government to develop as the centrepiece of its election campaign its own "mega-project" strategy. While pulp and paper and fertilizer had figured prominently in the economic development plans of the Roblin and Weir governments in the 1960s, the new proposals emphasized potash and aluminum smelting. But the logic of development remained the same: foreign capital would provide the spur while the province, rich in hydroelectric power, would provide the necessary energy.

The re-emergence of the "mega-project" strategy exhibited anew the tensions of a marginal political economy with a political culture that had in the past been strongly influenced by class conflict. The policies of the Lyon government, and in particular its efforts to reduce spending on social programmes, were highly controversial. In part, this controversy was the product of the unpopularity of Premier Lyon, who had gained national attention with his frequent abrasive personality and sharply right-wing views.[23] At the same time, however, it reflected the concern among many Manitobans that the Conservatives were insensitive to, or even hostile to, the aspirations of ordinary people. During the early stages of the government's term of office there had been public demonstrations against its proposed restraint programme and its position on labour questions, in particular its tough stance toward public sector workers. These demonstrations helped set the tone for the response given to many of the government's policies throughout its tenure. Even though the government reversed course somewhat during its last two years in power and increased its spending on social programmes, it never successfully shed its reputation as an ideologically motivated defender of the interests of the affluent.

The Conservatives thus succeeded, ironically, in stirring up the very class antagonisms they had resolved to suppress in the wake of eight years of "class" government by the NDP. In these circumstances, the resuscitation of the "mega-project" strategy was clearly understandable. Like its predecessor in the 1960s, the government hoped its proposed projects would shift attention from its apparent failure to stimulate economic growth.

The class antagonisms stirred up by the Lyon government helped a more rapid revival of the opposition that might otherwise have occurred. Under Ed Schreyer the NDP had become increasingly cautious, even conservative.[24] With the defeat of the Schreyer government, the party seemed a spent force. It appeared to lack new ideas and ideological zeal, and seemed doomed to a lengthy period of exile in the political wilderness. But the actions of the Conservative government were decisive in rekindling interest in the party. This interest was reflected in large increases in both party membership and financial contributions.[25] With his appointment in 1979 as Governor General, Ed Schreyer left the provincial arena and opened the way for the selection of a new leader. Howard Pawley, an important minister in the Schreyer cabinet, who had both close ties with the NDP organizational apparatus and the respect of members from all wings of the party, was chosen for the post. Thus by the 1981 election, the NDP was organizationally stronger than it had been for a decade and was in a solid position to capitalize on the vulnerability of the Lyon government.

However, while the NDP benefitted from the renewed significance of class questions, it did little to pose election issues in explicitly class terms. This was especially true with respect to economic development. No other issue reveals so sharply the contradictory qualities of Manitoba's political culture and the ambiguous role of social democracy in the province.

Given the political implications of the "mega-project" strategy, and hence province-building, in Manitoba, it is crucial to distinguish the Manitoba experience from the experience of the other provinces. For example, it differs from the more activist, if in their own way equally flawed, State programmes undertaken by the NDP in Saskatchewan, or even the Conservatives in Alberta. In formal terms, to be sure, the model of resource development used by the NDP in Saskatchewan before their electoral defeat in April 1982 was at the centre of the Manitoba NDP election platform. During the campaign the NDP stressed the need for a renewed public sector commitment to resource development. It advocated public-private joint ventures comparable to those mounted by Saskatchewan Oil and Gas Corporation. Indeed, the NDP promised to establish in Manitoba a similar company — Manoil — to explore and develop the limited oil reserves in the western part of the province. The party also strongly criticized the governing Conservatives who, it claimed, were "ready to adopt a 'do nothing' approach and wait for big companies to come in rather than seek joint ventures which [would] benefit Manitobans. They [had] no confidence in public investment."[26] In a like manner, the NDP attacked the Conservative "mega-project" strategy for its reliance on foreign capital and its apparent willingness to grant overly generous financial concessions to multi-national enterprises.[27]

But while the NDP rejected the Conservative strategy, it also made it clear that it would not follow radical paths of nationalization or of large-scale public spending. Extremely conscious of critics of the Schreyer government for its use of public funds to prop up marginal enterprises, Howard Pawley himself described the party's position on economic development as "cautious" relying less on large investments of public funds and more on the expertise and contacts of private companies working in concert with government.[28]

Thus at the centre of the NDP campaign appeal was a promise to reverse the economic decline that had occurred during the Lyon years. The

NDP hoped to fulfil this aim by building a more stable employment base and, hence, a larger surplus as a source of government revenue. Such additional revenue could then support new social programmes. In this sense the NDP position did not differ drastically from that of the Conservatives, who stressed that "mega-projects" would make possible a stronger economy. This would, in turn, broaden the tax base and increase the funds available for social services.

The apparent convergence of the two parties on questions of economic strategy is significant. What it reveals is the complex network of constraints that shapes the response of the party system to demands of economic development in a marginal province. Political culture is the vehicle which mediates perceptions of the issues at stake and the political-economic options available to deal with them. All too often political culture is the missing link in any coherent theory of economic development policy in a marginal jurisdiction. The institutional constraints on such development do not exist in isolation from the norms and values at the heart of public life in society. The "subjective" perceptions of the members of society form an integral element of its "objective" structures.

The issue of convergence in a party system in a liberal democracy and its relation to the political culture will be taken up again in the concluding section of the paper. Suffice it to say it is no accident that the PC party and the NDP have converged on certain questions of economic strategy, whatever ideological differences may exist between them: the pressures for convergence become more pronounced when class questions are relatively submerged. These pressures arise because the very threat of a class politics calls forth a response from the conservative forces in society. Such forces have considerable political, cultural, and economic resources at their disposal, particularly in a marginal political economy. Their deployment tends to impose political and economic orthodoxy on a social democratic government. *The character of any social democratic administration therefore depends, in the final analysis, on how thoroughly it comprehends the limits it faces and how imaginatively it challenges them.*

The paradox of convergence points to the ambiguous status of progressive class consciousness in a society without a mass will for fundamental change. In the absence of a mass base committed to change, the likelihood that a social democratic party will press forward with substantially different policies is reduced. This is particularly so when it encounters implacable opposition of the type that occurs in a polarized polity with a marginal economy. Under such circumstances, the unwillingness of social democratic leaders to advance radical proposals comes as no surprise. And its unwillingness to pursue new directions seems matched by its unwillingness to cultivate the mass support that would make that pursuit more possible.

Certainly in the context of the 1981 election in Manitoba, class issues did loom large. This is evident form a number of factors, but two seem particularly noteworthy: the collapse of the Liberal party and the regional polarization of the electorate.

The decline of the Liberal party in Manitoba reflects at the electoral level the historical changes in the political profile of the province (see Table III). Over the past fifteen years, the Liberals have suffered a massive erosion in their level of support that is startling in a party system as traditionally stable as that of Manitoba. For decades the party represented the once overwhelmingly dominant rural conservative ethos of the province. It failed, however, to adjust to the changing requirements of the Manitoba economy and the increasing political importance of the city of Winnipeg. As its position steadily worsened, the party wavered from a renewed commitment to its traditional conservatism to an attempt to construct a more contemporary urban liberal appeal.[29] Neither strategy worked. The Liberals rapidly yielded their former rural and south Winnipeg bases to the Conservatives, while failing to present a serious challenge to the NDP in the rest of the city.

By the 1981 campaign, the party's situation had become so desperate that it was able to contest just 39 of the 57 constituencies in the province. Its leader, Douglas Lauchlan, was a political unknown who had just returned to Winnipeg after many years in Calgary. Indeed, when chosen leader in November, 1980, he had not resided for a sufficient period of time in his constituency to be eligible for candidacy in an election (Bar-

Table III
Party Support Manitoba General Elections 1949-1981 (%)

	NDP/CCF*	*P.C	Liberal* Lib/Progressive	Others	Voter Turnout
1949	25.5	19.1	45.2	8.9	54.0
1953	16.2	20.6	43.1	18.0++	60.4
1958	20.0	40.6	34.7	3.9	61.0
1959	21.9	46.3	30.1	1.0	65.6
1962	15.2	44.7	36.1	3.1	61.0
1966	23.0	39.8	32.9	3.7	64.3
1969	38.1	35.4	23.9	2.2	64.4
1973	42.1	36.5	18.9	2.0	78.3
1977	38.5	48.6	12.3	0.3	75.6
1981	47.2	43.7	6.7	2.1	72.4

Source: *Report of the Chief Electoral Officer, Statement of Votes* Thirty-second General Election, 17 November 1981.
* The CCF changed to the NDP in 1961
** The Liberal-Progressive party changed to the Liberal party in 1961.
++ The larger percentage of the vote going to other parties in 1953 was due to the substantial support (13.1%) received by the Social Credit Party.

ber and Wiseman, 1981). The Liberals were never factors in the campaign and on election day failed to elect a single candidate. It is clear that the party may soon be simply a footnote to Manitoba's contemporary political history.[30]

More importantly, the collapse of the Liberals confirmed the full emergence in Manitoba of a two-party system. (The Thirty-Second Manitoba Legislature is the first since 1914 with representation from just two parties). Two-party systems tend to be the norm in liberal democratic polities. However, the character of that arrangement can and does vary. The social forces at work will gain expression in different ways depending upon the depth and endurance of the divisions between them. The party systems in all liberal democracies must manage the class relations endemic to capitalist societies. But this can be done through either of two methods. On the one hand, competing parties, although not themselves organized explicitly as class instruments, may draw support from class organizations, while continuing to act as brokerage parties (the American way). On the other hand, parties may serve as explicit class vehicles and campaign accordingly (the European model).[31] In Canada, party systems have displayed elements of both variants. In Manitoba, the system more closely approximates the European model than do the two-party arrangements common, for example, in the Maritime provinces. This indicates the relatively explicit role that class differences have played in the political life of the province.

The importance of class questions, and hence the conflict between neo-conservatism and social democracy, is also evident in the peculiar regional distribution of the vote in the 1981 election. As was noted earlier, Manitoba politics have been shaped by an economic and ethnic division between a prosperous, largely Anglo-Saxon business and agrarian community, and a more marginal agrarian and ethnically diverse urban working class. To a remarkable extent, this division is geopolitical as well as social. While the dominant classes are centred in affluent south Winnipeg ad the highly fertile southwestern region of Manitoba, members of the subordinate classes tend to be located in north Winnipeg and the much less fertile agrarian regions to the north and east of the city (Peterson, 1978; Wiseman, 1983). Under the circumstances it might be expected that the relative electoral strength of the Conservative party and the NDP would display a similar regional character — all the more so in the absence of a strong third party capable of winning votes from both major ones.

To a large degree the vote in the 1981 election was highly polarized along these regional, and thus class, lines. Given the regional concentration of the vote for the Conservatives and the NDP and the increased electoral importance of the city of Winnipeg,[32] it is clear that the NDP is now solidly entrenched as a major party. For their part, the Conservatives, even in defeat, managed to obtain almost 44 percent of the popular vote, a clear sign of the basic electoral strength and their roots in areas traditionally sympathetic to the political right.

The regional distribution of voter support in Manitoba has important implications for the pattern of party competition. One apparent conclusion is that, because of the distribution of its support, the Conservative party, to win office, must garner a significantly larger percentage of the popular vote than does the NDP. On the other hand, the NDP could, because of the more "efficient" distribution of its vote, particularly in urban areas, win a sufficient number of seats to govern even with an extremely narrow plurality of the popular vote. This tendency is strengthened by the current and possibly permanent absence of a strong third party in Manitoba politics.

There is considerable irony in this state of affairs. Since the first NDP electoral victory in 1969, some observers have believed that the party can win office only if two "free enterprise" parties split the opposition vote. It was just such a belief that lay behind the attempt to forge a right-wing coalition of Liberals and Conservatives in the 1973 election.[33] However, the apparent disappearance of the Liberal party in urban areas seems to have been accompanied by enhanced support for the NDP. Thus it appears that the Conservatives are more likely to win office if two (or more) parties split the centre-left vote.[34]

Less obviously, but more importantly, the vote in the 1981 election demonstrated a sharper degree of regional polarization than had been the case in 1977.[35] In large measure this resulted from the fact that the Liberal vote, or what was left of it, had by 1981 become almost totally concentrated in the city of Winnipeg. But much of the difference resulted from the greater concentration of the Conservative vote in those areas in which the party has historically been strong. This concentration outweighed the impact of the more evenly distributed support enjoyed by the NDP. Such a circumstance suggests a plausible hypothesis about party competition in Manitoba: *when the Conservatives are victorious in an election, and their chief rival is the NDP, the degree of political polarization along regional, and therefore class or ethnic, lines is smaller than is the case when the NDP is victorious and its chief rival is the Conservative party.* This would seem to come about because the relative increase in polarization for the PC when it loses, compared to the relative decrease in polarization for the NDP when it wins, is significantly greater. Thus it is plausible to argue that the NDP comes to power when class-based issues and/or ideological differences loom large in the society. Under such circumstances its vote appears to be less polarized because, given its character as a social democratic party, it can appeal to a larger proportion of the population. During the Lyon years, the neo-conservative quality of his government in effect polarized the electorate.

Conversely, the Conservatives win office when class issues lose some of their salience. This was conceivably the case during the final years of the NDP government of Ed Schreyer. As suggested above, Schreyer moved the party in a politically moderate direction in a manner that tended to dilute class questions. It is for this reason that political moderation, when pursued by the NDP, may well be self-defeating. And it is for this reason that it is possible to identify as an ongoing source of tension in liberal democratic political systems the potential numerical superiority of conservative ideas and political parties in the society. Given the political culture and history of Manitoba, this tension seems specially acute in that province.

The nature of the political culture, the pattern of party competition and the tension at work in the political order suggest broader theoretical issues at stake in the current debate between social democracy and neo-conservatism. Such issues provide the focus for the final section of this paper.

THE PRESENT AND THE FUTURE OF NEO-CONSERVATISM AND SOCIAL DEMOCRACY

This essay has been based on the assumption that it is possible to interpret the quality of public life — the interplay of polity and economy — in a capitalist society through an examination of its system of political parties and elections. It is nevertheless true that any attempt to relate the character of party politics and election outcomes to the broader array of forces at work in a liberal democratic polity faces serious problems. In the first place, election outcomes themselves are, as isolated political events, the products of individual vote responses. Hence, they turn in the first instance on factors affecting individual choice that cannot readily be linked to determinants of the political system as a whole. In other words there is in the polity, as in the economy, both a "micro" and a "macro" dimension. The problem of theoretically relating the two dimensions is the same for both economics and political science: the simple aggregation of individual choices does not necessarily result in a coherent macro theory of choice consistent with broad trends in the culture of the society.[36]

This difficulty is compounded by a further one. The relation between party system and the ideological alternatives that take root in a political culture is highly complex. It cannot easily be assumed that a specific party will bear in a pure form all the elements of the ideology from which it derives its name. As Gille Bourque has pointed out, "[a] party undertakes not only promotion of specific multiple and heterogeneous interests, but also the reproduction of the totality of the social formation" (1979: 130).

Under certain circumstances, however, it may be possible to identify a party more closely with its companion ideology than might otherwise be the case, and electors may well respond to specific ideological cues and symbols. Such a process seems to have been at work in the 1981 election in Manitoba. In this case an assessment of party fortunes, on the one hand, and the status of ideological alternatives, on the other, may come together.

Hence it is possible, in spite of these problems, to make some theoretically relevant observations about the Manitoba situation. These observations point to more general structural questions that have recently emerged both in Manitoba and in other governments. The most obvious point about the 1981 election, for example, was that it provided a clear test of a provincial government that had been committed to the principle of neo-conservatism. Throughout its term in office, the Lyon government considered itself representative of a new conservative force in Canadian politics. Its defeat could thus be seen as the electoral failure of neo-conservatism in Manitoba.

Such a consideration would be too hasty. What is further required to make sense of the Manitoba experience is a more broadly defined and if necessary, speculative, theoretical framework. Only with such a framework is it possible to "read" fully the implications of electoral politics for the character of the social and political order. At stake are the future prospects of social democracy, as represented by the NDP, and neo-conservatism, as embodied in the Progressive Conservative party.

As was suggested above, in a capitalist society characterized by class differentials in wealth and power, social democracy — the attempt to eliminate, or at least sharply reduce, the inequalities of capitalism through major structural reforms in the economy and society — has a contradictory status. On the one hand, it has potentially deep social roots because it attempts to address the needs of the non-propertied classes which comprise the larger majority of the population. On the other hand, in spite of its potential numerical strength, social democracy had, given the cultural realities of capitalism, a much more precarious basis of electoral support. Put in this way, the ambiguous position of social democracy reflects the apparent success of liberal democratic political systems in reconciling, or more properly masking, the inherent contradiction between liberalism *qua* capitalism and democracy, a contradiction that both nineteenth-century socialists and liberals believed irreconcilable (Macpherson, 1977: Chs. 1-3).

Of specific concern here is the significance of patterns of electoral competition for the definition and apparent resolution of this problem. In liberal democratic political systems, election campaigns are conducted in the context of a certain quality of political discourse. In a typical campaign various symbols, personalities and emotion-laden issues define the texture of the debate. This texture is not an unchanging given, but can be transformed over time as certain symbols are energized while others pass into obscurity.[37] However, the relation between the energized and exhausted symbols is not itself permanent. Symbols once believed moribund can, under certain historical circumstances, be recruited and pressed into service in the political arena. Neo-conservatism represents a clear example of an attempt to rescue (apparently) exhausted political symbols, norms and values (e.g., the free enterprise value of "rugged individualism") from the mists of nostalgia for a bygone era (i.e., that which prevailed in North American capitalism at the turn of the century).[38]

This born-again conservatism has emerged, however, in an historical setting very different from the "Gilded Age" of American politics. In societies in which social democratic politics has had some measure of success, either through the direct participation of a social democratic party in the exercise of power, or because of the demands of modern State capitalism, political debate takes place upon a foundation which American political scientist Ira Katznelson has defined as a social democratic minimum. This minimum comprises "state policies...required to ensure the accumulation process [i.e. the maintenance of capitalist economic growth] and to give it broad social acceptance" (1978:86). The character of social democratic policies is related directly to the needs of the State in advanced capitalist society. A social democratic minimum is thus the product of both political pressure from non-propertied classes and the need for a certain measure of rational planning in the service of capital accumulation.

Given its two-fold character, the idea of a social democratic minimum allows Katznelson to distinguish between social democratic movements or parties, and social democratic policies. Such a distinction roughly parallels the tension between the precarious electoral position of social democracy and its potentially deep and permanent roots in an unequal society. For this reason, the concept of a social democratic minimum provides a useful analytic tool in an account of the micro and macro political issues posed by the Manitoba experience.

A social democratic minimum, whatever its specific content in different social settings, involves the extent to which the three main elements of what Katznelson calls the social democratic programme are realized. These elements are "the extension of state planning mechanisms to interject social, as opposed to market, priorities in the capitalist accumulation process; the expansion of government programmes of service, social insurance, and other transfers (usually called the welfare state) to reshape and compensate for allocations of the market; and the use of macro-economic policy to minimize unemployment rather than inflation" (1978: 78). The significance of this perspective on social democracy is clear, given that neo-conservative ideology explicitly challenges all three elements of the programme. In fact, the Lyon government in Manitoba launched an onslaught on each of these areas in 1977.

In electoral terms, a social democratic minimum represents the conversion of formerly divisive political issues into matters of purely "technical" concern. These matters are generally accepted as "given" by all major political actors. Under "normal" circumstances, parties may differ in the emphasis each gives to this or that element of the technical problem. The broad consensus remains untouched.

However, the nature of a social democratic minimum, and especially the extent to which it remains consensually established, depends for Katznelson upon another process of political development in liberal democratic States. Under certain conditions, social democratic reforms may be moved forward more rapidly, to a point well beyond that normally associated with the mere "solution" of technical difficulties. In such circumstances it is possible to speak of a social democratic surplus (Katznelson, 1978: 78).

Thus, the "level of social democracy in a given moment is the sum of the reproduction minimum about which there is broad communal consensus, and the results of current contentious, factional group and class conflicts." (Katznelson, 1978:87). Normally, conservative parties of the right and centre (and this would include parties such as the Canadian federal liberal parties) attempt to check the growth of a social democratic surplus, while leaving the minimum virtually untouched. Neo-conservatism, however, represents an attempt not just to check the growth of the surplus, but also to roll back the level of a minimum itself. The simple prevention of the erosion of the social democratic minimum does not, therefore, by itself signify the eclipse of neo-conservatism and the triumph of social democracy. Genuinely social democratic governments cannot simply be managers of a social democratic minimum. They must seek to expand that minimum by entering the more contentious area of the social democratic surplus. Otherwise they are doomed to become conservatized through the exercise of power and, ultimately, to suffer electoral defeat. As suggested above, it is possible to view the defeat in Manitoba of the NDP government of Ed Schreyer in 1977 in precisely these terms. The key to electoral success for the NDP lies in a continuous effort, through the pursuit of a social democratic surplus, to maintain class inequalities as salient issues in political life.

Similarly, the rise to power of the Lyon government represented a successful electoral challenge to the social democratic minimum by the forces of a renascent free enterprise ideology. The defeat of this government, while apparently representing the defeat of neo-conservatism, still leaves open the question whether the social democratic minimum so defined in Manitoba will only be restored to its previous historical level, or will be moved to a new plateau under the Pawley government. Should the government fail to seek an expansion of the social democratic minimum via the pursuit of a social democratic surplus, it is likely to suffer the fate of the Schreyer ministry.

Hence the importance of the concept of "province-building" and the problem of applying it to Manitoba. The apparent convergence of both the NDP and the Conservatives on matters of economic development policy, notwithstanding their respective campaign appeals, reflects the imperatives of the Manitoba economy and their effect on both the character of political discourse and the level of the social democratic minimum. To be sure, this convergence should not obscure the real differences between the strategies of the two parties and the sectors of the public which would benefit from their implementation. This is what gives plausibility to those very ideological differences, even given the convergence. Nevertheless, it is still possible to see in both parties similar province-building aspirations.

But as has already been suggested, the province-building model does not apply totally to Manitoba. Attempts by province-building political and bureaucratic actors have always in the final analysis been constrained by the economic realities of Manitoba society. These constraints may well prevent the forces of social democracy in Manitoba from undertaking too thorough going a form of State intervention. The Saskatchewan model of social democracy may thus be irrelevant for Manitoba because the provincial economy and its resources base cannot generate the requisite level of surplus. Because a much larger share of the Manitoba economy is given over to manufacturing than in Saskatchewan,[39] State intervention has much more confining ideological boundaries. While intervention in the resource sector is acceptable as an element of the social democratic minimum, State involvement in manufacturing, except under conditions of perceived crisis, would fall under the rubric of the social democratic surplus. As such, it would be met with much fiercer political opposition.

It is somewhat ironic that the cautious, bureaucratic Saskatchewan-style approach should be adopted by the NDP in Manitoba and defended as the only plausible version of a social democratic economic strategy. Manitoba's marginal economic status may well require more strongly interventionist policies, precisely because the province, in a political system in which natural resources are provincial assets, does not possess an economy as resource-specialized as that of Saskatchewan. It is a geophysical accident that the resources in which Manitoba does specialize — hydro-electric power and nickel, for example — are either not in sufficient demand currently or not sufficiently concentrated in Manitoba for the economic rents flowing from them to be large enough to generate extensive economic activity.[40]

The defeat of the Conservative government in the end obscured what remains a fundamental truth about Manitoba politics: that both neo-conservatism and social democracy have a permanent, if ambiguous, presence in the province's political culture. Their precise future must await the unfolding of current events. To the extent that other jurisdictions in Canada share the structural features of the Manitoba polity and economy, they too face similarly uncertain features. In the end, no social democratic party can presume to sustain itself in power simply by virtue of its claim to being a more efficient manager of the political economy. The threat of its displacement from power by a neo-conservative party is very real. This argument is all the more true for a marginal political economy such as that of Manitoba.

APPENDIX

BREAKDOWN OF THE VOTE BY REGION AND PARTY, 1981

Manitoba Provincial Election

Tables IV and V break down the results of the 1981 election on a regional basis. The regions chosen are traditionally used in Manitoba politics and are distinguished by both class and ethnic divisions. Table IV presents party support as a percentage of the total popular vote in each region. It also includes statistics borrowed from regional economics: the location quotient and the coefficient of localization. The location quotient is a measure of the concentration of voter support on a regional basis. The coefficient of localization is a measure of the degree of dispersion or concentration of the vote for the parties as a whole, as well as for the electoral system as a whole. In general, it is a useful proxy for measuring the degree of political polarization, in this case along regional lines, of the electoral system. Given the fact that in Manitoba there is a correspondence between regional division, on the one hand, and ethnic and class divisions, on the other, this coefficient is useful for approximating the extent of polarization along class and ethnic lines as well.

Table IV demonstrates, for example, that the NDP has location quotients greater than one in Winnipeg North, Winnipeg Centre, Northern Manitoba and Central Manitoba for both 1977 and 1981. Location quotients greater than one indicate that the vote of the party is over-represented in the particular region as compared to the importance of that region in the overall vote. Interestingly, the location quotients of the NDP increased from the 1977 election to the 1981 election in Northern Manitoba, but decreased in Winnipeg North and Central Manitoba, while remaining virtually unchanged in Winnipeg Centre. The NDP has location quotients smaller than one in Winnipeg Southwest, Manitoba Southwest and, in the 1981 results, in Manitoba Southeast. Location quotients less than one indicate that the vote of that party is under-represented in the particular region as compared to the importance of the region in the overall vote. The location quotient for the NDP is equal to one — indicating a level of support exactly equal to the importance of the region in the overall vote — in Southeastern Manitoba in 1977. These location quotients reflect what is already known about the nature of the regional concentration of support for the NDP. The changes in the values of the quotients from the 1977 to the 1981 election suggest that the NDP became a relatively more broadly based party in the 1981 election. This is confirmed when the coefficients of localization for the NDP in both elections are compared. The value of this coefficient for 1977 is .130, while for 1981 it is .115. A smaller coefficient value indicated a more even regional distribution of the vote. This outcome is in fact, what one would expect given the NDP election victory. While all political parties have a certain concentrated base of voter support, a victorious party must broaden that base and penetrate marginal areas of support in order to win power.

By contrast, the Progressive Conservative party displays location quotients greater than one in Winnipeg South/West, Central Manitoba, Southeastern Manitoba and Southwestern Manitoba in both 1977 and 1981. Its location quotients increased in all of these areas. On the other hand, the Conservatives displayed location quotients of less than one in Winnipeg North, Winnipeg Centre and Northern Manitoba. These values all decreased from 1977 to 1981. Such results suggest that the Conservative party vote became more regionally polarized in the 1981 election as compared to the 1977 results. This impression is confirmed by a comparison of the coefficient of localization for the Conservative party for the 1977 election with the coefficient for the 1981 contest, which demonstrates a significantly greater polarization of Conservative support.

The Liberal party presented a difficult methodological problem because the Liberal contested only 39 seats. In the absence of a procedure for normalizing, the Liberal party results were normalized. They are detailed in Table IV. In general, they indicate that the liberal vote has become heavily concentrated in the city of Winnipeg. This concentration increased dramatically from 1977 to 1981 and is reflected in the large increase in the coefficient of localization for the party during those years.

Table IV
Party Support 1977 and 1981: Percentage of Popular Vote
Location Quotient and Coefficient of Localization

	1977		1981			1977		1981	
Winnipeg	%	L.Q.	%	L.Q.	Non-Winnipeg	%	L.Q.	%	L.Q.
North					Northern Manitoba				
PC	39	.77	29	.67	PC	42	.85	29	.66
NDP	53	1.36	62	1.30	NDP	48	1.17	62	1.32
LIB	8	.63	4	.56	LIB	11	.83	7	1.02
PROG	—	—	4	—	PROG	—	—	1	—
Centre					Central Manitoba				
PC	36	.79	31	.71	PC	49	1.01	45	1.04
NDP	43	1.14	54	1.15	NDP	44	1.14	50	1.06
LIB	21	1.15	13	1.93	LIB	7	.85	3	.73
PROG	—	—	2	—	PROG	—	—	1	—
South/West					Southwest Manitoba				
PC	60	1.20	54	1.24	PC	59	1.22	60	1.38
NDP	25	.65	34	.73	NDP	28	.72	33	.71
LIB	15	1.18	10	1.25	LIB	12	.99	5	1.18
PROG	—	—	1	—	PROG	—	—	1	—
Winnipeg					Southeast Winnipeg				
PC	46	.93	39	.87	PC	52	1.07	49	1.13
NDP	40	1.04	49	1.05	NDP	38	1.00	46	.96
LIB	14	1.08	9	1.08	LIB	10	.79	2	.41
PROG	—	—	2	—	PROG	—	—	3	—
Coefficient of Localization					PC	.090		.130	
					NDP	.130		.115	
					LIB	.134		.193	
(aggregate)Coefficient of Localization						.354		.438	

* The format of this table was adapted (with modifications) from J. Wilson, "The Decline of the Liberal party in Manitoba Politics," Journal of Canadian Studies 10 (1) (February 1975): pp. 24-41.

Table V
Party Vote — Winnipeg/Non-Winnipeg
as % of (aggregate) Party Vote

Winnipeg	1977	1981
PC	53	51
NDP	58	60
LIB	60	72
PROG	—	73
Winnipeg vote as % of (aggregate) Manitoba Vote	56	57
Non-Winnipeg	1977	1981
PC	47	49
NDP	42	40
LIB	40	28
PROG	—	27
Non-Winnipeg Vote as % of (aggregate) Manitoba Vote	44	43

NOTES

1. For an excellent series of essays that deals to a large extent with the relation of political culture to uneven development, see R.J. Brym and R.J. Sacoumen (eds.), *Underdevelopment and Social Movements in Atlantic Canada* (Toronto, 1979).
2. A cogent treatment of this capacity of the dominant class, undertaken in the context of Antonio Gramsci's notion of hegemony, is R.Williams, *Marxism and Literature* (Oxford, 1977), Part II.
3. For a good summary of the various implications of the idea of national policy for the Canadian political economy, see D. Smiley, "Canada and the Quest for a National Policy," *Canadian Journal of Political Science* Vol. VIII, No.1 (March, 1975), pp. 40-62.
4. The classic treatment of the "wheat economy" is of course F. Fowke, *The National Policy and the Wheat Economy* (Toronto, 1957). For an assessment of Fowke's work as a whole in the context of metropole-hinterland relations, see P. Phillips, *The Hinterland Perspective: The Political Economy of Vernon C. Fowke, Canadian Journal of Political and Social Theory*. Vol. 2, No.2 (Spring-Summer, 1978), pp. 73-96.
5. The idea of "defensive expansionism" was developed in a famous article by Hugh Aitken. It was intended to explain the response of the Canadian State as a whole, and especially the federal government, to the threat posed to Canadian political sovereignty by the aggressively expansionist American economy. Its application in this paper to provincial governments considered separately from the federal government seems to be consistent with Aitken's theoretical position. See H. Aitken, *Defensive Expansionism: the State and Economic Growth in Canada*, in W. T. Eastbrook and W.H. Watkins (eds.), *Approaches to Canadian Economic History*. (Toronto, 1967), pp. 183-221.

6. For Ontario, see C. Armstrong, *The Politics of Federalism: Ontario's Relations with the Federal Government, 1867-1942*. (Toronto, 1981). For Québec, see, for example, K. McRoberts and D. Postgate, *Québec: Social Change and Political Crisis* (2nd ed.) (Toronto, 1980); esp. Chs.6-9. Alberta is treated in C.B. McPherson, *Democracy in Alberta* (2nd ed.) (Toronto, 1962) and L. Pratt and J. Richards, *Prairie Capitalism*. (Toronto, 1979).
7. See A. Finkel, *Business and Social Reform in the Thirties* (Toronto, 1979) for an account of the effect of such pressures on the federal government during the Great Depression. At the same time, the fear of a serious working-class challenge to the dominant position of private capital was very real and the movement for social "reform" was in part a response to this perceived threat. However, economic rationalization on behalf of the dominant elements of the Canadian business community seems to have played an ever larger role than that played by working-class pressure.
8. The drive for increased participation in the Manitoba economy came from that element of the provincial business community which was entrepreneurial in orientation, relatively small in scale (albeit of sufficient size to be a substantial employer of wage labour) but interested in expansion, and geared to the domestic market. Given its particular qualities, this element had relatively more tenuous links to the national policy than had the older, dominant elite which had historically been aligned with the Liberal party. The push for an expansion of the State also developed in the context of an international environment in which economic growth was considered crucial in the Cold War struggle with the Soviet Union, whose successful space programme had been viewed as a humiliating setback for the United States.

    Much research remains to be done to establish the concrete links between fractions of the business community in Manitoba and the revived Conservative party under Duff Roblin. For some general observations on this issue, see H. Chorney, *The Political Economy of Provincial Economic Development Policy 1950-1970*, (unpublished M.A. thesis, University of Manitoba, 1970), ch.2.
9. During the 1966 provincial election campaign, several cabinet ministers from the old Liberal-Progressive government of the 1950s strongly criticized the Roblin government for its "socialist" direction (see Ibid., p.49).
10. In neo-Marxian terms: the accumulation function of the State took precedence over the legitimation function. The classic exposition of these categories is J. O'Connor, *The Fiscal Crisis of the State*. (New York, 1973).
11. The Roblin government's source of development programme for the North was conceived as a major source of new employment, especially for native people. The largest single project, the Churchill Forest Industries development, was lauded by the provincial Minister of Welfare as the "key which [might] unlock the door to the twentieth century for a large segment of the province's Indian and Métis citizens.

    Winnipeg Free Press, 9 March, 1966; cited in Chorney 1970a: p. 113. For a good overview of the history of resource-based development strategy in Manitoba, see A. Netherton, *The Opportunities and Limitation of a Hydro Development Strategy: The case of Manitoba 1960-1980*, paper presented to the annual meeting of the Canadian Political Science Association, U.B.C., June, 1968. See also J.Silver & J.Hull eds.*The Political Economy of Manitoba*, Regina: Canadian Plains Research Centre, 1990.
12. The specifically political implications of the Black and Cairns analysis were drawn out more fully by Cairns in an essay published a decade after the appearance of the original argument. This essay demonstrates the analytical problems arising from both an over-emphasis on the institutions of government and too great a reliance on an elite-based account of political change — two significant, if unexamined, elements of the original paper. See Cairns, "The Governments and Societies of Canadian Federalism," *Canadian Journal of Political Science*. X:4 (December, 1977), pp. 695-725.
13. Pratt and Richards explore this potential in their treatment of the development strategies of the provinces of Saskatchewan and Alberta in their important work, *Prairie Capitalism*.
14. Cf. R. Whitaker, "Images of the State in Canada," in Leo Panitch (ed.) *The Canadian State: Political Economy and Political Power*. (Toronto, 1977), pp. 28-68.

15. In an interview as recently as 1978, then Conservative Premier Sterling Lyon, the political voice of the "new right" in the province, assailed the NDP — and by implication any left-wing party — for what he saw as its commitment to "class warfare." He believed this commitment to be "really divisive," with "no place in modern society." *Winnipeg Tribune*, 29 December, 1978.
16. For an account of this period, see Wiseman, *Social Democracy in Manitoba*. (Winnipeg, 1983).
17. The concept of a "critical election" was first advanced by the American political scientist, V.O. Key Jr. See his *A Theory of Critical Elections, Journal of Politics*. 17(1955). For an application of the concept to federal elections in Canada, see D.E. Blake, *1986 and All That: Critical Elections in Canada, Canadian Journal of Political Science*. XII: 2 (June, 1979), pp. 259-79.
18. Provincial voters turnout, which in 1949 had been only 54.0 percent of the eligible electorate, had increased by 1969 to 64.4 percent. In 1973, when the Schreyer government stood for re-election, the turnout increased dramatically to 78.3 percent. It has remained well over 70 percent since then. These increases appear to have occurred disproportionately in less affluent constituencies. See Report of the Chief Electoral Officer, *Statement of Votes* Thirty-Second General Election, 17 November, 1981, pp. 10, 21ff.
19. Cf. Chorney and P. Hansen, *Manitoba: The Shape of Things to Come?* (unpublished paper, April, 1978). A version of this argument was published in a somewhat different form in *This Magazine*. Vol.12, No.3 (July-August, 1978), pp. 28-34.
20. The NDP caucus subsequently lost a sitting member, who left to serve as an independent.
21. Grubel argues further that "many of the policies initiated in an attempt to eliminate undesirable consequences of free markets have themselves resulted in costs that are greater than those they were supposed to eliminate.. [T]he very nature of the political and bureaucratic process must always produce unexpected costs" (p. 58).
22. For example, personal income increased in Manitoba by 7.9 percent in 1979 and 9.1 percent in 1980 (versus 11.0 percent and 11.3 percent in Saskatchewan and 18.2 percent and 16.0 percent in Alberta). In each year the Manitoba increase was significantly below the national average increase. For these and other indices of Manitoba's economic performance, see Canada, Department of Finance, *Economic Review*, April 1981, esp. pp. 54, 124ff.; *Economic Review*, April, 1982 esp.. pp. 67-8; 13ff.
23. Premier Lyon's assault on what he saw as the "socialist menace" of the NDP became during his term in office a central feature of the Manitoba political vocabulary. In particular, he believed that what he called "secular humanist government," including of course socialist government, had usurped the proper role of religion, with baleful moral consequences: "To be a committed Marxist, for example, I don't think a committed Marxist can be a Christian. Marxism has to the anti-Christ." *Winnipeg Tribune*, December 29, 1978).

This capacity for ideological purity and rhetorical zeal was clearly demonstrated during the 1981 election campaign. At one point Lyon labelled the NDP and the newly created Progressive party, led by a former NDP cabinet minister, "the two socialist parties," whose presence was "sort of like having a case of double pneumonia." In the same speech, the Premier referred derisively to the policy of the former NDP government of employing Soviet-built turbines in a northern Manitoba hydro project as an example of the New Democrats' "sordid history," with "their Russian engineers up there…Crawling all over the turbines like a bunch of monkeys trying to make them work." Lyon concluded that, as result of the "sordid" past, the "same socialists who got their behinds whacked with leather by the people of Manitoba are going to get them whacked again" (Winnipeg Free Press, 13 November, 1981).

The Premier's strong hostility to an entrenched charter of rights in the new Canadian constitution brought him and his views to national attention during the constitutional negotiations of 1980 and 1981.
24. James McAllister has argued that, during the NDP's years in office between 1969 and 1977 on the basis of public revenue and expenditure trends, there was little evidence

of a policy direction significantly different from that of other provinces with non-social democratic governments - or even the NDP's Conservative predecessor in Manitoba. McAllister goes on to suggest certain political-economic constraints that tend to restrict the options available to social democrats in office provincially, including the structure of the Canadian federal system and the reliance on foreign capital markets for government borrowings. J. Mcallister, "The Fiscal Analysis of Policy Outputs," *Canadian Public Administration* Vol. 23, No.3 (Fall, 1981), pp. 458-86.
25. On the basis of available evidence, the NDP had on the eve of the 1981 election 23,000 paid up members.
26. See *Winnipeg Free Press*, 30 October, 1981.
27. Among other things, during the campaign the New Democrats vigorously questioned the terms of an impending agreement with the Alcan Corporation over the development of a Conservative "mega-project": an aluminum smelter earmarked for Manitoba's Interlake region. Under the agreement, Alcan was to have purchased a minority interest in a new hydro-electric generating station, a concession which the NDP believed to be excessive. The project was subsequently abandoned altogether soon after the New Democrats took office.
28. See *Toronto Globe and Mail*, 10 March, 1982.
29. This ambiguity over the proper direction for the party was reflected in the choices for liberal leader during this period. The party was led in the 1969 campaign by Robert Bend, a rural ultra-conservative veteran of the Liberal-Progressive governments of the 1950s, and in 1973 by Winnipeg lawyer and venture capitalist I.H. Asper, who similarly echoed the party's traditional ethos. By contrast, the leader in 1977 was Charles Huband, a liberal Winnipeg lawyer with a great concern for social issues and questions of civil liberties.
30. The 1981 campaign also saw the birth of a new political formation, the Progressive party. This party was a disparate collection of disgruntled former New Democrats, as well as scattering of supporters from other parties. It presented itself as a moderate social democratic alternative, free of the "big labour" domination which it claimed characterized the NDP. The party was largely the personal creation of its leader, Sidney Green, long a maverick NDP MLA and a controversial cabinet minister in the Schreyer government. Its performance during the campaign tended to reflect these origins. it lacked a real electoral base and hence never posed a serious threat to the NDP and the Conservatives. On election day, Progressive candidates fared poorly in all 35 of the 57 provincial seats they contested.
31. This classification of party systems is drawn from the work of C.B. Macpherson. See his *Democracy in Alberta*, pp. 243 ff., and *The Life and Times of Liberal Democracy* (Oxford, 1977), pp. 64-9. For Macpherson, the management of class tension in liberal democratic States involves both the expression of, and simultaneously the blurring of, class divisions.
32. As a result of a major electoral redistribution following the 1977 election, the city of Winnipeg was for the first time in Manitoba history allotted a majority of legislative seats in the province — 29 out of 57. Rural areas in the province continued to enjoy modest overrepresentation.
33. This coalition called itself the "Group for Good Government." For an account of its im pact on the 1973 campaign, see M. Debicki, *Why Voters Didn't Play the Game* (paper presented to the annual meeting of the Canadian Political Science Association, University of Alberta, Edmonton, June, 1975).
34. There were suggestions, ultimately unfounded, that the presence of the Progressive party could create such a split in the 1981 election.
35. This appears to be confirmed by the fact that, for the electoral system as a whole, the coefficient of localization in 78the 1977 election is smaller than it is in 1981. See Appendix
36. For a cogent theoretical treatment of this question, see Macpherson, "Market Concepts in Political Theory," in *Democratic Theory: Essays in Retrieval* (Oxford, 1973), pp. 185-94. In addition, there are students of voting behaviour who are aware of this problem and have seen the need to situate the study of election outcomes within the

broader context of history and political theory. Prominent among them is the American political scientist Walter Dean Burham. His writings are voluminous, but see, for example, "The Changing Shape of the American Political Universe, *American Political Science Review* 59:1 (March, 1965), pp. 7-28; *Critical Elections and the Mainspring of American Politics* (New York, 1970); and *The 1980 Earthquake: Realignment, Reaction or What?* in T. Ferguson and J. Rogers (eds.), *The Hidden Election: Politics and Economics in the 1980s Presidential Campaign* (New York, 1981), pp. 98-140.

For an illuminating debate on the theoretical implications of voting behaviour, and indeed the relation between theory and the study of voting behaviour, see the exchange involving Burnham, Philip Converse and Jerrold Rusk in *American Political Science Review* 68:3 (September, 1974), pp. 1002-57.

37. This discussion does not deal with the social roots of discourse, i.e. The fact that the very pattern of discourse is itself weighted. For a more elaborate treatment of this issue, see the important work of Murray Edelman, especially *Political Language: Words that Succeed and Policies that Fail*, (New York, 1977).
38. Cf. Hansen, *Neo-conservatism as Political Ideology* (unpublished paper presented to "Conference on the State," Department of Economics, University of Manitoba, Winnipeg, February, 1980).
39. In 1974, for example, manufacturing in Manitoba accounted for 15.3 percent of the labour force. By contrast, the comparable figure for Saskatchewan is 4.6 percent and for Ontario, 26.6 percent. *Canada Year Book 1976-77* (Ottawa, 1977).
40. Of course, as may well happen in Saskatchewan and Alberta, excessive dependence upon resource rents without the development of a manufacturing base is inherently unstable and ultimately vulnerable to changes in world demand. It also risks the very real possibility that high prices will stimulate the development of substitutes in consuming markets.

REFERENCES

Armstrong, C. and H.V. Nelles, 1973. *Private Property in Peril: Ontario Businessmen and the Federal System, 1898-1911*. Pp. 2-38 in G. Porter and R. Cuff (eds.), *Enterprise and National Development*. Toronto: Hakkert.

Artibise, A., 1975. *Winnipeg: A Social History of Urban Growth*. Montréal: McGill-Queen's University Press.

Barber, P., and N. Wiseman, 1981. *The 1981 Manitoba Election*. Unpublished paper (November).

Black, E.R., and A.C. Cairns, 1966. " A Different Perspective on Canadian Federalism." *Canadian Public Administration* IX (1) (March): 27-45.

Bourque, G.,1979. *Class, Nation and the Party Québecois, Studies in Political Economy* No. 2 (Autumn): 129-58.

Chorney, H., 1970a. *The Political Economy of Provincial Economic Development Policy 1950-1970*, Unpublished Master's dissertation, University of Manitoba.

____ 1970b. *The NDP Meets Big Business: A Case Study of the Manitoba Development Fund*. Pp. 81-104 in W.E. Mann (ed.),

Social, Political and Cultural Change in Canada (vol. 2). Toronto: Copp-Clark.

____ 1977 *Regional Underdevelopment and Cultural Decay*. Toronto:Between the Lines.

Doern, G.B. (ed.), 1978. *Modernization and the Canadian State*. Toronto: Macmillan.

Government of Canada, 1981. Canada Census, 1981, Population Statistics, Preliminary Estimates. Ottawa: Minister of Supply and Services Canada.

Government of Manitoba, 1978. Report of the Task Force in Government Organization and the Economy (2 vols.) Winnipeg: Queen's Printer.

Grubel, H., 1982. "Reflections on a Canadian Bill of Economic Rights." *Canadian Public Policy* VIII (1) (Winter): 57-68.

Katznelson, I.1978. "Considerations on Social Democracy in the United States," *Comparative Politics* 11 (October): 77-99.
Macpherson, C.B., 1977. *The Life and Times of Liberal Democracy.* Oxford: Oxford University Press.
Mathias, P., 1971. *Forced Growth.* Toronto: James, Lewis and Samuel.
Nelles, H.V., 1975. *The Politics of Development.* Toronto: Macmillan
Peterson, T., 1978. "Ethnic and Class Politics," pp. 61-119 in M. Robin (ed.), *Canadian Provincial Politics* (2nd ed.). Toronto: Prentice-Hall.
Wiseman, N., 1973. *The C.C.F. and the Manitoba "Non-Partisan" Government of 1940.*
Canadian Historical Review 59: 173-95.
1983. *Social Democracy in Manitoba.* Winnipeg: University of Manitoba Press.

3

THE FALLING RATE OF LEGITIMATION

by Harold Chorney and Phillip Hansen

This essay was written on the floor of an apartment on Bathurst Street in Toronto, in the midst of moving, on an old electric typewriter and polished in an apartment on Pembina Highway in Winnipeg.It was presented as a paper to the Canadian political Science Association at its annual meeting in 1979 at the University of Saskatchewan in Saskatoon. It was later published in *Studies in Political Economy* in Autumn, 1980. It was intended to be a critical examination of the then current notion of legitimation crisis against the backdrop of both the rise of neo-conservatism and the development of increasingly sophisticated theories of the State. Obviously we are no longer wedded to its language and conceptual methodology. Nevertheless, the essay raised important questions about the nature of Canadian democracy and the susceptibility of Canadian society to neo-conservative pressures. At the time the essay was strongly criticized for its alleged pessimism. In fact, as events have shown since it was perhaps too optimistic. It presupposed that the post-World War Two social contract, (even while under severe attack), was more resilient than it has turned out to be. Even more importantly, it argued that the cultural preconditions for such a social contract and for the very concept of legitimacy itself were much less developed than is commonly assumed. Indeed, most analysts ignored the fact that the problem was not the nature of the State but the absence of public life and community.Because of this absence we believed that neo-conservatism was going to be politically successful for some time. The essay was written in the spring and early summer of 1979. It would nice to hear from our critics now.

There now does appear to be growing resistance to the damage to our social contract that neo-conservatism has wrought but it has taken over a decade for that resistance to have positive political consequences. It remains to be seen if the rebirth of liberalism and social democracy will vanquish the forces of neo-conservatism and its impact on the social contract. Because it has held sway for more than a decade many neo-conservative ideas have penetrated the conventional wisdom. In this respect socialist and social democratic parties and movements have not been immune to its influence. In the end, much as we predicted, neo-conservative politics have had a profound effect on Western societies.

* * *

The recent work of a number of neo-Marxian thinkers has focused on problems of ensuring mass loyalty in capitalist society.[1] It is argued that there is a growing crisis tendency as the State exhausts its political alternatives in its continual efforts to balance the claims of legitimation against those of accumulation. The growing decline in loyalty to traditional pluralist political institutions has been accompanied by a politicized interest in areas of social life traditionally considered marginal to politics. The State apparatus in advanced capitalist society has, at the same time, assumed an ever expanding role in its drive to channel democratic pressures into paths compatible with continued accumulation. With the politicization of previously marginal areas, the exhaustion of traditional political alternatives and the increasing challenge to capitalist hegemony, it is argued that a major crisis of legitimation becomes likely, if not unavoidable.

In Canada, at least, the appropriateness of this analysis seems open to question. We are currently in the midst of a major assault on State welfare institutions, apparently without the development of any politicized centres of resistance to this offensive. There does not, in other words, appear to be an impending crisis of legitimacy: the fundamental erosion on a massive scale of the authoritative character of existing social and political institutions, and the consequent emergence of mass pressure for social transformation. It seems possible that Canadians will witness a fundamental restructuring of their "social contract" without legitimation problems of the type described most accurately by Jurgen Habermas. This position clearly raises important questions about the nature of Canada's political culture — its political norms and values — and the theory of legitimation crisis itself.

What we wish to argue in this essay is that it appears to be a tendency over time for a decline in the need for the State to justify its increasing, and increasingly obvious (to the population as a whole), efforts in aiding the accumulation of capital by the business class at the expense of other classes. Rather than the legitimacy of the capitalist State being increasingly called into question it would appear to the contrary, that there is, in fact, a declining need for State legitimation activities, per se. As a result we may speak of a falling rate of legitimation as a characteristic of late twentieth century capitalism in Canada, a characteristic that may apply to other contemporary capitalist societies as well.

By the term "falling rate of legitimation" we do not of course mean to imply that the future is inescapably determined and that nothing Canadian working people may be forced to endure will promote resistance to regressive developments in Canadian society. Rather, our purpose in developing this category is to throw into critical question the neo-Marxian work on legitimation problems in late capitalism. In particular, we wish to suggest that the nature of political culture in Canada — that is, the quality of the political experience in everyday life; the self-images of citizens and their critical attitudes toward capitalism, democracy and institutions of government; and most importantly their aspirations for a different kind of social order — must be a critical factor in any challenge to the legitimacy of late capitalist institutions. Any economic crisis which may be unfolding in Canada cannot automatically be translated into a political crisis, the resolution of which would resemble Marx's cataclysmic transformation of society. In fact, political crisis must be seen as an autonomous phenomenon whose genesis lies as much, if not more, in the nature of political culture as it does in the structure of capital reproduction. Without an analysis of political culture in Canada, it is impossible to understand the role of the State in contemporary Canadian society, the manner in which the State balances the demands of accumulation and legitimation.

Our reference to the autonomous character of political crisis is not intended to suggest what Nicos Poulantzas and Ralph Miliband, for example, have meant by the "autonomy of the political": the existence of a phenomenally and conceptually distinct sphere of bureaucratic relations that stands in some sense "above" civil society, while serving the interests of capital, and is the focus for precise scientific analysis. Rather, we wish to recall the now suppressed and almost forgotten classical moral vision of politics as the simultaneous development of the good man and pursuit of the good society — that is, the harmonious development of the individual in the context of the realization of community. This uniquely human need for political association has persisted, albeit in radically different forms, throughout history. Even capitalist society meets, in however a mystified, inadequate and ultimately manipulative way, the need for political community. This fact has surely contributed to the ability of capitalism to survive. In this context we discuss the significance of what Alan Wolfe has called "alienated politics": the peculiar form of false community that addresses the need for genuine political association. Thus one of the purposes of our analysis is to suggest a possible basis for a critical theory of the politics of contemporary capitalism.

There can be little doubt that in the past decade in Canada there has been a growing chorus of opposition to the role of government in the economy, the growing size of the federal deficit, the "uncontrollable" growth of government spending and the accompanying size of the State workforce.[2] Opposition by Canadian business to big government in Canada is not, of course, of recent vintage. What must be explained is the seemingly more persuasive effect that such opposition has today by comparison with the recent past. Undoubtedly one reason for the growth of this opposition is the general state of the Canadian economy, whose poor performance over the past decade has generated increased economic hardship. The failure of the economy to respond to government management has greatly disturbed professional economists[3] — indeed many now speak of a "crisis of economic theory" — and it has stimulated the always latent opposition to a large State sector within the ranks of the Canadian political and economic elite.

For its part, the traditional Marxist interpretation of economic crisis has been somewhat refurbished.[4] However, despite revisions, the analysis as a whole has not moved beyond the position which holds either that there is a tendency for the rate of profit to fall or the organic composition of capital to rise, or, that in the long run, there is a realization crisis rooted in the problem of surplus absorption. While these theoretical positions may have explanatory value in delineating the dimensions of what might be called the current economic crisis in Canada, they have far less value in explaining how such a crisis will be resolved. The fact remains that even after the most sophisticated analysis of the current economic crisis of capitalism is attempted, most analysts are left without a clear conception of political transformation, or indeed of the "political" itself.[5]

Thus, for example, we have in the most recent collection of Canadian neo-Marxist articles on the state the following statement by its editor, Leo Panitch:

> Most important of all will be the question of whether the generation of marxist theory itself will continue to be by and large divorced from the working class in Canada. For without a working class helping to identify the "significant problems" by its own actions, and taking up cultural as well as political and economic struggle by re-examining its history and developing a theory and practice for future change, marxist theory will lack a social base, which is the final sine qua non for the sustenance of any body of ideas. Whether marxist theory in Canada will prove capable of generating its own further development will in no small measure depend on the future development of the Canadian working class.[6]

We think Panitch's analysis begs a very critical question, one to which, until fairly recently, very little Canadian analysis has addressed itself: How has it become possible for the industrial capitalist world, of which Canada is clearly a part, to have survived in capitalist form despite all the predictions of the demise of the system? At the same time, throughout this long period of survival, how has the working class changed its composition, its outlook, its self-preservation, its consciousness of itself as a class "for itself"?[7] Perhaps it is time to reconsider the utility of the very concept "working class" as a meaningful category of radical political analysis.

It is from this perspective that we will examine in this paper the work of Jurgen Habermas, who in many respects rejects Marxist orthodoxy and whose insights bear significantly on the problem of legitimacy in capitalist society. What is at stake here is not the economics of capitalism — though we could discuss this at some length as well — but the socio-political and cultural thrust of traditional Marxism. For it was, after all, political and cultural transformation which concerned Marx in his attempt to develop a critical science of capitalist society.[8]

Our starting point, then, is that capitalism has survived and will continue to survive the falling rate of profit, the rise in the organic composition of capital, the failure of capital to be realized, the problem of surplus absorption and, indeed, what has come to be identified as the fiscal crisis of the State if such tendencies — each on its own, or in concert — do not generate critical political consciousness. Such consciousness would express the refusal by the vast majority of the population to accept the continued existence of an unreformed economic system that brings them so much unhappiness. In this sense, we argue that the current possibility for a crisis of legitimacy, and the attempt to eliminate it in a manner which is both more authoritarian and less materially satisfactory that we have become accustomed to expect in the last thirty years, is the consequence of the existence of a political culture in which the possibilities for the emergence of what we might still call class consciousness have been attenuated. Later in this paper we will specify those elements of Canadian political culture which have worked most strongly against the emergence of a critical political consciousness. For now, we only wish to note that while the economic crisis may be the driving force behind the changes that have taken place at the level of State accumulation and possible legitimation strategies, the resolution of this restructuring, the degree to which it will continue and the new social contract which may be established depend directly on these political factors. Class struggle (and we need a better concept than this), political consciousness and the quality of political life will determine the final outcome. The internal dynamics of the capitalist economy can at best only create certain possibilities for the development of crisis tendencies. The state of the legitimacy of the system itself, will determine whether such tendencies are actually realized.

We should make it clear that our argument is intended to be an opening statement in what we think is a long overdue and much needed debate on the character of political culture and the real, as opposed to imagined, fetishized or religiously believed possibilities for social transformation in Canada. To that end, much of what we present in this paper is necessarily speculative and hence tentative. Many of the points we raise are not here empirically verified. We hope, however, that this essay will be received as essentially a series of hypotheses which could serve as a guide to empirical research and further theoretical debate.

THE PARAMETER OF STATE INTERVENTION

What is increasingly clear about the nature of political culture in Canada is the decline in the level of quality of public life. Recent election campaigns confirm that politics at the electoral level has been reduced to widespread manipulation of public opinion with a heavy reliance upon professional pollsters, media specialists and advertising techniques.[9] Not even the supposedly alternative party, the New Democratic Party, has avoided this approach. In fact, the New Democrats employ an advertising agency which specializes in bringing relatively little known consumer products with a small share of the market to wider prominence and a much larger market share. The emphasis in recent campaigns on "leadership," the superficiality of popular journalism, and the influence of dress and style on public perception confirm this decline. This is not to suggest that this transformation in how the political parties campaign has met with the complete approval of the electorate. Undoubtedly a significant portion of the electorate which longs for a more substantive and meaningful politics is quite dissatisfied. This dissatisfaction was to some extent reflected in the federal elections of 1979 and 1980 in the large number of undecided voters. Nevertheless, the reduction of elections to carefully stage-managed advertising campaigns with all the political punch of a campaign for deodorants is a very real phenomenon.

Normative issues about the justice and equity of government and economic policy in particular have ceased to be important. While both the Conservative and Liberal parties have moved to the right, appealing to the immediate and selfish interest of affluent voters and pitching their campaigns at the "middle class" suburban vote, the NDP for its part has moved toward the centre, adopting a nationalistic technocratic approach to current political questions. Hence we see a fundamental coalescence of all three of the major political parties around such pithy normative issue as leadership.

The process has not been a totally smooth one, however. All political parties live in constant fear of the electorate and search their collective egos, and unconscious ids for the clues about how to pacify resentments, sooth hostilities and slake expectations. There is a sense of unease that the electorate cannot be expected to confront the parties' true plans for the economy, or face the "reality" that "there is only so much government can do." There is indeed the increasingly widespread perception that perhaps democracy itself is not sufficiently flexible to deal with the problems facing capitalist economies.[10] Political parties have for the most part avidly, almost desperately, sought a set of policies that would ensure electoral success, much as product packaging ensures market receptivity. Concern for the material of legitimation, if it exists at all, generally has come later, almost as an afterthought.

The increasing similarity of political parties in their approach to politics, the pervasiveness of technocratic ideologies and the veritable collapse of radical opinions have all been conditioned by the post-war State intervention into the capitalist economy of such a massive proportion as to have almost justifiably spawned the notion of "state capitalism."

The notion of State capitalism was most cogently developed in the 1940s by Friedrich Pollock. According to Pollock, State capitalism in all of its variants assumes important functions of the private capitalist, while at the same time the interest of profit still plays a significant role. In its democratic form, the form under which the State apparatus is in some sense controlled by the people, State capitalism has the following characteristics. 1) The market is deposed from its ruling function to co-ordinate production and distribution. This function has been taken over by a system of direct controls. Freedom of trade, enterprise and labour are subject to governmental interference of such a degree that they are practically abolished. With the autonomous market the so-called economic laws disappear. 2) These controls are vested in the State which uses a combination of old and new devices, including a "pseudo market" for regulating and expanding production and co-ordinating it with consumption. Full employment of all resources is claimed as the main achievement in the economic field. The State transgresses all limits drawn for peacetime State activities.[11]

According to Pollock, the rise of State capitalism was the result of the failure of the market enterprise system during the Depression of the 1930s. This depression was accompanied by the growing domination of the market by giant firms operating a system of administered prices and financed internally out of their massive funds of retained earnings. At the same time, large unions made substantial wage cuts difficult, if not impossible. These developments made it inevitable that the State would assume an ever-expanding and more central role in the system.

Pollock's model of State capitalism was intended as the Weberian ideal. Clearly the so-called "economic laws" which Pollock suggested had disappeared cannot be so easily abolished. In fact the State capitalism which has come to prevail in the real world, even in as sophisticated a variant as Western Europe, has never attained the level of conscious political direction and economic co-ordination that Pollock's model both presupposed and saw as inevitable.[12]

Nevertheless, Pollock emphasized the crucial significance of economic and social planning, and all of the ramifications of such planning for the further development of economic systems that could still be called capitalist. Particularly important here is his discussion of the emergence of new ideological and institutional elements in capitalist social orders, such as the universalization of the principles of scientific management and the substitution of bureaucratic structures for market forms of social integration. Given these concerns, Pollock's argument is of obvious significance for the most recent efforts to understand the evolution of the State in advanced capitalism. However the universalisation of scientific management and the substitution of bureaucratic for market integration via the achievement principle has not in practice been fully realized. In other words, newer forms of capitalist rationalization have not by any means fully displaced older forms of bourgeois rationality (i.e. economic irrationality) that governed earlier phases of the historical development of capitalist systems. More importantly, radical analyses of the structures of advanced capitalism that accept capital's own claims to effective rationalization concede to capital too much — a point made respectively by Thorstein Veblen more than a half century ago.

Studies of the growth of the State in Canada and the introduction of the welfare system suggest that certain key sectors of the Canadian business community welcomed the heretofore reviled presence of a State whose intervention was no longer apparently restricted to the facilitation of capital accumulation.[13] Other sectors, however, never accepted it ideologically. This revulsion had never prevented the private sector in Canada from actively seeking massive State support for schemes of economic development, tax incentives and the supply of basic infrastructure.[14] State intervention has always occupied an ambiguous position in business ideology. On the one hand, State interference with trade has always been strongly rejected and the right to accumulate privately without interference in the management of capital and labour strongly upheld.[15] On the other hand, the political consequences, and ultimately the business consequences, of private dominance of the accumulation process were such that a stronger role for the State was actively sought.

Stanley Aronowitz has described this divided approach in terms of the two phases of capital accumulation: the accumulative and disaccumulative. The accumulation phase coincides with the emergence of monopoly capitalism in its earliest form. This period was characterized by the massive expansion of the means of production and the creation of mass markets fostered by the simultaneous transformation of business organizations into large national and subsequently multinational firms, and the emergence of the mass culture industry. The disaccumulative phase, as Aronowitz understands it, involves the disposal of the social product in ways that foster neither "the consumption of workers and capitalists in the productive sector, nor...the expansion of...real capital. Instead it is disposed of in purely 'wasteful' ways from the point of view of accumulation."[16] The disaccumulative phase, which has its roots in the earliest features of a maturing corporate capitalism and the growing importance of the realization problem, ultimately entails the creation of a much expanded public sector as a major vehicle for the absorption of surplus capital. As Aronowitz notes:

> The creation of the public sector as a major form of capital absorption protects productive capital in two ways: First, it establishes an outlet for the past accumulated capital that has been prevented from use in the private industrial sector...At the same time, public sector employment generates personal income that can be used to stimulate production of commodities without itself creating new commodities that compete with the productive sector. Second, it maintains the ideological legitimacy of the capitalist system by providing

employment for those who would be otherwise redundant and services such as education, health and welfare payments for the whole population.[17]

Thus, during the accumulative phase, when the hegemony of the American capitalist economy was being established, there was little interest in a strongly interventionist State. During the disaccumulative phase, however, with the accumulation process undergoing a major realization crisis, the state and expansion of its activities was seen as the salvation of the system. In both Canada and the United States, the massive expansion of the State sector, occasioned by huge increases in war materials expenditures, was the basis of the economic recovery at the end of a decade of severely retarded accumulation. While the military sector in the United States continued to serve this role, in Canada the social welfare system was more extensively developed to take up the slack. However, this entire expansion of the State sector was premised upon the assumption that the problem faced by the capitalist sector in both countries was one of capital realization: an excess of surplus capital seeking to be realized in ways that were not themselves surplus generating.[18]

According to Aronowitz, for the last forty years American capitalism in general has been in its disaccumulative phase. However, with the rise to competitive prominence of the European and Japanese economies, complete with their own multinationals, and the emergence of the oil crisis, American capitalism no longer faces a crisis rooted solely in inadequate disaccumulation outlets.[19] Rather, it now faces instead a renewed crisis of accumulation itself, a crisis aggravated by excessive non surplus-generating production. What was established by the State to realize capital must now be restructured by the State to rationalize capital. Despite the widespread belief that the entire social welfare apparatus was born solely out of the struggle of the working class in the depths of the Depression, to the extent that members of this class no longer — if they ever did — view these social programme as hard-won achievements that must be defended as popular victories against the onslaught of conservative regimes, the contradiction of the welfare society will proceed.

In terms of Aronowitz's argument, it seems that a legitimation crisis is not likely as a result of the dismantling of the welfare State for the simple reason that it was never established wholly as a legitimating strategy in response to class-based opposition. It was as much a crucial element in the attempted solution to the problem of surplus capital absorption.

To be sure, the welfare State was also the outcome of a certain level of class conflict that emerged during the Depression era. The acceptance of the welfare system was based, in part, on the fear concerning the ultimate survival of capitalism itself. Nevertheless, to the extent that the degree of class militancy found during the Depression has subsided or, more importantly, has been reduced to the status of economic interest group bargaining, without wider normative appeal to the population as a whole, it has become increasingly possible for a rationalization of the welfare State in the interests of accumulation to be attempted. On the other hand, to the extent that such marginalized militancy does threaten to become widespread and the electorate refuses to respond to manipulated appeals to reject social equality as merely the pleading of special interest groups, it has encouraged precisely the growing belief within inner corporate business circles, and the State sector itself, that democracy is becoming increasingly inflexible, a "luxury" we may no longer be able to afford.

STATE INTERVENTION IN CANADA

The switch in the nature of the North American economy from the accumulative to the disaccumulative, and now to a new accumulative stage, must be situated within the context of the peculiar nature of the accumulation process in Canada, a process governed by the massive American domination of the Canadian economy. In fact, this foreign control has always signalled the apparent relative shortage of capital in Canada. "Apparent" is the operative word here, for the problem increasingly has not been one of a true shortage of capital, but rather one of the enormous leakage of capital through the repatriation by multinational firms of dividends, interest charges and other fees. The latest data on our balance of payments confirms this process. The net outflow of interests and dividends and service charges amounted to some $6.2 billion on our current account in 1978.[20] Without such a negative balance, our current account deficit, which was $5.2 billion in 1978 would have been a surplus.

It seems difficult to accept then that the Canadian problem is one solely of realization rooted in surplus capital. Instead, the Canadian problem might better be regarded as one of accumulation in an economy with both a high degree of foreign control and a large State sector. An examination of recent profit data for Canadian corporations and banks and other financial institutions reveals that the long-term problem of excessive foreign ownership and an excessively expanded State sector was aggravated by the short-term cyclical problem of increased wage militancy. Thus a militant labour sector cut into profit margins to such an extent that wage controls were required to restore them. The success of the wage controls programme is reflected in the latest data on corporate profits which for the first quarter of 1979 were 58 percent higher than the preceding quarter, when in turn they were 26 percent higher than in the final quarter of 1977. For their part, bank profits in the third quarter of 1978 were 41 percent higher than in the preceding quarter, the largest such gain in three years.[21]

The impact of the federal wage and price controls programme clearly was to reduce wage compensation and prevent the fall in profits which normally accompanies recovery by wages during the course of the business cycle.[22] In terms of the relation between compensation, labour productivity and inflation, in the period of 1974-1976, during which the clamour for controls and the implementation of the programme itself occurred, compensation exceeded inflation plus productivity gains. The controls programme worked to reverse this situation, and by 1977, compensation had once again fallen behind productivity and inflation increases — a situation which has prevailed in twelve of the last seventeen years in manufacturing and ten of the last seventeen in the commercial sector. Annual percentage increases in labour compensation have only exceeded inflation plus productivity gains, in manufacturing sector in the years 1967, 1970 and 1974 to 1976, and in the commercial sector in 1965, 1966, 1967, 1970 and 1974 to 1976.[23]

A study of the impact of the controls programme by the Conference Board of Canada, a private sector economic forecasting body, has revealed that the programme was responsible for holding down wages by 7.7 percent while prices fell by only 2 percent points. The Board argues that the controls programme prevented profits from falling by a considerably larger amount because of the downturn in the business cycle during the length of programme. In the absence of the controls programme, profits before taxes would have fallen by 9 percent more than they actually did. The overall result of the programme was to shift income from labour to capital, dampen labour's expectations and, with the increase in unemployment which accompanied the programme — the rate rose from 5.4 percent in 1974 to 8.5 percent in 1978 — allow accumulation to take place, thereby, it was hoped, laying the foundation for a new round of capital investment. Capacity utilization rates over the last eight years also point to this role for the controls programme.

The wage control programme also formally signalled the end of the post-war commitment to the central management of the economy with the goal of full employment, stable prices, steady economic growth and a sound balance of payments as well as a commitment to moderate income redistribution. These goals of course were never attained. Whereas the Keynesian era heralded the potential achievement of these goals through a sophisticated use of fiscal, and to a lesser extent monetary policy, complete with automatic stabilizers and fine tuning, the era of direct controls makes it clear that conventional Keynesian techniques have been exhausted. The neat trade-offs which the Phillips curve analysis had suggested about the relation between money wage rates and the rate of unemployment seem completely out of kilter. In order to reduce the inflation rate one or two percentage points, very significant increases in the rate of unemployment seem to be required. One study has pointed out that the nature of the short-run and long-run Phillips curve in Canada is such that "while policy makers can trade off some unemployment for a lower inflation rate, the terms of the trade-off may be very painful."[24]

Virtually all important government figures at every level, and many academic analysts, share a similarly pessimistic view of the possibilities for effective implementation of Keynesian policies of economic management.[25] The Ontario Economic Council's approach is not all unrepresentative:

> The Council believes that fiscal policy has become a much less flexible instrument because of continued high rates of government spending and because of the monetary implications of financial deficits. If growth in the size of the public sector were more limited expansionary fiscal policy could emphasize tax reductions rather than increased government spending. Indeed, without expenditure restraint, in the short run the need to finance the revenue losses arising from tax cuts can have adverse monetary consequences.[26]

This monetarist position has its intellectual roots in the work of the classical depression economics of Pigou, Hayek, Hawtry, Von Mises and Robbins, among others, who in the face of overwhelming evidence to the contrary, still argued that the Great Depression was solely the result of excessive monetary contraction and the failure of workers to accept substantial enough money wage cuts.[27] The monetarist position now most strongly identified with Milton Friedman, the Nobel Prize-winning advisor to the Pinochet regime in Chile, is the rapidly emerging new orthodoxy of the day in academic and governmental economics.[28] The monetarists consider inflation as the result of excessive increases in the money supply. Unemployment is the result of poor monetary management and monopoly practices by unions. A certain "natural" rate of unemployment is to be expected in a free enterprise economy. Further unemployment in Canada is considered to be no real hardship, the monetarists argue, for many of the unemployed come from the families with more than one income earner, receive substantial benefits while unemployed and therefore must be voluntarily unemployed.

The current practices of the Bank of Canada are direct evidence of the increasing prominence of the monetarist position in Canadian economic circles. The Bank's policy of drastically restricting the money supply, thereby generating higher unemployment, in order to prevent "irresponsible" unions and corporations from validating wage and price increases through an increase in the supply of money, is a step in the direction of more direct and permanent interference in the collective bargaining process. As Gerald Bouey, Governor of the Bank of Canada, has put it: "No group in the community should count on the Bank of Canada to float off its inflationary activities with a wave of monetary expansion."[29] Certainly the wage control programme must be seen in this light as well.

There can be little doubt that Keynesianism has been eclipsed. The monetarist counter-revolution is reflected in the economic thinking of the two major political parties and, to a certain extent, even that of the NDP. If, for example, we examine the NDP platform in the 1979 election, it did not, aside from its commitment to maintain Medicare and increase pensions, advance a single significant social programme oriented toward income redistribution. Rather, the promise of better economic management and greater national autonomy provided the thrust for its proposals.[30]

Ironically, ideas which had supposedly been discredited by the Great Depression are now presented as the crowning achievements of economic "science." It is as if Keynes has stepped into the closet of history and reemerged as Herbert Hoover. While "bastardized Keynesianism" may be a highly inadequate medicine for an actually ill patient, monetarism is equivalent to cutting off the respirator and seeing if the patient will survive.

When we actually look at the federal government deficits and surpluses since 1930 and the percentage of the Gross National Expenditure they constitute, the neo-conservative cry of continuous revenue deficit is simply without historical support. In twenty of the last forty-nine years, there has been a surplus and not a deficit. The deficits during the Depression were basically the result of the collapse of government policy. In fact, most of the government deficits that have occurred since then were primarily the result of lagging government revenues rather than deliberately counter-cyclical spending. If provincial government expenditures are taken into account the overall impact of the deficit, excluding the Depression, is lessened.

Furthermore, the deficits which generated such an outcry in the past five years, (on the basis of constituting between 2 and 5% of Gross National Expenditure) pale in comparison to those of the period 1943-1946 (when the Federal deficit hovered around 20% of Gross National Expenditure).[31] What was acceptable, of course, in wartime for reasons of State, has now become quite unacceptable in peacetime. Businessmen will support an enormous increase in government expenditures during wartime for military and even certain social purposes. In peacetime, however, when such a military spending is relatively unimportant (Canada not being the United States) even one-third the relative level of government deficits is apparently intolerable.

It is curious that one central tenet of monetarism — that persistent government deficits are inflationary — has also emerged in a number of Marxist analyses of the current crisis of capitalism. This is clear in the work of Paul Sweezy and Harry Magdoff in *Monthy Review*, Paul Mattick in *Marx and Keynes* and Andrew Gamble and Paul Walton in their work, *Capitalism in Crisis*. It also forms part of the analysis that James O'Connor presents in *The Fiscal Crisis of the State*. The argument is essentially that deficit financing, which has been central to the expansion of the State sector, is a form of State appropriation of private capital through the inflationary process to which it gives rise. For instance, Paul Mattick argues:

> Public consumption does not add to the formation of capital. It does, however, increase the national debt. The cost of the

debt, that is the interest paid to the bondholders, must come out of the profits of the relatively diminishing private sector of the economy...

These profits Mattick argues once taxed cannot function as sources of private investment. As such they can no longer function capitalistically. Instead, he claims they are "expropriated" by the State:

> There must then be a limit to the expansion of the non-profitable part of the economy. When this limit is reached, deficit financing and government-induced production as policies to counteract the social consequences of a declining rate of accumulation must come to an end. The Keynesian solution will stand exposed as a pseudo-solution, capable of postponing but not preventing the contradictory course of capital accumulation as predicted by Marx.[32]

In this sense Marxists like Mattick mirror the neo-conservatives in their predictions of inevitable breakdown should unrestrained deficit-financing continue. This may be a comforting stance for it presupposes the kind of economic determinism in which nineteenth century liberalism (i.e. modern neo-conservatism) and orthodox Marxism alike have their roots. Consequently, most Marxists positions on Keynesian prescriptions for the stabilization of the business cycle in capitalist economies are pessimistic. They range form the argument of Ernest Mandel — who suggests that the capitalist economy has entered a long period of economic downturn — to the Sweezy and Magdoff position that the expansion of the State sector is limited both by the inflationary pressures which deficit financing and credit expansion entail, and by the competitive relation of State expenditures to private accumulation.[33] Paradoxically, current business ideology is in many respects in agreement with this analysis. A careful reading of the business press suggests that the hostility in business circles to government spending and deficit financing has now reached epidemic proportions. Yet, as Mattick and other have pointed out, a return to a policy of State retrenchment, monetary contraction and fiscal non-interference can only result in massive unemployment. The business cycle and its cleansing impact upon unprofitable invested capital will return with a vengeance. In its own way business ideology accepts this analysis and its consequences.

That major Marxist theorists and neo-conservative monetarists share a certain intellectual common ground does not, of course, mean that each draws the same political conclusions from their respective analyses. Nevertheless, the structural similarity of views that characterizes both Marxist crisis theory and monetarism suggest a real problem: How do economic crisis tendencies inform political consciousness and political practice, particularly the consciousness and practice of those who might be expected to rebel against an exploitative, and frequently oppressive, social system when their expected and habitual living standards are eroded? How, in other words, can a Marxist economic analysis of even the most sophisticated and subtle kind, provide us with an explanation of how such an economic crisis will translate itself into a political and cultural crisis of sufficient dimensions that social transformation can seriously be considered as a potential outcome?[34]

It is to precisely these questions of social transformation and class consciousness that we wish to devote our attention. While the work of theorists of legitimation vary as to how central a role they allocate to the problem of economic crisis — in Habermas's case a classical economic crisis is largely ruled out as a likely possibility — nonetheless they are all in agreement that there are socio-cultural limitations to the possibilities for non-normative systems legitimation even in the absence of an economic crisis along classical Marxist or neo-Marxist lines.

LEGITIMATION AND CANADIAN POLITICAL CULTURE

The concept of legitimation, and the concrete political and social questions with it, must first of all be understood as the properties of a particular socio-historical formation: liberal (democratic) society. While "legitimacy" has a long and distinguished intellectual history, dating back at least to the work of Jean-Jacques Rousseau, developing through the insights of thinkers such as Weber and Parsons, and culminating in the work of Habermas, Wolfe, et al., its recent emergence as an important theme in the literature on the tensions and problems of the State in advanced capitalism parallels the growth over the last half-century of large scale State intervention in the economies of Western societies.[35] This intervention, encroaching as it has on the operation of a social system that previously appeared to its unwitting members as the product of unplanned, nature-like processes, could not have proceeded without a significant shift in perceptions of the proper role for the State, and the political generally, in this self-reproducing social order. In other words, the "objective" need for an active State required for its historical fulfilment a "subjective" commitment, at least on the part of the dominant classes in Western societies, to such an expansion of State power.

This subjective acceptance of State intervention may have arisen out of the recognition by far-sighted members of the capitalist class of the need to foster social harmony.[36] Or it may have developed as an unintended consequence of corporate strategies designed to preserve stable markets and profits. That is, the interventionist State may have resulted either from class conflict and the desire to defuse it, or from corporate attempts to rationalize the crisis-prone market system. Whatever its basis it cannot, of course, be assumed that support for an expanded State has ever been totally understood self-reflexively by all save a few representatives of national and international capital. Thus in all Western democracies, even in those Western European states in which social democracy has deep political roots, business leaders are currently promoting both a contraction of State spending on social programming and an expansion of State accumulation.[37] This ambivalence suggests the extent to which even a State-managed, "rationalized" capitalism continues to function as a blind force operating behind the backs of both its architects and its victims, with the added problem that the sources of occlusion can no longer be comprehended adequately by the classical critique of political economy.

More simply, classical, orthodox Marxism, focusing as it does on the critique of political economy, is no longer capable of illuminating clearly and comprehensively the operating principles of advanced capitalism. This is particularly the case with respect to the manner in which advanced capitalism has thus far more or less successfully presented itself to people as a natural, eternal phenomenon: though the medium of culture.

It is precisely for this reason that theories of legitimation problems were developed. Jurgen Habermas, the thinker most closely associated with the notion of a crisis of legitimacy, argues that capitalism requires for its successful functioning the continual ability to feed off the remnants of bourgeois, and even prebourgeois, cultural traditions which go beyond the requirements of simple capital reproduction.

These traditions have a two-fold and contrary character. On the one hand, they relate to the possibility, at least at the level of articulated values, for the emergence of full participation in the political life of society, i.e., they express the classical conception of the citizen. On the other hand, bourgeois and pre-bourgeois traditions maintain values which reinforce on the part of citizens a differential attitude toward political authority.[38] This dimension of tradition includes the upholding of the paternalistic yet harmonious family; the widespread acceptance of a fatalist religious view of the world; and the vitality of an aesthetically noninstrumental body of art that expresses the longing for harmony — never realized — with nature, group solidarity and beauty itself. Habermas, in turn, links these traditions with what he sees as the twin motivational patterns through which bourgeois society reproduces itself: civic and familial-vocational privatism.[39] Further, with the erosion of such traditions, a "motivation crisis" which threatens the reproduction of the system becomes possible. By motivation crisis, Habermas means a state of affairs under which the socio-cultural system of an advanced capitalist social formation could no longer adequately generate the requisite quantity of what he calls "action motivating meaning."[40] More simply, the cultural system could no longer provide people with readily believable reasons for doing what the system of social labour requires. In fact, the output of the cultural system itself could become directly dysfunctional if it generated values and norms hostile to the maintenance of capitalist social relations (as it did in the sixties with respect to certain elements of the counter-culture, the new left, the ecology movement, etc.).

In this context it seems to us that three interrelated questions pose themselves. First, to what extent is the erosion of what Habermas calls the achievement principle (the competitive quest for wealth and status), the bourgeois family and religion actually taking place? Second, even if it is occurring, to what extent can these traditions still serve to sustain the system? Finally, if they can no longer sustain the system, why must a crisis of motivation occur and in what political space might it occur?[41]

The assumption underlying Habermas' theory of legitimation crisis is that a motivation crisis is a possible outcome of certain social and political tendencies because, and insofar as, the State cannot indefinitely regenerate the cultural traditions required for it to maintain the diffuse mass loyalty it needs to manage successfully the contradictory demands of capitalist production. In other words, there is for Habermas an area of social life that cannot readily be converted into an unambiguous, unproblematic basis of support for capitalism because it has traditionally been immune to administrative intervention. Although Habermas does not make the argument in quite these terms, we believe that the mass acceptance of democratic norms and values — what Habermas calls "a truth dependent mode of socialization"[42] — cannot be just the goal of radical social transformation. Such norms and values must be implicit in the self-understanding, everyday practice and political experience of the liberal democratic citizen if concepts such as "crisis tendencies," let alone social transformation itself, are to have any meaning. That is, democratic values and norms must, at least in principle, be capable here and now of practical appropriation (i.e., according to the requirements of substantive reason) such that they are implicated in the very structures of meaning within which people understand themselves and their world.[43] If it can be shown that societies evolve independently of normative structures possessing practical significance, the whole legitimation problem may well be called into question.

In essence this means that the role of State intervention is both more ambiguous and, potentially at least, more expansive than either orthodox analysis, or even Habermas's position, assumes. Modern State intervention, occurring as it does in the context of societies which in a fundamental sense (with regard to the process of private capital accumulation) reproduce themselves blindly, is not a smoothly harmonious process. Habermas refers to this problem in his discussion of the possibility of a crisis of administrative rationality.[44] By means of this concept, he wishes to specify the problems the State in advanced capitalism necessarily encounters in meeting successfully the requirements of stable economic growth. Indeed, according to Habermas, a likely form of political crisis in advanced capitalism is a crisis of rationality which, in the context of a crisis of motivation, could develop in tandem with, while simultaneously fuelling, a crisis of legitimation.

But the rationality involved here is the formal or technical reason — the utilitarian logic of the choice of efficient means for the attainment of ends not themselves determined according to standards of reason — that provides both the basis for and operating principle of bureaucratic organization. A crisis of rationality may be seen then as a crisis of efficiency. And such a crisis could well trigger legitimation problems of a sort, although not, to be sure, of the kind that Habermas discusses. A crisis of efficiency, of technical rationality, need not be resolved in a "progressive," i.e. anti-authoritarian, way. It will be resolved in that fashion only if democratic norms are deeply embedded in a society's political culture. Otherwise, a crisis of legitimacy may well terminate in the establishment of a more not less authoritarian politics.

In fact, Habermas does acknowledge that from a purely functional point of view, the administrative system of advanced capitalism could be replaced by a less democratic variant. This could be a "conservative-authoritarian" State. The latter would operate with a high degree of mobilization while the former would attempt to reduce political participation on the part of the citizens to a minimum. In either case the boundaries of the welfare State would be strictly managed. However, Habermas suggests that neither of these options would be as compatible in the long run with advanced capitalism as a system based on representational mass democracy, complete with political parties. According to Habermas, this kind of mass democracy is more likely to prevail because "the socio-cultural system produces demands that cannot be met in authoritarian systems."[45]

It seems to us that Habermas' assertion that the conservative-authoritarian option is "obviously less compatible with developed capitalism" is highly questionable. This may have once been the case, but there are signs that with growing decay in political and cultural life, particularly in Canada, the conservative-authoritarian option cannot be ruled out.

The significance of the legitimacy issue for an understanding of these developments on the Canadian political and social scene follows from this brief attempt to underscore the ambiguous character of the legitimacy question in contemporary capitalist society. In Canada, as we have suggested here and elsewhere,[46] those democratic values which are both the basis and outcome of the existence of any significant degree of class consciousness do not appear to be deeply embedded in the political culture. At least since the defeat of the radical labour movement in Canada in the earliest decades of the twentieth century, the mass base of support upon which the possibility of a critical and not merely formal notion of legitimacy rests has for the most part been absent.

By a critical notion of legitimacy we mean one which is rooted in standards that actually govern both the moral self-understanding and actual conduct of the individual. These standards would not be abstract imperatives, but central elements in lived, sensual experience such that challenges to them could lead to demands for a radically re-organised social order that would be in harmony with the claims these standards advance. By a formal notion of legitimacy, we mean a concept which emphasizes the structural roots of social stability as an abstract property of a social system, without reference to individual goal states or actual lived experience. It is purely formal because in its concern for system maintenance in general, it obscures the historical roots, and hence dynamics for change, of particular (especially advanced capitalist) social formations. It cannot therefore successfully address the possibilities for qualitative change in social relations of the kind that a genuinely radical theory of social transformation must incorporate. The ambiguity in both the definition and use of the concept of legitimacy will remain as long as the real fate of democracy, and hence radical social change, is historically unsettled.[47]

Certain Marxist theorists, notably Claus Offe, argue that a crisis of legitimation is still possible even in the absence of a mass-based socialist movement. Offe refers in particular to the possibility that previously marginalized groups on the political spectrum will, either because of their strategic position in society or because of the reconstitution of certain previously non-politicized areas of social life, serve as catalysts for a challenge to capitalist hegemony.[48] What is partly at stake here is the validity of the concept of the new working class, a concept advanced most notably by Serge Mallet and André Gorz.[49] In addition, the emerging critical importance of ecology and a concern for the quality of everyday life raises the possibility that previously depoliticized areas of private as well as social existence can now become, in Habermas's terms, the basis of discursive will-formation, i.e. a substantively, and not simply procedurally, democratic politics. Certainly the nuclear "accident" at Three Mile Island, Pennsylvania in the spring of 1979 raises the spectre of this kind of challenge to the heretofore almost unquestioned application of technical rationality.

Some interpreters of this argument go so far as to suggest the likelihood of a new populist politics as a consequence of these developments. However, we believe that this analysis still presupposes the real existence of a political culture that can sustain the kind of commitment implied. We may recall that for Marx, the key issue involved in the attempt to specify the character of political consciousness was its critical foundation, i.e., its capacity to pinpoint possibilities in the current society for a qualitatively new kind of social order. He believed, following Hegel, that the bearer of such consciousness would be a universal class as Hegel understood it. The proletariat could serve as the vehicle for universality only insofar as it abolished itself as a proletariat. Clearly the experience of the twentieth century has taught us that at least in North America, if not elsewhere, the proletariat as a class has failed in its historic mission. As an empirical entity the working class does of course exist in capitalist society. But the empirical existence of the working class says nothing about its role as a critical and conscious agent of social change. And that, for Marxists, has been central to their claim that the point of social theory is not simply to interpret the world but to change it in a revolutionary way. Its empirical presence notwithstanding, that the working class in advanced capitalism remains a class incapable of transcending its class-based interest to realize what Marx understood to be human universality, is an indication not of its strength as orthodox Marxism would have it, but its real weakness: its continued existence as the object and not the subject of history.

Even if it could be shown that in Canada we have witnessed in the last hundred years a good deal of class conflict (and it can be),[50] that of itself would be insufficient to justify a belief in the immanent possibility of a radical politics. Capitalism is built in, and progresses through, conflict: it is, in Marx's apt expression, the final antagonistic form of social production. Such conflict, at least in controlled doses, can even foster social integration.

To put it another way that calls into question the frequently careless use of the term "crisis" that we have come to witness recently: capitalism has succeeded in domesticating potentially disruptive conflict by displacing it from the economic sphere to more marginal reaches of social life, where it is experienced either as a failure of scientific-administrative control or, even more tellingly, as the disintegration of a coherent individual personality structure. As Habermas notes, the central question from the point of view of advanced capitalism's current economic difficulties concerns "whether economic problems will become of such magnitude that this model thriving on "small crises" will be unable to function any longer and, consequently, precipitate a crisis of classic dimensions.[51] In short, capitalism can survive, and many indeed require, a measure of opposition in order to maintain itself. And this opposition may even evince a significant element of critical political consciousness.[52]

In Europe the reality of such integrative conflict has traditionally been more or less accepted. In Canada, however, we are faced with a double-barrelled problem. Quite apart from the fact that class conflict in and of itself need not result in a radical challenge to the social system, Canada's political culture makes it difficult for conflict even at the interest group, let alone class, level to emerge as an acceptable mode of social expression. And we do not exempt Québec from this analysis. Canada itself combines all the integrative tendencies (with the exception, of course, of allowable conflict) of modern capitalism with all the repressive fury of the nineteenth century bourgeois personality. In Habermas's terms we have not witnessed a serious erosion of those traditions on which capitalism must feed on order to survive. In this sense we have the worst of all possible worlds at both the purely economic and cultural levels: integration and repression, accumulation and disaccumulation.

The reasons for this double barrier to the development of a radical, critical politics lie as much in the predominantly hierarchic, anti-democratic, anti-egalitarian character of both our political and social systems, and our dominant values, as in the fragmented and retarded nature of our economic development.[53] The nature of the accumulation process in Canada has required that the State serve not simply as the passive guardian of, but as an active partner in, the promotion of capital expansion. This "statist" tradition has been the object of much analysis in Canadian political economy, history and social theory. But such analyses have tended to view this activist State in purely formal terms without paying attention to the impact of statism upon politics in Canada. In its most obvious expression this blindness has been at the heart of Canadian social democracy, which identifies socialism with statism, socialization with nationalization.

The limitations of social democracy have, of course, been clear to segments of the Canadian left for a long time. What has not been so clear are precisely its cultural-political, as well as economic, implications. A crisis of legitimation in Canada, premised upon the dismantling of the welfare State, would presuppose some sort of social democratic consciousness among significant sectors of the Canadian population. And yet, paradoxically, the very nature of social democratic consciousness, particularly in its Canadian form, is fundamentally at odds with an emancipatory politics. That is, social democracy in Canada had in its own way reproduced, under the guise of a radical political movement, the paternalistic values which are at the centre of Canada's political culture.

What is significant about social democracy and the politics of the capitalist class in this context is that the battle over social contract has been fought largely over the heads of most ordinary Canadians — in corporate boardrooms, at federal-provincial conferences and to a much more limited extent, union meeting halls. The "struggle" has been so waged because our statist tradition has created a particularly strong variant of what Alan Wolfe has called "alienated politics."[54] Alienated politics, as Wolfe defines it, is a politics designed to reinforce the competitive separation of people in objectively identical circumstances who might otherwise be capable of generating modes of collective action. This is possible because the State, and political institutions and practices generally in capitalist society, expropriate the common social power that individuals possess as potential members of a moral and political community and re-impose that power as an alien force directed against those from whom it was expropriated. Wolfe intends this to be the political (i.e., communal) equivalent of Marx's notion of alienation as the expropriation of labour's product and its conversion into an alien objectified world: capital. In Canada the very elements of the political culture facilitate a thoroughgoing kind of alienated politics that functions by means of the ability of our traditions and institutions to promote the false community of essentially antagonistic but rarely, and then only sporadically expressed, class interests — interests which if not a sufficient, are certainly a necessary, condition of a radical politics.

And it is here that the real significance of Canada's political tradition lies: in its ability to promote, as the highest expression of the public interest, forms of bureaucratically controlled interdependence without substantive community.[55] The success of any form of alienated politics lies in the ability of that politics, and the institutions that sustain it, to promote form but not the substance of community. The fact that large numbers of Canadians believe that "excessive" wage demands on the part of labour constitute an assault on the "public interest" must be seen as more than simply false consciousness, although it certainly is that. It has objective roots in the very success of our political and social institutions and traditions in fostering a bureaucratic vision of social reality. At the same time, however, the destruction of the real possibilities of community implicit in the homogenizing tendencies of modern urbanistic capitalism reinforces the continued existence of the false community that the uniquely Canadian political and social system has provided.

In Canada this false sense of community has been promoted in large measure by the ongoing concern with the challenge posed by Québec to the survival of federalism, and the emotional angst which Québec's threatened separation has wrung from the Canadian psyche. This ersatz ideology of community has been cleverly manipulated by politicians to mask certain fundamental features of contemporary capitalism in Canada.[56] In this sense the promise of both Québec and Canadian nationalism is a deeply flawed promise, necessary because of its historic roots but also false because of its unwillingness to come to terms with economic class questions. As such the phenomenon of nationalism is ideological in terms of T.W. Adorno's conception of ideology: it is necessary but false consciousness.[57]

The problem of false consciousness is in this sense inextricably linked to the historical meaning of class consciousness and its universalizing role in the context of the nature of the State and the changing character of possible sources of delegitimation. The laissez-faire State could successfully "destaticize" its function (i.e., mask, if not render invisible its altogether "visible" hand) because breakdowns did not have the universal consequences they would have under the logic of advanced capitalism. That is, "disturbances and undesired side effects of the accumulation process did not have to result in the withdrawal of legitimation so long as the interests harmed could count as private interests and be segmented."[58] This constituted the objective basis of legitimacy; the subjective basis lay in the acceptance of market justice as natural fate, i.e., as "private" and "segmented."

With the emergence of interdependence, however, the increased susceptibility of these once-private domains to disturbances turned them into matters of general, i.e., political concern and called for a more obviously substantial role for the State. What Habermas has elsewhere called "the repoliticization of the relations of production" was the recognition through institutional change that bourgeois society had not in its liberal capitalist period eliminated classes, but rather altered the character of class rule such that it was only mediately and not immediately political. That is, class domination took the anonymous form of market justice normatively sustained by the principle of exchange equivalence. To the extent this is still true — and we think it is — the need to develop a meaningful political theory remains a paramount task.[59] The recognition of this state of affairs, which is simultaneously the recognition of the structural, and not simply contingent, basis of the disruptive effects of capitalist growth, is at the core of class consciousness. Or to put another way, class consciousness is an historically universal force (Lukacs' Hegelian instincts were well grounded).

As is the case with Québec nationalism, regionalism in Canada is a contradictory phenomenon. On the one hand, it promotes a sense of meaningful community essential for the emergence of class consciousness. On the other hand, insofar as it involves the presentation and preservation of an abstract particularism (e.g. the West) which masks a substantive universal (the logic of capital reproduction), it thwarts the ability of social subjects to grasp the genuinely universal character of their situation and to act on that recognition.

In short, the problem of alienated politics is one of false consciousness. But as alienated politics is in an important sense, meaningful and justifiable, as it is "political" in its ability to create an intelligent, perceptible yet false communal world, so false consciousness is likewise the true understanding of a false reality. That is, false consciousness can orient people toward successful strategic behaviour in a world governed by the dictates of capitalist rationality (the prevalence of interest group bargaining is relevant here), but cannot point beyond the given structure of power and authority toward a new form of social organization. The tenacity of false consciousness, which orthodox Marxism has tended to underestimate, follows from the fact that demands for a revolutionary transformation of society are, from the point of view of such consciousness, literally "unreal."[60] The tyranny of the given, in Marx's words, literally does "weigh like a nightmare on the brain of the living."[61] There is much evidence to suggest that the capacity for the Canadian State and political culture to reproduce alienated politics remains very strong. The continued existence of more or less stable political party preferences despite the increasing ideological similarity of the parties and their movements toward market commodification is one indication of this capacity. Another sign of the resilience of the State in its current Canadian form is the continued relevance and acceptance on the face of all apparent evidence to the contrary of the ideology of possessive individualism, symbolized by a commitment to private enterprise and the work ethic.[62] What, finally, is the consequence of all this for legitimation and the possibilities of a legitimation crisis? Simply this: if legitimation and legitimation crisis presuppose a fundamental commitment to the egalitarian and communal values of democracy, there are strong reasons to believe that such a commitment is in many fundamental respects absent in Canada. If this is so, rather than speak of the falling rate of profit, we may more accurately speak of what we called at the outset of this paper a falling rate of legitimation. Thus the legitimating activities implicit in welfare State programmes become more marginal. It does not matter much here that this is done through the generalized acceptance by large masses of people of apparently apolitical technocratic values that legitimize our social system as the expression of universal necessity. While this problem is of obvious importance in analyzing the widespread prevalence of false consciousness, the fact remains that, as we have already suggested, such consciousness does exist as a real and potent force. [63]

If the falling rate of profit suggests the inability of capital to realize itself and is hence potentially a source of crisis, the falling rate of legitimation suggests the success of the dominant class in Canada in realizing the political capital that comes in the form of the appropriated communal power that is the source and substance of alienated politics, and hence thwarts the development of crisis. If the falling rate of profit implies the erosion of capital, the falling rate of legitimation implies an accumulation of political capital. And finally, if the falling rate of profit suggests the transcendence of the proletariat, the falling rate of legitimation entails its abolition as an agency of social emancipation — although not of the task or possibility of emancipation itself.

APPENDIX

Table 1

Selected Economic Indices, 1971-1979

(all figures in percentages)

	1	2	3	4	5	6	7
1971	12.8	—	2.9	7.6	8.6	6.2	84
1972	24.4	28.9	4.8	6.8	8.4	6.2	87
1973	42.8	50.2	7.6	10.0	7.5	5.5	91
1974	30.1	25.9	10.9	14.1	11.0	5.3	90
1975	-1.8	-5.9	10.8	17.0	14.2	6.9	81
1976	2.9	4.9	7.5	9.7	12.2	7.1	83
1977	10.1	15.7	8.0	7.7	9.6	8.1	82
1978	16.7	19.1	9.0	6.9	6.2	8.4	86
1979*	35.8	36.8	9.9	—	—	7.9	87

* 1979 figures are either first of second quarter results or latest monthly figure available.

Sources: 1, 2, 3, 4, 5, 6: *Economic Review*, April 1979, Department of Finance, Ottawa.

7: *Statistics Canada Daily*, March 1, 1979.

1. Corporate profits before taxes — annual rate of increase
2. Corporate profits after taxes — annual rate of increase.
3. Rate of increase in the consumer price index.
4. Rate of increase in negotiated wage settlements.
5. Rate of increase in average weekly wages.
6. Unemployment rate.
7. Capacity utilization rate in manufacturing.

Table 2
Federal Government (-) or Surplus
as a % of Gross National Expenditure (G.N.E.)

	1 G.N.E. (in millions $)	2 Deficit or Surplus (in millions $)	3 2 as % of 1
1930	5348	48	.9
1931	4480	-84	-1.9
1932	3718	-114	-3.1
1933	3468	-221	-6.4
1934	3962	-134	-3.4
1935	4285	-116	-2.7
1936	4644	-160	-3.4
1937	5279	-78	-1.5
1938	5165	-18	-.4
1939	5598	-51	-.9
1940	6772	-119	-1.8
1941	8434	-377	-4.5
1942	10507	-397	-3.8
1943	11297	-2137	-18.9
1944	11887	-2558	-21.5
1945	11732	-2559	-21.8
1946	11863	2123	-17.9
1947	13375	607	4.5
1948	15509	765	4.9
1949	16800	484	2.8
1950	18491	650	3.5
1951	21640	971	4.5
1952	24588	195	.8
1953	25833	151	.6
1954	25918	-46	-.2
1955	28528	202	.7
1956	32058	598	1.9
1957	33513	250	.7
1958	34777	-767	-2.2
1959	36846	-339	-.9
1960	38358	-229	-.6
1961	39646	-410	-1.0
1962	42927	-507	-1.2
1963	45978	-286	-.6
1964	50280	345	.7
1965	55364	544	1.0
1966	61828	231	.4
1967	66409	-84	.1
1968	72586	-11	.02
1969	79815	1021	1.3
1970	85685	266	.3
1971	94450	-145	-.2
1972	105234	-566	-.5
1973	123560	387	.3
1974	147528	1109	.8
1975	165428	-3802	-2.2
1976	191492	-3201	-1.7
1977	210132	-7409	-3.5
1978	231835	-10677	-4.6

Source: Canada Statistical Yearbook, Ottawa, 1948, 1949, *Public Finance*, Tables 8 and 9 and *National Accounts*, Table 2; Department of Finance, *Economic Review*, Ottawa, 1979, Tables 54, 55, 2.

NOTES

1. See, for example, J. Habermas, *Legitimation Crisis* (Boston: Beacon Press, 1975); J. O'-Connor, *The Fiscal Crisis of the State* (New York: The Free Press, 1977); A. Wolfe. *The Limits of Legitimation*. New York: The Free Press, 1977; C. Offe, *The Theory of the Capitalist State and the Problem of Policy Formation*, in L. Lindberg, et. al. (eds.), *Stress and Contradiction in Modern Capitalism* (Lexington, Mass.: Heath and Co., 1975, pp. 125-144; A. Gamble and P. Walton, *Capitalism in Crisis* (London: Macmillan Press, 1976). For assessments of some of the recent literature on various theories of capitalist crises, see J. Keane (ed.), *Reviews in Crisis Theory*, *Canadian Journal of Political and Social Theory*, Vol. 3, No. 2 (Spring Summer, 1979), pp. 183-211.
2. See Hugh Armstrong, *The Labour Force and State Workers* in L. Panitch (ed.) *The Canadian State* (Toronto: University of Toronto Press, 1977), and C. Gonick, *Out of Work* (Toronto: James Lorimer, 1978).
3. Economists generally agree that this failure is a failure of Keynesian management. But for an evaluation of Canadian economic policy which sees the problem not in Keynesianism itself, but rather in the relative absence of genuinely Keynesian measures, see W. Irwin Gillespie, *Postwar Canadian Fiscal Policy Revisited, 1945-1975*,*Canadian Tax Journal*, Vol. 27, No.3 (May/June 1979), pp. 265-76.
4. See, for example, Gamble and Walton, op.cit. E. Mandel, *Late Capitalism* (London: New Left Books, 1972); P. Mattick, Marx and Keynes (New York: Pantheon Books 1972); P. Baran and P. Sweezy, *Monopoly Capital* (New York: Monthly Review Press, 1966); E.K. Hunt and J. Schwartz, *A Critique of Economic Theory* (Middlesex: Penguin, 1972)
5. See however, R. Miliband, *Marxism and Politics* (Oxford University Press, 1977) for an interesting if not wholly successful, attempt to deal with this problem.
6. L. Panitch (ed), *The Canadian State, Political Economy and Political Power*. (Toronto: University of Toronto Press, 1977), p. x.
7. See H. Chorney, et. al., *The State and Political Economy*, *The Canadian Journal of Political and Social Theory*, Vol. 1, No.3 (Fall 1977), pp.71-85.
8. See especially, K. Marx, *Private Property and Comunism, Economic and Philosophic Manuscripts* (1844), in L.D. Easton and K.H. Guddat (eds.), *Writings of the Young Marx on Philosophy and Society* (New York: Anchor Books, 1967), pp. 301-14; see also Agnes Heller, *The Theory of Need in Marx* (Allison and Busby, London, 1974).
9. See D. Camp, *Points of Departure* (Ottawa: Deneau and Greensberg, 1979) for an excellent account of this process at work, by one of its principal architects.
10. See M. J. Crozier et al., *The Crisis of Democracy: Report on the Governability of Democracies to the Trilateral Commission* (New York: New York University Press, 1975), esp. Ch.V, and D. Bell, *The Cultural Contradictions of Capitalism* (New York: Basic Books, 1976).
11. F. Pollock, *State Capitalism: Its Possibilities and Limitations*, in A. Arato and E. Gebhardt (eds.), *The Essential Frankfurt School Reader* (New York: Urizen Books, 1978), pp. 73ff.
12. While Pollock's model of democratic as opposed to totalitarian State capitalism should not be seen as a corporatist one, its applicability nevertheless raises issues discussed in recent debates on corporatism. See L. Panitch, *Corporatism in Canada, Studies in Political Economy*, I (1979), and *The Development of Corporatism in Liberal Democracies*,*Comparative Political Studies*, Vol. 10, No. 1 (April 1977); P. Schmitter, *Still the Century of Corporatism?*,*Review of Politics*, Vol. 36, No. 1 (January 1974); A. Wolfe, op. cit.
13. See, for example, A. Finkel,*Business and Social Reform in the Thirties* (Toronto: Lorimer, 1979).
14. See, for example, H.V. Nelles, *The Politics of Development* (Toronto: Macmillan, 1974).
15. See H.C. Pentland, *The Socio Economic Background of Industrial Relations*. Unpublished background paper for Government of Canada, Task Force on Industrial Relations (Ottawa, Queen's Printer, 1967).
16. S. Aronowitz, *Crisis and Confrontation: Developments in U.S. Capitalism in the 1970s*, unpublished manuscript, p. 14.
17. Ibid., p. 12.

18. See Baran and Sweezy, op. cit., for the now classic statement of the surplus absorption problem.
19. See also A. Carlo, *The Oil Crisis and the Iron Law of Underdevelopment,Telos*, No. 31 (Spring 1977), pp. 534; *Imperialism, Monopolies and Inflation, Telos* No. 34 (Winter 1977-78), pp. 89-110; *Unemployment,Telos*, No. 38 (Winter 1978-79), pp. 5-31.
20. See *International Payments, Current Account*, in Government of Canada (Department of Finance), *Economic Review*, April 1979. See also J. Britton and J. Gilmour, *The Weakest Link: A Technological Perspective on Canadian Industrial Underdevelopment*, Background Study No. 43, Science Council of Canada (Ottawa: Queen's Printer, 1978).
21. Toronto Globe and Mail, February 7, 1979, p. 131. Cf. C.L. Barber and J.C.P. McCallum, *Unemployment and Inflation: The Canadian Experience* (Toronto: Canadian Institute for Economic Policy, 1980). Barber and McCallum argue that many of the recent gains in the 1970s were illusionary because they reflected greatly inflated values in inventories, rather than increased profit margins.
22. See A. Chester (ed.),*Inflation and Democracy in Canada: 30 Years of Stop and Go* (Kitchener, Ont.: Dumont Press Graphix, 1976), and L. Panitch,*Workers, Wages and Controls* (Toronto: New Hogtown Press, 1976).
23. Source: Department of Finance, *Economic Review*, April 1979, Ottawa, ref. Tables 38, 41.
24. D.A.S. Auld et al.,*The Determinants of Negotiated Wage Settlements in Canada, 1966-75* (Ottawa: Government of Canada, 1979), p. 5.
25. But see, however, A. Lerner, "From PreKeynes to Post Keynes," Social Research, Vol.44, No.3 (Autumn 1977), pp. 387-415, for an argument by an important Keynesian setting out the basis of a reconciliation between the competing claims of Keynesianism and Monetarism. For a spirited series of commentaries on Lerner's position see "Comments on Abba Lerner's From PreKeynes to PostKeynes" *Social Research*, Vol. 46, No. 2 (Summer 1979), pp. 207-54.
26. Ontario Economic Council, *The Ontario Economy to 1987* (Toronto: Queen's Printer, 1977), p. XV. See also the Anti Inflation Board, *Inflation and Public Policy* (Ottawa: Government of Canada, 1979).
27. For a review of the classical positions, see G. Haberler, *Prosperity and Depression* (Geneva: League of nations, 1941); L. Robbins,*The Great Depression* (London" Macmillan, 1934); and M. Friedman and A. J. Schwartz, *A Monetary History of the United States 1867-1960* (Princeton, N.J.: Princeton University Press, 1963).
28. See M. Friedman,*The Counter Revolution in Monetary Theory* (London: Institute of Economic Affairs, 1972), and *From Galbraith to Economic Freedom* (London: Institute of Economic Affairs, 1971).
29. Quoted in C.L. Barber, *Recent Canadian Economic Experience*, and Address delivered to the conference Practical Economics for Executives, Gull Harbour, Manitoba, October 2, 1977, p. 13. See also the address by G. Lawson, Senior Deputy, Bank of Canada, to the Institute of Canadian Bankers in *Bank of Canada Monthly Review*, April 1979.
30. On the new monetarist orthodoxy in Canada, See A. Donner and D. Peters,*The Monetarist Counter Revolution: A Critique of Canadian Monetary Policy 1975-1979* (Toronto: James Lorimer and Co., 1979). As for the NDP, the editorial support given to the NDP by the Toronto Star during the 1979 election campaign may be relevant in this context. The Star strongly favours a nationalist economic planning strategy for Canada and apparently sees the NDP as a logical stabilizing political influence under which a gentle rationalization of the social welfare State, coupled with increased economic planning, can be carried out. (The Star's support of the Liberals in the 1980 election campaign, motivated as it was by tactical considerations, would not seem to contradict this). In this view the State is joined by relatively few Canadian businessmen. For some exceptions, at least insofar as economic planning is concerned, see the following: "Government Must Take Big Role in Providing Industrial Direction," *Toronto Globe and Mail*, May 23, 1979, p. 32; *Plan Urged to Bolster Manufacturing Sector,Globe and Mail*, March 23, 1979; see also J. Britton and J. Gilmour, op. cit.

31. These figures are derived from: *Canada Statistical Yearbook*, Ottawa, 1948, 1949: *Public Finance*, Tables 8,9 and *National Accounts*, Tables 2; and Department of Finance, *Economic Review*, Ottawa, 1979, Tables 54,55,2.
32. P. Mattick, *Marx and Keynes: The Limits of the Mixed Economy* (Boston: Porter Sargeant, 1969), pp. 160-3. Cf. D.S. Yaffe, *The Marxian Theory of Crisis, Capital and the State, Economy and Society*, Vol.2 (1973), pp. 186-232. Yaffe argues that Marx underconsumptionist and disproportionality theories of crisis incorrectly separate the circulation process of capital expansion from the production process itself, thereby confusing the possibility of crisis with its causes - a failing to which, in their own way, neo-conservative monetarists succumb.
33. Mandel, op. cit., and H. Magdoff and P. Sweezy, *The End of Prosperity: The American Economy in the 1970s* (New York: Monthly Review Press, 1971).
34. Cf. Yaffe, op. cit., whose argument, as careful and detailed as it is, does not escape this problem.
35. See J. Keane, *The 'Decline of the Individual and the Problem of Legitimacy*. Paper presented to the annual meeting of the Canadian Political Science Association, University of Saskatchewan, Saskatoon, May 1979, for a comparable, if somewhat different, interpretation of the roots of the concept of legitimacy.
36. J. Weinstein, *The Corporate Ideal in the Liberal State: 1900-1918*(Boston: Beacon Press, 1968); Finkel, op cit.
37. See*Acta Sociologica*, Vol. 21 (1978), especial issue on the Nordic welfare States.
38. Cf. H. Marcuse, *A Revolution in Values*, in J.A. Gould and W.H. Truitt (eds.), *Political Ideologies* (New York: Macmillan, 1973), pp. 33-16.
39. Habermas, op. cit., p. 75.
40. Ibid., p. 49, et seq.
41. For a discussion of the problem of political space and social transformation see H. Chorney, *Amnesia, Integration and Repression: the Roots of Canadian Urban Political Culture* in this volume Part One. and P. Hansen, *Hannah Arendt: Politics, History and Citizenship*.Cambridge: Polity Press, 1993. Speech and the Public Space of Appearances, paper presented to the annual meeting of the Canadian Political Science Association, University of Western Ontario, London, May 1978.
42. Habermas, op. cit., p. 142.
43. See. Habermas, *Legitimation Problems in the Modern State*, in Habermas,*Communication and the Evolution of Society* (Boston: Beacon Press, 1979), pp. 178-205.
44. Habermas,*Legitimation Crisis*, pp. 61ff.
45. Ibid., p. 75.
46. G. Janosik and R. Voline, *Bloodbath in the Red River Valley, This Magazine*, Vol. 12, No. 3 (July-August, 1978), p. 28-34. "Janosik" and "Voline" are pseudonums for Chorney and Hansen.
47. Cf. Also J. Keane, loc.cit., esp. Part I.
48. C. Offe, *The Separation of Form and Content in Liberal Democratic PoliticsStudies in Political Economy* 3, 1980. Cf. J. Keane, *The Legacy of Political Economy: Thinking With and Against Claus Offe, Canadian Journal of Political and Social Theory*, Vol.2, No. 3 (Fall 1978), pp. 49-92.
49. S. Mallet, *Essays on the New Working Class* (St. Louis: Telos Press, 1975); A. Gorz, *Strategy for Labour* (Boston: Beacon Press, 1967); *Socialism and Revolution* (New York: Anchor Press, 1973); A. Gorz, *Ecology as Politics* (Montréal: Black Rose Books, 1980).
50. See, for example, S. Jamieson,*Times of Trouble: Task Force on Labour Relations*, Study No. 22 (Ottawa: Queen's Printer, 1967).
51. *An Interview with Jurgen Habermas, Telos* No. 39 (Spring 1979), p. 17.
52. Relevant here is the notion of "artificial negativity," advanced by Paul Piccone, the idea that the capitalist system needs to generate sources of opposition, or negativity, if its essential irrational bureaucratic structures are to have a focus for the instrumental logic of bureaucratic rationality — or, to put it more directly, bureaucracy needs, "something" to bureaucratize. See P. Piccone, *The Crisis of One Dimensionality*,*Telos* No. 38 (Spring 1978), pp. 43-54.

A similar point is made somewhat differently by Alan Wolfe, who argues that, in the United States at least, the benefits of liberalism were extended to ever larger sections of the population — and by implication the successful transition to a corporate liberal society both made possible and guaranteed - by the frequently radical activities for groups that were not themselves liberal (e.g.,The International Workers of the World). A, Wolfe, *Waiting for Righty: A Critique of the 'Fascism' Hypothesis,Review of Radical Political Economics*, Vol. 5, No. 3 (Fall 1973), pp. 46-66.

53. John A. Macdonald put it clearly during the Confederation Debates: "While the principle of representation by population is adopted with respect to the popular branch of the legislature, as I stated before, not a single one of the representatives of the government or of the opposition...was in favour of universal suffrage. Every one felt that in this respect the principle of the British Constitution should be carried out and that classes and property should be represented as well as numbers." Parliamentary Debates on the Subject of the Confederation of the British North American Provinces (1865) (Ottawa: King's Printer, 1951), p. 39.
54. A. Wolfe, *New Directions in the Marxist Theory of Politics, Politics and Society* 4 (Winter 1974), pp. 148 ff.
55. For an intelligent discussion of the nature of genuine political community see Robert Paul Wolf, *The Poverty of Liberalism* (Boston: Beacon Press, 1968), Ch. 5.
56. At times Garth Stevenson's important work on Canadian federalism appears to lose sight of this process. See G. Stevenson,*Unfulfilled Union* (Toronto: Macmillan, 1979).
57. T.W. Adorno, *Ideology* in Frankfurt Institute for Social Research, *Aspects of Sociology* (Boston: Beacon Press, 1972), pp. 189, 197-9.
58. Habermas, *Legitimation Problems in the Modern State*, p. 195.
59. Cf. J. Cohen, *Why More political Theory?, Telos* No. 40 (Summer 1979), pp. 70-94.
60. At stake here is the power of "common sense." For an insightful account of the trap of common sense and its failure to correspond to "good" sense on the past of what he calls the "subaltern class," see A. Gramsci, *The Prison Notebooks*, edited and translated by Q. Hoare and G.N. Smith (New York: International Publishers, 1971), pp. 419-25.
61. K. Marx, *The Eighteenth Brumaire of Louis Bonaparte*, in R.C. Tucker (ed.), *The Marx and Engels Reader* (New York: W.W. Norton, 1978), p. 595. The full expression Marx uses here is generally translated as: "We believe that Marx has something like what Gramsci was later to call 'common sense' in mind here, especially given the contrary and ambiguous character of tradition, and Marx's view that revolution was an act of anamnesis, of recovery, 'a confession, nothing less.' Recall, too, Marx's claim that Bentham was "the genius of bourgeois stupidity."
62. This commitment to traditional beliefs is also found in the area of religious beliefs. For instance, the most recent annual Gallup Poll on the religious beliefs of Canadians indicates that the level of support for religious belief in Canada is stable, at close to 60 percent of the population. Furthermore, the Church and organized religion generally, is the most respected social institution (by 60 percent of those polled), followed by the Supreme Court (57 percent), public schools (54 percent), House of Commons (38 percent), newspapers (37 percent), large corporations (34 percent), political parties (30 percent) and labour unions (23 percent). See Canadian Institute of Public Opinion, *Church Ranks Highest*, July 1979.
63. Cf. Adorno, lo.cit., and R. Jacoby, *A Falling Rate of Intelligence? Telos*, No.27 (Spring 1976),pp.141-60.

PART TWO

ECONOMICS AND POLITICAL ECONOMY

4

THE POWER OF REASON AND THE LEGACY OF KEYNES

Harold Chorney

This essay was written in response to Robert Campbell's provocative essay on Keynes.[1] I was convinced then and remain convinced today that Maynard Keynes' work was badly misunderstood and distorted both by his neoclassical critics and by many interpreters on the left. Indeed, the fashionable dismissal of Keynes and the power of his insights into the workings of the economic system was a fad shared by both the left and the monetarist right during the late seventies and early 1980s. In recent months there has been a renewed interest in his work and his general approach to macroeconomic management.

The United Nations Commission on Trade and Development has recently called for an abandonment of monetarism and a return to Keynesian approaches on a co-ordinated world scale to overcome the current economic slump. The Japanese have recently launched a $100 billion economic recovery package that is clearly inspired by Keynesian ideas. It is only a matter of time before similar policy shifts occur in Canada and the United States and Europe.

A large part of the reason for the temporary eclipse of Keynes was that while many dismissed him, few had read his writings carefully and in the spirit in which they were written. Over the past decade I have worked with Keynes' ideas and his writings extensively and found them the single best guide to understanding the behaviour of the modern economy. Although his approach inevitably requires some updating, his fundamental arguments are still sound and humane — a far cry from those of the monetarists and the zero-inflation rational expectationists who now dominate the conventional wisdom. The ideas of these neo-conservative economists are simply the recycling of the ideas of writers like Friedrich Von Hayek and other economists from the pre-Keynesian epoch that were discredited by the depression of the 1930s.

The monetarism and sound finance of the right has been regrettably matched by the monetarism of the left. While Campbell, in his own work demonstrates a partial, if uneven appreciation of Keynes, his essay gave me the opportunity to begin a defense of the man and his work. It seems increasingly clear that the luminous spirit of Maynard Keynes and the sheer brilliance of his intellectual imagination will once more come into his own during the 1990s as we move to escape from the nightmare years of the 1980s and the wreckage that monetarist policies and politics have brought about. If you have any doubt about the contemporary relevance of Keynes' ideas just reread his essay "The Economic Consequences of Mr.Churchill" in the context of the Bank of Canada's insistence on keeping the Canadian exchange rate high and opting for zero inflation or the Bank of England's refusal to lower interest rates in order to conform to the demands of the European exchange rate mechanism.

The decision in September 1992 of Britain to suspend its membership in the exchange rate mechanism, when faced with the prospects of 15 percent or higher interest rates to defend the pound is a haunting echo of the decision in September of 1931 to suspend the gold standard. In 1931 Keynes welcomed this decision as the vindication of his opposition to the return to the gold standard. He had opposed this decision in 1926 on the grounds that the gold standard would cause deflation and a slump. He was right. In a similar fashion one can make the argument that the system of fixed rates under the European exchange rate mechanism has been responsible for the sharp rise in unemployment experienced in Britain and in most of Western Europe during the 1980s. So despite the passage of time, Keynes' ideas are still important for understanding the damage that monetarism and laissez-faire economics has caused in the world economy.

The works that will succeed in pointing the way out of our contemporary dilemma will not be based on a simple return to the ideas that Keynes promoted in his work but they will be a logical extension of them and stand on the shoulders of his achievements during the dark days of the 1930s.In the pantheon of humanist political economy none can achieve higher rating than the Cambridge boy from Harvey Road and later Gordon Square, Bloomsbury and the beautiful south Downs near Brighton; husband of a ballerina, collector of books and fine art, intimate of statesmen and artists alike, confidante of Vanessa Bell and Virginia Woolf and defender of the premodern tradition against the onslaught of immoral unreason.

* * *

It is fashionable these days to announce that "Keynesianism is dead." Both the right and the left have been trumpeting this conclusion with ever increasing volume. Robert Campbell's "Post-Keynesian Politics and the Post Schumpeterian World"[2] incorporates this notion as the starting-point for his analysis and critique of the eclipse of Keynesianism and the current state of the political economy of public policy.

Perhaps a clear disavowal of past orthodoxy is a healthy beginning to the process of constructing a new and improved theory of the complex political economy of advanced capitalism. Such a new theory is all the more important in light of the current recession, the recrudescence of previously bankrupt ideologies about the virtues of laissez-faire, the apparent successful ideological revival of nineteenth century market liberalism and the tragic circumstances of the unemployed. But in our haste to dispose of the corpse of Keynesianism we may well be discarding prematurely a number of extremely valuable insights associated with the original theorist, as opposed to with his interpreters.

As is often the case in human endeavour and, in particular in intellectual work, progress is rarely linear. Rather, it moves in a lurching step function manner. Furthermore, the inevitable, if regrettable tendency to distort ideas once they have left the hand of the original developer must be taken account of in any wholesale abandonment of ideas or conceptual system. This is critical in particular where the perilous state of economic theory is concerned.

It is precisely this problem of distorted interpretation that surrounds the work of John Maynard Keynes. It is always, of course, much easier to rely upon preconceived conceptions or accepted conventional sources of interpretation than to return to the original source in an attempt to deal with the work of an original thinker. The currently fashionable dismissal of Keynes by contemporary Philistine technicians of neoclassical economics notwithstanding, Keynes was above all else a great thinker. Indeed, a number of his contemporaries, including Bertrand Russell, thought of him as the smartest man they had ever met. His unwillingness to be bound by any artificial disciplinary borders and his capacity for employing imagination in the search for truth ensured that he would be no mere mechanic in the practice of the discipline of economics. Having said this any interpretation of Keynes' writings is bound to be altered by the peculiar prisms through which an interpreter encounters his work. It could not be otherwise. Furthermore, precisely because Keynes was a great thinker as well as a great polemicist, his ideas were in a constant state of flux.

It is not surprising therefore that there are contradictory tendencies in his work. This is to be expected in the work of someone who was emerging out of one dominant paradigm and beginning the process of establishing another. As it turned out this alternative paradigm was an aborted revolution. It fell victim to the forces of reaction, both intellectual and political, that shaped the reception of Keynes' work. The fact that Keynes' ideas were never truly implemented was masked by the particular circumstances of the post-war period. The destruction of the competitive Japanese and European national capitals that occurred in the Second World War permitted the post-war period of reconstruction and the long boom of the business cycle recovery that lasted more or less uninterrupted until the early 1970s, despite the failure to fully implement Keynes' ideas.

In order to understand why it is misleading and ultimately damaging to the cause of social reform to speak of Keynes, as Campbell does, as a "hyper rationalist" who believed that "a little clear thinking" was all that was required, and to hold him accountable for the bureaucratization of economics and the "trivializing and tranquillizing" of political life, it is necessary to recover the core of his original argument. In doing so we must place it in the context of his personal biography and that of his times.[3] Only by doing this can we appreciate just how badly Keynes' project was distorted and deformed by his interpreters, in particular, those neoclassical economists who popularized Keynesianism as it came to be taught in the standard economics text books and understood by governments.

What began as a truly revolutionary challenge to orthodoxy within the walls of the establishment, rather quickly and perhaps not surprisingly, was shorn of its radical content. Insofar as Keynes' work represented a radical challenge, it is not surprising that the establishment and rentier class were unwilling to participate in their own euthanasia. Nevertheless, the fact that governments in varying degrees did accept, albeit reluctantly, a role for State intervention in the economy in the interests of economic stabilization, did give observers the illusion that Keynes' ideas were actually implemented. As such, once the work of Keynes had become transformed into Keynesianism the die was cast for the inevitable discrediting of his work once the business cycle returned with vengeance.

The distortion of Keynes into what Joan Robinson called bastardized Keynesianism[4] is a matter of more than purely hermeneutic importance. As Keynes himself argued, ideas are important: both in terms of the role they play in influencing actual policy making and in terms of their hegemonic power. Once a given ideational system has been established and entrenched it is extremely difficult to dislodge. This is all the more critical in times of social crisis when ideas once vulgarized have a way of becoming embodied in social and political movements and thereby assuming a dynamic of their own.

The willingness of neo-conservatives to master this lesson more thoroughly than the left explains, in part, their extraordinary success in recent years. There is perhaps nothing more deadly and disarming than the economic orientation shown by certain analysts on the left towards ideas as distinct from material forces. For peculiar historical reasons, the very real threat posed by Keynes to the ideological dominance of classical laissez-faire as the principal explanatory system for the operation of the "free market" economy was under-estimated. Had Keynes' ideas been communicated in an undistorted form and absorbed by those who were part of the socialist and social democratic movements, politics would have developed in a very different fashion than was in fact the case.

Of course, one cannot ignore the role which other powerful cultural and environmental factors played in shoring up the ideological hegemony of the prevailing social order. Nevertheless, as Michael Kalecki[5] long ago argued Keynes' full employment economic policies could never have been implemented without fundamental change in the capitalist social order. It was just because of their radical nature that they were to be bastardized and a "political" cycle of unemployment complete with the appropriate neoclassical rationalizations established.

It is in the above sense that Robert Campbell and others are correct in arguing that ultimately, the solutions to the economic crisis lie in the realm of politics rather than technique, but incorrect in asserting that Keynes' prescription was purely technocratic and hyper-rationalist. To be sure, Keynes did believe in a kind of Edwardian liberalism in which the eventual triumph of good will assisted by a neutral State beholden to no one particular class, but dedicated to the public good was assured. Nevertheless, his proposals involved the definite restriction and eventual diminishing of upper class rentier wealth and power.[6]

Campbell chooses to interpret Keynes in terms of two versions of Keynesianism, supply side and demand side. Neither of these versions as they are described are undistorted variants of Keynes' work. In reality, Keynes approached the operation of the capitalist economy from a far more holistic point of view in which both the insufficiency of aggregate demand and the instability of the investment function were key ingredients in the diagnosis of the causes of economic depression. Keynes was able to show that full employment, rather than being an *expected* outcome, was actually an *accidental* outcome of the system. The explanation for the tendency of the economy to produce less than full employment and for the business cycle itself lay deep within the structure of the capital accumulation process.

It thus makes little sense to speak of Keynes as a demand side or supply side theorist. In reality he was both. Furthermore, he was not a believer in the idea that has come to be associated with his name, namely that simple State intervention in the economy on the side of demand stimulation in the absence of other more fundamental changes would be sufficient to sustain cycle free economic growth. He regarded such a summary of his views as nothing more than crude reductionism.

In order to better understand the critical role that the investment process played in Keynes' theory, it is necessary to understand in some detail his personal background. Keynes came from a middle class family. His father was a well-established professor of economics at Cambridge. His mother was a social reformer and successful local politician. Unlike many of those who were born to privilege, Keynes was also brought up with a profound commitment to reason and truth, and no less importantly to social responsibility and justice. Because of his intellectual talents which were considerable and went far beyond his brilliance in economics, Keynes rather early on became a star in the British establishment. His book on the treaty of Versailles, *The Economic Consequences of the Peace*, was a world wide best seller, selling more than 100,000 copies in 1920. Because of the fame that the book brought him and his war-time experience in the British Treasury, Keynes had access to ministers of the crown, bankers and diplomats. Nevertheless, because of his critical spirit he was often regarded with distrust by insiders. Thus when he did break with the establishment of the economics profession it was an event that automatically received considerable attention.

Keynes was also an expert in matters of logic and probability. Indeed, he wrote a major dissertation on the logical foundations of the theory of probability in which he explored the role of uncertainty and the impossibility of quantifying it in probabilistic terms. His approach to uncertainty was to play a key role in his later theory of the investment process.

Finally, Keynes had an intimate knowledge of the capital accumulation process and, in particular, its highly speculative, uncertain and risk taking character. Indeed, he made a fortune out of speculating in the commodity markets. He was also successfully involved in running a major British insurance company. Keynes' intimate knowledge of the financial side of capitalism, his connections with the British political and business establishment and his intellectual training equipped him to understand better than most of his contemporary economists how inherently risky, uncertain and prone to miscalculation the process of capital accumulation might be. In much the same way as Marx regarded capitalism as grounded in the anarchy of private production, Keynes eventually came to view the capital accumulation process as fundamentally irrational and therefore incapable of consistently producing socially rational results.

One of the bastions of economic orthodoxy that Keynes struggled to demolish was Say's law. Despite Keynes' best effort to destroy Say's law forever, it has recently resurfaced again with the revival of laissez-faire. Why should the economic theory of an otherwise obscure early nineteenth century French economist Jean Baptiste Say, still be influential in economic theory and thereby indirectly in public policy? The ironies of history are many. Say achieved lasting fame in economic theory on the basis of a small aspect of his *Treatise on Economics*, the notion that supply creates its own demand. Despite it becoming the target of considerable criticism at the time of its original formulation, it has continued to trouble economists to this very day.

The reason is not hard to find. If supply truly did create its own demand then a free market economy would tend toward a full employment equilibrium. Gluts of unemployed resources such as labour could be eliminated so long as they were prepared to adjust their prices, that is their wage, downwards to the point where they would be hired. Hence, the claim that we still hear today from those who espouse the zero inflation doctrine — if only workers would ask for more reasonable wages all would be well. This notion, which still has considerable currency, rests upon the fantasy that simply adding up all the buyers and sellers in a market and adjusting the prices of the goods bought and sold appropriately, will result in a market clearing equilibrium.[7] Should temporary gluts appear the explanation is less than perfect foresight in judging the correct price. In such circumstance the solution is easily at hand. Cut the price of the goods in excess supply until the market clears. Thus Say's law has had enormous ideological appeal because it supports the free market fantasy: the perfect vision of eighteenth century enlightenment, the frictionless equilibrium, the idyll of capitalist goodness.

Of course, reality was far more unkind and unforgiving. Persistent gluts of unemployed workers appeared and reappeared throughout the history of capitalism. Attempts to solve the problem by cutting wages often only prolonged the depression. In the face of the depression of the 1930s, classical economists simply retreated further into their own cocoons spinning new and more elegant refinements of Say's law. Serious critics of the tendency toward gluts of unemployed workers were banished as cranks or outsiders.[8]

It was to this traditional classical orthodoxy that Keynes addressed himself when he broke from their blindness to reality in the face of the moral crisis surrounding the massive market failure and catastrophic unemployment that struck England as early as the late 1920s. The first major proposition that Keynes overturned was Say's law. He showed precisely that a cut in real wages would not necessarily clear a glut on the unemployment market. In other words, even if wage prices are flexible downwards, unemployment may persist. This is one of the first propositions that Keynes established in his work *The General Theory of Employment, Interest and Money*. And yet this is precisely what the neoclassicals refused to acknowledge in their bastardized interpretation of Keynes' work. Instead they argued that Keynes' theory was really a special case of the more general classical model in which prices were flexible. In other words, they claimed that Keynes' argument rested upon rigid money wages, something that Keynes explicitly refuted.[9]

Keynes was able to show in his work that even if workers accepted wage cuts there was no guarantee that the level of employment that would be offered would correspond to the full employment level. Indeed wage cuts would just as likely result in price cuts without any expansion of employment. For Keynes, the explanation as to why wage-cutting was not a solution lay in the fundamental character of capital accumulation itself.

All investment decisions which ultimately are associated with employment creation involve, according to Keynes, a very firm-specific or even individual calculation of the expected rate of return, the turnover time for the invested capital: in other words, how long it takes to make back the initial outlay, the risk involved, and the degree of uncertainty about whether the expected rate of return will actually occur. Each economic actor makes this calculation alone, as opposed to in concert with others. Thus, there is absolutely no guarantee that when we add up or aggregate all these private autarkic decisions that they will total up to economic activity resulting in offers of jobs corresponding to the level of full employment. (This is true irrespective of the nature of technological labour displacement associated with new capital investment). Indeed, the full employment result is quite simply a random one among many other alternative outcomes. Much like a lottery, the chances of any one set of decisions resulting in the jackpot are statistically low.

Furthermore, the investment decision is complicated by what Keynes rather unfortunately chose to call the marginal efficiency of capital. This notion corresponds to that rate of return on capital that will just induce wealth holders to invest their savings in a project of capital accumulation. If the marginal efficiency of capital is very high — it will always be a few percentage points above the rate of interest — there is a risk that capitalists will choose not to invest their savings because there are not enough projects with a sufficient rate of return in which to invest. Instead, they may hoard their money or speculate with it in a non-productive manner. Much of the international currency exchange trading that our financial institutions indulge in today is highly speculative and falls into this category. This hoarding potential increases as the degree of risk and uncertainty increase in the economy. It was here that Keynes' intimate knowledge of the commodity markets served him well. Unlike his contemporaries Keynes developed a speculative theory of the investment process which linked it to the financial markets.[10]

It was on account of these factors and the psychological traits associated with the act of consumption that Keynes was able to show that contrary to the classical economists, savings did not automatically translate themselves into productive investment. Instead, hoards of unproductive wealth could be and were amassed in the form of jewelry, real estate, objets d'art or simply held as cash. Hence, it was a critical aspect of Keynes' theory that the social class which was most closely bound up with hoarding and speculation, the rentier class, exercised far too much power in the economic system. It was this enormous power that had to be broken if capitalism ever were to be reformed.

In Keynes' view, the "euthanasia of the rentier class" could only come about after a long period of full employment in which State intervention and the specific targeting of investment would produce an economy in which there was no longer any shortage of capital and the marginal efficiency of capital would therefore tend toward zero. Keynes believed, rather naively it would seem, that a period of twenty to thirty years of full employment might produce a sufficient abundance of capital to accomplish this. He expected this capital investment to be of a peaceful, rather than military nature. Here Keynes quite clearly misread the growth and consumerist fixation of modern capitalism.

Furthermore, Keynes argued strongly for a serious structural redistribution of wealth and income so as to ensure the weakening of rentier power. Keynes, understood in his own terms, did represent a serious challenge to capitalism. While it is a serious distortion of his views to see him as a radical socialist, the fact is his "saviour role" for capitalism has hidden the extent to which his ideas represented a very fundamental reform of the power and class structure of capitalist society.

Hence, Kalecki's warning that Keynes would never be implemented precisely because of his radicalism makes sense. The need for a fundamental redistribution of wealth, income and power of the rentier class is greater than ever. Their power has been aided by a number of perverse "reforms" designed to stimulate saving and accumulation. It is no wonder that the business cycle has returned with a vengeance. Of course, much has changed since Keynes wrote the *General Theory*. The transnational nature of capital and the disruptive nature of new technologies certainly complicate the problem of achieving full employment. But we ought to remember that neither of these factors are totally new. Indeed they were both powerful factors in the 1930s.

I am not arguing that all will be well if we simply return to Keynes properly understood. Rather I am suggesting that a new theory of economic management that builds upon Keynes' insights is required. We ought to develop an economic system that enables us to detach ourselves from the irrationalities of unecological growth, the hardships imposed by business cycle swings and the alienation of excessive commodification. We need a far less bureaucratic and much more participatory mode of political and economic organization than that associated with the post-war welfare State.

In the end, if we are to be successful in reconstructing a new vision of a better society it is rather important that we pay proper respect to the courageous personal and intellectual efforts of those who have come before us. It is in this sense that it is essential to understand that Keynes, however imperfectly, did grasp the essentials of what was flawed in the capitalist system.

It is true, of course, in the end that power and politics can never be banished by appeals to reason. And yet it is also true that reason does play a critical role in history. For it is the power of ideas and the visions of justice that accompany them, rather than brute force or crass privilege that come back time and time again to inspire and inform political action. It is an ancient legacy that we would do well to respect.

NOTES

1. The essay appeared in the *Canadian Journal of Political and Social Theory*, Vol.8, No.3, Fall, 1984. Campbell's essay appeared in the previous issue see note 2.
2. *Canadian Journal of Political and Social Theory*, Vol. 8, Nos. (1-2) 1984, pp. 72-91.
3. The following are particularly useful in this regard:
    R.Skidelsky, *John Maynard Keynes*, London: Macmillan, 1986; D.Moggridge, *Keynes*, London: Macmillan, 1976., *Maynard Keynes, An Economist's Biography*, London: Routeledge, 1992; Charles Hession, *John Maynard Keynes: A Personal Biography of the Man Who Revolutionized Capitalism and the Way We Live*, New York: Macmillan, 1983. London: Routledge, 1992; E. & H.Johnson, *The Shadow of Keynes*, Chicago: University of

Chicago Press, 1978; Fausto Vicarelli, *Keynes: The Instability of Capitalism*, Philadelphia: University of Pennsylvania, 1984.

For the theoretical controversies surrounding his work see: D. Moggridge, ed. *The Collected Writings of John Maynard Keynes*, Cambridge, Macmillan, Cambridge University Press, 1973.; S. Weintraub, *Keynes, Keynesians and Monetarists*, Philadelphia: University of Pennsylvania Press, 1978; P. Davidson. *Money and the Real World*, N.Y.: John Wiley & Sons, 1972.; J. Hotson, *Stagnation and the Bastard Keynesians*, Waterloo Press, 1976; A. Leijonhufvud. *On Keynesian Economics and the Economics of Keynes*, N.Y.: Oxford University Press, 1968.; H. Minsky, *John Maynard Keynes*, London: Macmillan, 1976.; Joan Robinson, *Contributions to Modern Economics*, Oxford: Basil Blackwell, 1978; *Economic Heresies*, N.Y.: Basic Books, 1971.; A. Coddington, *Keynesian Economics: The Search for First Principles*, Boston: George Allen & Unwin, 1983. A.Fitzgibbons, Keynes' Vision, Oxford: Clarendon Press, 1988; Peter Clarke, *The Keynesian Revolution in the Making*, Oxford: Clarendon Press, 1988.
4. See J. Robinson, *Economic Heresies*, Cambridge: Cambridge University Press, 1974.
5. M.Kalecki, "Political Aspects of Full Employment" 1943 in *Selected Essays on the Dynamics of the Capitalist Economy*, Cambridge: Cambridge University Press, 1971.
6. See J.M.Keynes, *The General Theory of Employment*, Interest and Money, London: Macmillan, 1964. bk.IV, ch.16,p.221; bk.V. ch.20, p.290, ch.19, p.262; bk.VI, ch.24, p. 376.
7. See discussion of Say's law in J.Schumpeter, *History of Economic Analysis*, N.Y.: Oxford University Press, 1954.
8. See ch.23 in Keynes' *General Theory* and Keynes' note on Marx pp.81-83 and his letter to J.A.Hobson, pp.210-211 in vol.XXIX, *The Collected Writings*.
9. See the discussion of this in A. Leijonhufvud, *On Keynesian Economics;* For a classic example of contemporary distortion of Keynes see M. Parkin, *Modern Macro-economics*, Scarborough: Prentice-Hall, 1982. This is a Canadian text from a monetarist point of view which is becoming a standard offering in undergraduate courses. The text suggests that unemployment is caused by minimum wage laws, labour unions and excessive unemployment compensation. A case of "rigid wages" with a vengeance. This "rigid wage" approach however persists in even non-monetarist texts see for example, R.V. Cherneff, *Macro Economics: Theory & Policy*, Scarborough: Prentice-Hall, 1983, pp.69, 203-204, 221-222.
10. See H. Minsky, *John Maynard Keynes and the General Theory*. Bk. IV and ch.22 and reference to Marx (see note 6) in *Collected Writings*.

5

The Deficit: Hysteria and the Current Crisis

Harold Chorney

This essay was first published in 1984 as a monograph for the Canadian Centre for Policy Alternatives, a progressive think tank in Ottawa supported by the labour unions, a number of non-governmental organizations and individuals. I attempted in this essay to puncture the myths that lay behind the hysteria that the new Conservative Government of Brian Mulroney was stirring up about public sector deficits. Much of what I warned about in this essay has come to pass.

Instead of a decade of prosperity the 1980s and early 1990s have been marred by two very serious recessions and a drastic rise in the rate of long term unemployment. In many respects the decade resembles the slump of the 1930s. Indeed, at the time of writing, fall 1992, it appears likely that the current recession will drag on with little or no improvement in the rate of unemployment until 1994. In fact, the situation may worsen. Because of the worldwide nature of the recession and the absence of serious recovery, despite the recession having lasted over two years and the accompanying financial instability ranging from the collapse of stock prices in Japan, the savings and loan scandal in the United States and the crisis over the exchange rate mechanism in Europe, it is more accurate to call this a slump rather than a simple business cycle recession.

The average rate of unemployment for the past twelve years in Canada is close to 10 percent, the highest average rate since the great depression of the thirties. Similar rates now prevail in Great Britain, France, Belgium, Australia and Italy. The official rate in the United States is somewhat lower but there are many more discouraged workers that are not counted as unemployed in the U.S. than in other countries. Japan and Germany, which have avoided recessions up to now, both appear to be on the edge of the slump themselves.

The Japanese have attempted to buck the anti-Keynesian trend. Their have recently announced $100 billion programme of public sector investments financed by expanding their deficit. They did so to the applause of both their own business federation and Wall Street. The contrast with Canada could not be greater. We shall see if this counter-cyclical strategy is enough to move the Japanese economy away from the precipice of recession. The Germans, on the other hand, despite substantial expansion of their public sector deficit, primarily to finance economic reconstruction in the former East Germany, still stubbornly stick to their policy of excessively high interest rates and may well lapse into recession later in the year.

Indeed it was the German policy of excessive high rates that ultimately forced Britain to leave the exchange rate mechanism. However, as the *British Observer* commentator William Keegan pointed out, they deserved a medal of gratitude from Britain for this feat, for the exchange rate mechanism was simply a monetarist device for forcing Britain to deflate and raise unemployment to discipline wage demands. The British are well to be rid of it. Much like the gold standard of the late 1920s, it depressed British manufacturing and lowered prices by creating a recession. One might call it "exchange rate monetarism" to go along with "deficit reduction monetarism" practised here at home.

The Bank of Canada has also practised exchange rate monetarism in keeping our interest rates higher than the American rates in order to ensure a higher exchange rate on the U.S. dollar. This has had the effect of deflating the Canadian economy more than would have been the case had our real rate of interest been more sensible. In both Britain and Canada the dogma of zero inflation monetarism has dominated public policy. The policy has now accomplished its goal with the following results: Inflation is now (September, 1992) 1.2 percent. If we subtract tax increases we now have negative inflation. This is similar to the situation during the depression of the thirties when falling prices reflected the weakness in the economy. Pessimism about the future of the economy abounds everywhere. Businesses continue to go bankrupt. Unemployment continues to rise and may yet reach 12 percent or more. What a Pyrrhic victory over inflation. Zero inflation has come to mean zero economic growth and zero employment prospects for more than one and a half million Canadians. It is hardly a policy to crow about!

Alas no one in power listened to what I warned about if a policy of sound finance and deficit reduction through austerity were pursued. Sound finance and deficit reduction became conventional wisdom. Instead of prosperity, these policies have produced a decade of lost dreams and despair for several million Canadians. Unemployment has become a chronic problem and we still have not succeeded in eliminating the debt.

Sound finance, eternally popular with lawyers and chartered accountants turned politicians, is once more the scourge of the unemployed and a definite obstacle to economic recovery. Since this first essay I have published several other monographs on the problems of debt management and monetarism, including *The Deficit and Debt Management: An Alternative to Monetarism (1989)* which is still available from the Canadian Centre for Policy Alternatives in Ottawa. A book length revision of that work should be available in 1993.

For me the deficit controversy has proved to be a rich intellectual ore body, but for many of the general public and the unemployed, in particular, it has proved to be nothing less than a disaster and in some cases a tragedy. The controversies of public policy and economics may seem dry and technical but the decisions that are made on the basis of these arguments and debates involve real blood, sweat and all too often tears. I can think of no more important arena in which to practice a humanist political economy than around the controversy that rages over the question of the debt.

* * *

INTRODUCTION

The tragically misguided economic "wisdoms" of the 1930s have once again come back to haunt us. Then, as now, faced by chronic and catastrophic rates of unemployment, the federal and provincial government, most of the business community, and many professional economists argued for "sound" conservative public finance. The cry was for deficit reduction and balancing the budget.

The result then was the continuation of the Depression with its awful impact upon personal and social life right up until the Second World War offered deliverance. Can we be so foolish as to repeat this massive failure of public intelligence? Must yet another generation of Canadians suffer the painful fate of a "lost generation"?

Much of the current debate about deficits seems to ignore the lessons of the 1930s. Instead, we hear calls to cut the deficit, to reduce government expenditure, to let the private sector flourish. On the whole, this chorus of opinion has its base in the corporate and financial community. But, as in the 1930s, they have been joined by voices from the academic community. The combination of corporate special pleading and academic legitimacy has been irresistible for the Canadian media. The move to deficit reduction has become the conventional wisdom of the day. The correctness of such a policy is projected as being beyond dispute. To question it is to reveal oneself as unfashionable, out of touch and certainly suspect.

The new Progressive Conservative federal government promises the people of Canada a new deal. How cruel will be the disappointment of the electorate if their mandate for change is wasted upon the discredited policies of the past. Let the new government recall the fate of R.B. Bennett, the Conservative Prime Minister from 1930 to 1935. It was Mr. Bennett's insistence upon sound finance that ultimately saddled the Conservative party with its reputation for inflexibility and inability to manage the economy.

If the new government is to avoid making the same mistake, it ought to reconsider the advice it is receiving from the corporate community that deficit-cutting is the only road to restoring prosperity. The recent Economic

Statement by Finance Minister Wilson, "A New Direction for Canada," unfortunately has committed the new government to the bankrupt policies of the past.

The result of these policies will be continued economic stagnation rather than economic renewal. Mr. Wilson argues that "the need for action" on reducing the deficit "is not a matter of ideology. It is an inescapable reality we have to deal with." Yet, the facts show otherwise.

It is time then to re-examine the deficit issue more closely. This short essay will look at some of the issues and some of the major myths in the debate about deficits. It will be critical of some of the economic "wisdom" regarding deficits that has been taken for granted until now.

THE DEFICIT: WHAT EXACTLY DOES IT MEAN?

Much of the current debate uses the term "deficit" without ever defining precisely what it means. Many people believe that public sector deficits are comparable to their own personal financial situation when they are in debt. As many business people are so fond of repeating, "you can't run a business constantly in the red. Eventually you're going to go bankrupt." It is this kind of logic that is often incorrectly applied to government.

Some people confuse the public sector deficit with the current account deficit or surplus on our balance of payments. Finally, many people believe that the deficit has reached an all-time high in Canadian history. As we shall see, all of these notions are quite inaccurate and misleading.

The term "deficit" when used with reference to government finance means simply the difference between government expenditure in total and government revenues. When government expenditure exceed government revenues there is a *deficit*. When government revenues exceed government expenditure there is a *surplus*.

Because of the federal nature of the country, provincial and local government expenditure and revenues are a part of this calculation. As well, the hospital sector and the Canada and Québec Pension Plans are also part of the calculation. In order to gauge the overall impact of deficits or surpluses upon the economy economists calculate the deficit or surplus from information made available in the National Accounts. The calculation is done this way in order to include information from the public accounts about government expenditure and revenues, and information from the National Accounts about changes in expenditures and revenues from "specified purpose funds" which are excluded from public accounts.[1]

Unfortunately, media reports about the deficit rarely pay any attention to these complications. As a consequence much of the information presented about the deficit is distorted or misleading. The actual economically significant deficit is the consolidated government deficit (or surplus) calculated on a National Accounts basis, as follows:

Table A

Federal deficit on a National Accounts basis (N.A. basis)	=	Federal expenditures on a N.A. basis (including deficits by specified purpose funds	−	Federal revenues on a N.A. basis
+		+		+
Deficit of the (P) provincial -(L)local -(H) hospital sector on a N.A. basis	=	Expenditures of the P-L-H sector on a N.A. basis	−	Revenues of the P-L-H sector on a N.A. basis
+		+		+
Net change in CPP and QPP balances	=	Benefits paid by CPP and QPP	−	Revenues of CPP and QPP
Deficit of the consolidated government sector (CGS) on a National Account basis	=	Expenditures of the CGS on a N.A.	−	Revenues of the CGS on a N.A. basis

When the term "deficit" is used one must ask, "which deficit?" On what basis has it been calculated? Is it strictly the federal deficit? Or is it the consolidated government deficit including the hospitals and the Canada and Québec pension plans? Calculating the deficit itself involves several important steps and assumptions. When the word "deficit" is used without qualification or explanation one should be dubious about any policy conclusions drawn about the figure.

The deficit (or surplus) applies to a given budgetary year. The accumulation of deficits year after year less any surpluses year after year yield the accumulated *debt* of the consolidated government sector. The best way of gauging the size and importance of this public debt is to measure its size in relation to the size of the overall gross national product. The ratio of these two figures has been rising and falling and then rising again over the past 50 years. Contrary to popular mythology it is not currently near its historic peak over the past 50 years. That peak occurred during the period immediately following World War II. For example, in 1952 the total net *federal* debt alone as a proportion of the GNP was 51.7 percent. In 1983 it stood at 33.5 percent of GNP.

Total government debt as a proportion of GNP was also higher in the early 1950s than the present level of 63 percent. On the other hand, the total *private sector* debt as a proportion of GNP in 1983 was 98 percent.[2] Yet, you would never know this from the hysteria about government debt in the business community.

During the war years 1942 to 1945 the annual consolidated government deficit averaged 16.9 percent of the GNP. The debt to GNP ratio

Table 1
Net Federal Government Accumulated Debt
National Accounts Basis as a % of G.N.P. (%)

1926-27	45.6		
1931-32	50.6		
1936-37	66.6		
1941-42	48.3		
1946-47	106.6		
1952	51.7	1972	19.9
1957	34.3	1973	18.8
1962	37.2	1974	17.2
1963	36.2	1975	15.5
1964	36.2	1976	17.2
1965	33.8	1977	18.0
1966	30.2	1978	21.4
1967	27.5	1979	24.6
1968	26.7	1980	26.0
1969	25.0	1981	27.4
1970	22.1	1982	28.0
1971	21.0	1983	33.5

Source: Department of Finance, Annual Review, April 1984, p. 185.

peaked in 1946 when it reached 106 percent of the GNP! Despite a level more than the three times that reached in 1983, the economy survived. Indeed, the post-war years were years of prosperity. The rate of inflation during the war averaged 1.9 percent and the rate of unemployment 1.9 percent. In 1983, the consolidated government deficit was 5.9 percent of the GNP, the rate of inflation 5.8 percent and the rate of unemployment 11.9 percent. So in very crude terms it would appear that increasing the deficit significantly as a proportion of the GNP has a positive effect in reducing unemployment. It is not possible to say this about inflation as price controls prevailed during World War II. I will return to this relationship between the deficit, inflation and unemployment in later sections.

At this point let me clarify two common misunderstandings about the deficit: the relationship between the current account deficit, and the comparison of public sector deficits and debt to household debt.

The current account deficit (or surplus) refers to the balance that results in our international trade in goods and services. Like the public sector deficit (surplus) the calculation of the balance involves a number of components and is a little complicated. The only connection that our balance of payments has with the public sector deficit is the extent to which the latter is financed by borrowings from abroad. As I explain later, foreign borrowings are of relatively little significance in the financing of the federal government deficit, although they do play a much more significant role in financing provincial government deficits. The only other complication that ought to be identified is the connection between the exchange rate on the Canadian dollar and interest paid on the debt. Just as deficits in the balance of payments can affect the value of the dollar, so too can interest rate differentials between Canada and the U.S. If the Government wishes to pursue an independent and lower interest rate policy from that of the U.S. this difference in interest rates may have exchange rate implications. I discuss these implications in section VI below.

It is often suggested that the most important difference between public sector and household debt is the fact that whereas the household must finance its debt from private financial sources such as chartered banks, trust companies and credit unions, the public sector has the power to tax, and in the case of the federal government it has access to the Bank of Canada.[3] The Bank of Canada has considerable influence over the money supply and can finance federal government debt by creating money. Where a private householder may face the real risk of financial insolvency it is almost never the case with the public sector. It is certainly not the case today. This fundamental difference between the household and the government sector is very important but it is not the whole truth.

The fact is that government debt represents investment in public assets. The total wealth of our public sector in Canada, our roads, expressways, rapid transit system, hospitals, airports, ports, power plants, public buildings, universities, schools, crown lands and natural resources represent enormous wealth-producing assets. It is the collective wealth of these assets that stand behind the liabilities associated with the debt. If one has lost confidence in the net worth of these assets there can be little doubt that long before this point one lost confidence in the net worth of the private sector.

It is simply ideological blindness not to recognize that public sector assets represent the most secure assets in the land. Furthermore, most government debt is used to finance the expansion of this asset base, either directly through additions to the physical stock of capital, or indirectly through producing and maintaining a healthy, educated and skilled workforce.

Government investments in the physical plant and social overhead capital of the nation are investments which generate wealth bearing assets that may last as long as 50 to 100 years. It would be foolish indeed to attempt to finance these assets on a pay as you go basis. No private corporation would dream of doing so. At the level of household finance, the notion of financing the purchase of a home through a 25-year mortgage is normally accepted as a sound financial decision. Similarly, a portion of government expenditure through debt is at least equally sound. Indeed, there is considerably less risk involved.

Finally, it must be understood that the vast bulk of government debt is owed to ourselves. Anyone who purchases a Canada or Provincial Savings

Bond or whose pension plan buys government bills and bonds is participating in funding Canada's debt. There may well be questions about income and wealth distribution that arise from these transfers, but on the whole, the effects are benign. If one is concerned about these effects than the answer lies in changing the tax policy that affects them and ensuring that interest paid on the debt is as low as possible. Let us now examine in detail how Canada's public sector debt is financed.

HOW IS THE DEFICIT FINANCED?

When governments run deficits in their expenditure-revenue accounts they have to finance their expenditures somehow. Generally this occurs in one of two ways. Either the government borrows money from the public or the chartered banks, or in the case of federal deficits, the Bank of Canada finances some of the government's debt. The former is by far the more common route taken. The latter is called "monetizing" the debt and generally involves direct expansion of the money supply.

When the federal government finances its deficit by borrowings it sells either a Canada savings bond, a Treasury bill or a marketable bond to individual members of the general public or institutional savers or the chartered banks. The length of term to maturity of each of these debt instruments varies from 91, 182 or 365 days for Treasury bills, to seven years for Canada saving bonds to anywhere from two to as long as twenty years for marketable bonds.

The vast bulk of these debt instruments are held by the chartered banks and the general public. For example, in 1982 Treasury bills amounted to $25.7 billion, marketable bonds $47.9 billion and Canada Savings Bonds $33.7 billion. Of this total of $107.3 billion of outstanding debt, $15.4 billion was held by the Bank of Canada. In other words, in 1982, 86 percent of the outstanding debt of the federal government was held by the general public and the chartered banks. The general public itself held 73 percent of the outstanding debt.

The principal difference between financing the federal debt through borrowings from the general public and financing the debt through direct purchases by the Bank of Canada is the effect upon the money supply. Selling bonds to the general public reduces the money supply. But if the Bank of Canada buys the securities and prints additional money to pay for them, it is expanding the money supply or monetizing the debt. On the whole, this happens only a small percentage of the time. In recent years because of the adoption by the Bank of Canada of very conservative policies, this has happened hardly at all. It is one of monetarism's contentions that monetizing the debt is always inflationary. In fact, this is not so and depends upon the circumstances in which monetization takes place. It must be remembered that selling bonds to the chartered banks also monetizes debt. The difference is that the Government must pay interest to the chartered banks.

In the case of the Bank of Canada the Government is paying interest to itself.

Provincial and local governments and the hospital and pension plan sectors do not have recourse to the Bank of Canada. Their debt must be totally financed by private pools of savings. In the case of provincial governments it is not uncommon for them to borrow on foreign, as well as domestic money markets. Nevertheless, the vast bulk of all federal government debt (over 86 percent of it as of 1984) is held in Canada by Canadians. If too much of the debt were held abroad this could create problems such as exchange rate complications. (In 1992, 79% of federal debt was still held in Canada.)

While the debt represents an obligation for the federal and provincial governments that they must service by paying interest on it, for those holding the debt it represents an important secure asset. However a number of quite conservative economists have recently suggested that government debt affects the expectations of savers and taxpayers about their future lifetime tax obligations to pay for the debt. This argument suggests that government debt does not truly represent a wealth bearing asset, despite the payment of interest associated with it. As such, they say, debt financing through the sale of bonds has the same effect as financing the debt through the levying of taxes. If this is so, it is argued that deficit financing cannot have a stimulative effect upon aggregate economic demand. They claim the private sector anticipates these future tax liabilities and reduces its consumption and investment by amounts equal to the increased government expenditure. This argument, however, makes a number of quite critical and heroic assumptions which are quite unrealistic about the long term rational planning activities of savers.

For example, it suggests that individual savers behave as perfectly rational, far-seeing calculators of their own interests, anticipating as far ahead and as comprehensibly as is possible, all likely market outcomes. As such, they are part of an overall economic system that behaves in a far-seeing, rational and relatively certain manner. Yet, as we know from present experience, the economy is a far cry from this ideologically inspired vision of a world of pure reason. In fact, uncertainty and decision-making in the absence of information and rational expectations are the rule rather than the exception. As such, the argument that taxpayers repudiate debt because they rationally have come to expect the future tax consequences seems far-fetched and at odds with actual behaviour. Finally, it assumes quite wrongly that private sector economic activities are inherently more productive of wealth than public sector activities financed by the deficits.

When one compares the role played by hospitals, day-care centres, the school system, universities, highways and airports with that played by private sector firms it is rather difficult to sustain this conclusion. Obviously wealth is created by the application of labour, technology and organization to the production of goods and services in the private or public sector. To argue that only the private sector creates wealth because it produces profits is very much at odds with the facts in a modern economy. Indeed, it smacks of pure ideological assertion.

One of the problems with current economic policy is the excessive influence of neoclassical market dogma. Many neoclassical economists stubbornly insist upon the sanctity of the market, its stable tendency toward perfect market clearing equilibrium and the rational expectations that prevail. In such an environment the role of State intervention can only be one of shock and disturbance. This idealized utopian model would be harmless if it were not for the fact that these same economists confuse it for the real world and attempt to prescribe policy from this perspective. It is because of their deeply held set of beliefs, largely at variance with reality, that so many neoclassical economists are prepared to attack public sector deficits as destabilizing influences upon the economy. Among leaders in the business community, this attack contests the very legitimacy of the public sector itself.

Far too often, the media are unaware of these dogmatically held ideas that lie behind neoclassical policy prescriptions. As I have already suggested these religious beliefs lead to perverse policy prescriptions. One is the notion that the deficit has grown far too large in recent years.

HAS THE SIZE OF THE DEFICIT GROWN TOO LARGE?

In order to answer this question it is necessary to compare the current deficit and debt situation with what it was in past years. As well, it is useful to make international comparisons and to assess the burden of the debt in terms of interest payments. (See Section V.)

When we consolidate the federal government, the provincial and local government and hospital sectors and the Canada and Québec pension plan accounts, we get an overall picture of the total consolidated government deficit (or surplus). If we compare this deficit (or surplus) to the total gross national product on an annual basis since 1930 it becomes quite clear that the size of the deficit in historical terms is high but nowhere near the levels it reached during the Second World War. Rather, what is striking is that the consolidated deficit as a proportion of the gross national expenditure (GNE) — in other words in relation to the size of the economy — is roughly comparable to what it was during the 1930s.

The consolidated deficit today as a proportion of the total economy pales in significance when it is compared to the years 1942 to 1945 when it averaged 17 percent of the GNE. During that period of massive government expenditure both inflation and unemployment were less than 2 percent. More recently, the consolidated deficit as a proportion of the GNE has grown from 1.2 percent in 1981 to 6.4 percent in 1983. During this period of time inflation fell from 12.5 percent to 5.8 percent. The deficit has continued to grow and the rate of inflation continues to fall. *There is clearly no direct or necessary connection between the deficit and inflation.*

On the other hand, high rates of unemployment, because of the nature of our tax and expenditures system, do cause the deficit to rise. If our deficit did not behave in this manner our rate of unemployment would grow even higher. Further, in order to reduce the rate of unemployment and eventually the deficit in the longer term it is necessary to greatly increase the gap between government expenditure and revenues. This is clearly what happened during World War II when the deficit rose from less than 1 percent of the GNE in 1939 to 21.7 percent of the GNE in 1944. The unemployment rate fell from 11.4 percent to 1.4 percent during the same period. In a period of less than 3 years after these enormous deficits, the resulting economic recovery produced a surplus in 1947 of 5.7 percent of the GNE. This surplus position continued until 1954.

Table 2

Federal and Consolidated Government surplus or deficit (-) in relation to the Gross National Expenditure

Year	Consolidated deficit	Year	Consolidated deficit as a percentage
1930	-3.9	1957	-0.06
1931	-7.1	1958	-3.1
1932	-7.3	1959	-1.6
1933	-5.0	1960	-1.7
1934	-4.7	1961	-2.1
1935	-4.0	1962	-1.6
1936	-0.7	1963	-1.4
1937	-0.6	1964	0.2
1938	-2.8	1965	0.4
1939	-0.8	1966	0.7
1940	-1.0	1967	0.2
1941	0.7	1968	0.7
1942	-15.3	1969	2.4
1943	-16.1	1970	0.9
1944	-21.7	1971	0.1
1945	-14.3	1972	-0.03
1946	-1.2	1973	1.0
1947	5.7	1974	1.4
1948	4.7	1975	-2.4
1949	2.0	1976	-1.7
1950	3.0	1977	-2.4
1951	3.8	1978	-3.2
1952	0.2	1979	-1.9
1953	0.3	1980	-2.1
1954	-1.0	1981	-1.2
1955	-0.1	1982	-5.3
1956	0.8	1983	-6.4

Source: Department of Finance, Economic Review 1984 and Canada Statistical Yearbook, 1948-1949.

What is significant about this first period of surplus in the post-war period is the fact that it contained two years of significant inflation; 1948 and 1951. In 1948, inflation was 14.2 percent, in 1951, 10.6 percent. Once again inflation appears to have little connection to deficits. A similar situation occurred in the period 1973 and 1974 when inflation hit 7.5 percent and 10.9 percent despite the fact that the consolidated financial balance was in surplus from 1964 to 1974.

If there is demonstrably no necessary connection between deficits and inflation then why has the public been led to believe the contrary? In the first place it is argued, wrongly, that deficits always lead to expansion of the money supply and that expanding the money supply inevitably leads to inflation. Again, the reasons have to do with the theoretical and ideological framework that informs both neoclassical economics and the business community. Neoclassical monetarist economists, in particular, who have dominated the economics profession for a number of years, rely upon some variant of the "quantity theory of money" as a guide to explaining inflation. On the basis of this theory they argue that the behavioural characteristics of people with regard to the length of time they hold on to cash is a relatively constant factor. Or if it is not constant it changes so slowly as to be predictable. If this is so, they claim, then there is a direct relationship between the money supply and the rate of inflation and the number of transactions in the economy. If the total number of transactions can be held relatively constant then controlling the money supply can control inflation. Since transactions are simply another way of describing output, and output always tends to full employment in their model the problem of inflation simply involves the money supply.

The problem with this very old doctrine (it goes back to the sixteenth century) is that it ignores the fact that behavioural preferences for cash are variable and that transactions themselves are highly sensitive to the supply of money. Put simply, Say's law does not hold. Markets do not always clear. Involuntary unemployment is possible in a market economy.

Furthermore, the monetarist model confuses changes in the money supply that are the *results* of inflationary pressures with the *causes* of the inflation itself. It also ignores the role of market imperfections such as large oligopolies, cartels and the collective bargaining process in industries that can act as transmission belts for inflationary pressures. Perhaps most important, the theory pays no attention to price shocks such as occurred with OPEC and the rise in world commodity prices in the early 1970s. The theory in its present form also operates with a distorted understanding of John Maynard Keynes' original model of the economy which had a very well developed dual sectoral theory of the inflationary process. Finally, to repeat my message, it ignores the empirical evidence that there is virtually no consistent correlation between inflation and deficits.

Because of the sensational nature of media reports on the deficit many people are under the impression that the consolidated government balance is always in deficit. Of course this is not so. Indeed, over the past 53 years there has been a surplus rather than a deficit in eighteen of these years.

DOES THE DEFICIT CONTRIBUTE TO ECONOMIC RECOVERY?

The deficit is the outcome of the balance of expenditures and revenues. In difficult economic times the tax and expenditure structure is designed to increase the deficit dramatically. If this were not the case the upward pressure on unemployment rates would even be greater. During a period of economic decline there is a tendency for productive investment activity to decline and for pools of savings to accumulate without being invested. In general, there is no necessary connection between the decision to save as opposed to the decision to invest. These are separate decisions taken by separate sectors of the economy under conditions of uncertainty. But during hard times, when economic stimulation is needed, the conversion of savings into productive economic activity finances the deficit.

This savings pool, particularly that portion that is in the form of tax sheltered income, large accumulations of wealth and, as is increasingly the case, pension funds, all too often finds its way into excessively short term ventures that frequently involve no job creating productive investment in our economy. Some of the savings pool is also committed to speculative activities. As well, in recent years growing chunks of Canadian savings have been funnelled by our banks into international money markets. Much of this money is involved in the casino like international exchange market where billions of dollars of currency are traded daily for no other reason than a speculative one. Hence, arranging for the public sector to tap more of these funds is a way of ensuring that a higher proportion of savings are invested in the production of jobs in the Canadian economy.

Contrary to much of the current rhetoric about wasteful government expenditure, government in modern society is an important producer of wealth and economic activity. The government sector can be wasteful, and excessively bureaucratic and it sometimes acts in a harmful way from the perspective of the economy or social welfare. Clearly all large hierarchical bureaucratically organized institutions can display these characteristics, whether public or private. But it is largely a myth that government institutions are inherently more bureaucratic and wasteful than private corporations. What is needed is a restructuring of bureaucracy, decentralization and the promotion of greater public access and participatory control over these institutions. As far as the corporate sector is concerned, particularly because of the growing concentration of ownership of corporate assets in a few hands, public accountability of the corporate sector is considerably more limited. And yet consumers are asked to absorb corporate sector waste through the price system. The discipline of market competition is often nowhere to be found. What competition does exist is that found between giant oligopolies that are quick to arrive at price leadership and market share solutions to ensure that profits are maximized. In the case of government, at least the electorate gets the opportunity to vote political leaders out of office. No such recourse is available in the corporate sector as shareholders are often disbursed in comparison to the controlling group of managers.

WHAT IS THE DIFFERENCE BETWEEN DEFICITS AND OUTSTANDING DEBT?

It is important to understand the difference between deficits and debt. The cumulative total of government deficits less the cumulative total of government surpluses yields the total accumulated debt. This accumulated debt can be calculated on a federal level, or at the provincial, local and hospital level or at the consolidated level. The composition of this debt is constantly changing as governments "retire" debt by redeeming debt instruments such as bonds and treasury bills by paying to their holder their face value. The government then refinances its debt by issuing new securities.

As Table 1 above shows, the ratio of net federal government debt as a percentage of the GNP has been rising in recent years after falling from a peak of over 90 percent of the GNP that it reached in the immediate post-war period.[5] It reached a post-war low of 15.5 percent in 1975. Since then it has been rising steadily. In 1983 the ratio stood at 33.5 percent, a figure still well below the post-war peak. The rise in the ratio of debt to GNP reflects, of course, the enormous rise in the rate of unemployment. In 1974 unemployment was 5.3 percent. Today (1984) it stands at 11.3 percent. (Unemployment in 1992 has averaged 11.0% as of July, 1992.)

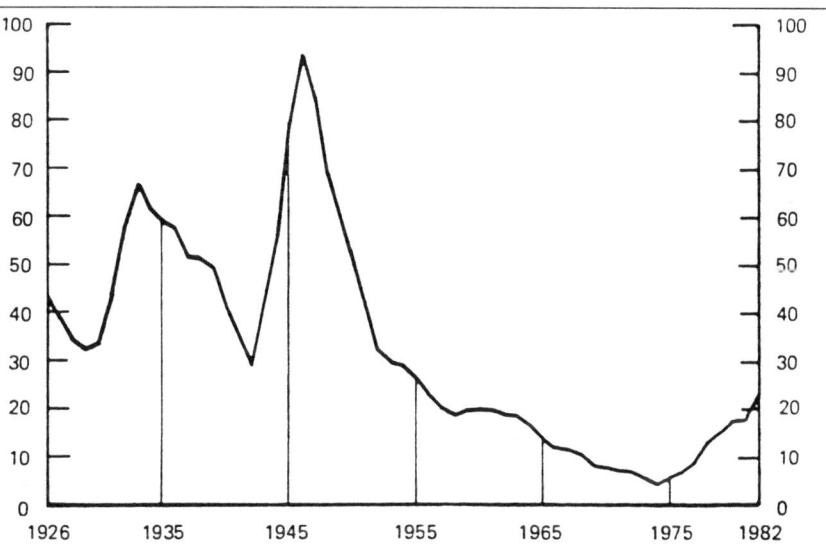

Federal Net Liabilities (As a percentage of GNP)

Source: The Honourable Marc Lalone, Minister of Finance, *The Federal Deficit in Perspective*, April 1983, p.2.

Furthermore, the ratio of net federal debt to the size of the economy is not dramatically at odds with experiences in other major industrial economies. For example, in 1981-1982 both Japan and the United Kingdom had a considerably high ratio of central government debt to the Gross Domestic Product that did Canada. During the period 1975 to 1981 the average ratio of the federal deficit to the GNP was lower than in Germany, the United Kingdom, Japan and Italy.[6]

If the size of the debt is nowhere near the historical peak that it reached in the post-war period then why all the fuss? Well, quite clearly, part of the reason is that far too few people have examined the issue from a historical and dispassionate perspective. The recent dominance of very conservative economists over the economics profession is also partly responsible. These economists essentially prefer as little government intervention in the economy as possible; they prefer "free enterprise." They argue that government debt "crowds out" private investment and develops pessimistic expectations about future taxation to finance the deficit. These theories are based on very dubious assumptions.

A final part of the reason for the outcry over the deficit has to do with a more legitimate problem — the interest burden of the debt. The interest paid by government on the debt cannot be ignored. Because of the extremely high *real* interest rates (the difference between the actual interest rate and the rate of inflation) that the Bank of Canada has fostered by its tight money policies and unwillingness to go separate ways with the American Federal Reserve the burden of the debt has risen sharply in recent years. For example, in 1983 interest payments on the consolidated government debt in Canada amounted to $27.7 billion or over 7 percent of the GNP. This ratio is the highest since the 1932 to 1934 period. This fact is no coincidence. During the years 1930 to 1933 real interest rates were even higher than they are today. The combination of high unemployment, large government deficits and excessively high real interest rates was exactly parallel to the current situation. Then, as now, the cry was to reduce deficits, restore "sound public finance" and let the private sector promote economic recovery. Then as now, this policy was doomed to fail.

The real problem posed by large deficits is the burden of high interest payments. This burden is both a direct one — high rates of interest discourage investment — and an indirect one — they impose a hardship on small businesses. Conservative economists claim that high real interest rates are the product of large deficits in the first place. But this argument ignores the role that a tight conservative money policy plays in pushing the rates up.

The current high real interest rates of over 8 percent reflect this kind of excessively restrictive policy. A reduction of real interest rates of 5 percentage points would both reduce the burden of the debt and contribute to economic recovery by stimulating economic activity.

Table 3
Real Long Term Interest rates (%)

1930 - 1935		1979 - 1984	
1930	8.2	1979	0.1
1931	10.8	1980	1.1
1932	14.4	1981	4.6
1933	6.3	1982	3.9
1934	2.6	1983	6.4
1935	3.3	*1984	7.5

Note: Real rates are calculated by substracting the rate of increase in the G.N.E. price deflator from the nominal long term interest rate. Long term rates refer to 15-year-and-over bonds for 1939-1935, and 10 years-and-over bonds for 1979-1984.
* 1984 is for the first quarter.

Source: Statistics Canada, Current Economic Analysis and M. Parkin, Modern Macro-Economics (Scarborough: Prentice-Hall, 1982)

Table 4
Interest on the Consolidated Public Debt as a Percentage of the G.N.P. (%)

1930 - 1935		1978 - 1983	
1930	4.3	1978	5.0
1931	5.4	1979	5.3
1932	7.2	1980	5.7
1933	8.1	1981	6.5
1934	7.2	1982	7.2
1935	6.5	1983	7.5

Source: Department of Finance Economic Review 1984 and Canada. Statistical Yearbook, 1948-1949.

The role of lower interest rates in reducing debt burdens is clear when we examine the period 1942 to 1945. During this period the consolidated deficit averaged close to 17 percent (or about double the current ratio) as a percentage of GNP. Yet, interest costs were considerably smaller than today (about 1/2 the size) as a proportion of the GNP. Real interest rates during this period averaged less than 2 percent. Clearly, then it is the policy of high interest rates *and not the deficit* that is the source of the problem.

DOES THE DEFICIT ITSELF CAUSE HIGH INTEREST RATES?

Contemporary conservative economists argue that the deficit causes high interest rates. Actually, this theory and the concept of "crowding out" that it has spawned were also circulated during the Great Depression of the 1930s. Like many of the myths that surround the issue of deficits, it is an old notion. During the 1930s many economists and businessmen believed financing government deficits by borrowing would displace or "crowd out" private investment projects by pushing up the rate of interest.

This argument misrepresents how interest rates are established. In fact, the Bank of Canada can exercise considerable influence over interest rates through its "open market operations." These operations refer to the bank's role in buying and selling bonds and Treasury bills.

Some economists argue that reducing interest rates in this way will lead to inflation. In fact, as I have explained above, the theory depends upon a number of assumptions which may not hold. Furthermore inflation is currently not the problem, however, unconscionable excessive unemployment is. It is certainly not beyond the Bank of Canada's capacity to pursue a less rigid money supply in order to lower interest rates. Also, such a policy of monetizing more of the debt than it now does need not last indefinitely. Rather, it is a temporary measure to ensure that the deficits have an opportunity to stimulate economic recovery and a greater supply of savings to retire the debt further down the road as the economy recovers and the deficit declines. Thus, the timing, as well as the actual financing policy, used by the Bank is of importance in managing the debt. Other things being equal, if the central bank allows a lag of sufficient time during which it monetized a certain portion of the debt before turning to the money markets to reduce the monetized portion through borrowings it will both reduce interest payments *and* unemployment. Unfortunately, the Bank has not been following this policy.

Instead, the Bank has been following a restrictive monetary policy and not monetizing any significant portion of the debt before borrowing from the money markets on the federal government's behalf. The result, ever since 1975 when the Bank first declared itself in favour of these policies, has been rising interest rates and rising unemployment. While price inflation has been dramatically reduced the cost in terms of increased unemployment has been disastrous.

The supposedly "tolerable" level of unemployment that these restrictive policies were to have created was grossly underestimated. Unfortunately, for Canadians the Bank's policies have seriously harmed the welfare of millions of citizens and contributed to the current malaise in our economy.

Of course, Canada's interest rate policy is complicated by our excessive economic dependence upon the U.S. Since the U.S. Federal Reserve is also committed to a tight money, high interest rate policy, the high U.S. rates have acted as a barrier to reducing Canadian rates. First of all, it should be pointed out that the U.S. central bank has actually pursued since 1981 a slightly less restrictive monetary policy than our own central bank. Nevertheless, American interest rates have still been very high and have encouraged the Bank of Canada to keep our rates up in order to prevent speculative outflows of Canadian savings to the U.S. money markets. These outflows tend to erode the exchange value of the Canadian dollar. The Bank of Canada has argued that if it allows too great a gap to develop between interest rates in Canada and the U.S. rates we will experience too rapid and too large a depreciation in our currency vis à vis the U.S. dollar.

This fear of excessive exchange rate depreciation however, ignores the enormous cost in higher rates of unemployment that result from excessively high interest rates. There are alternatives to this policy which would improve our economic situation. These alternatives include an interest equalization tax which would tax away the benefit of the interest rate differential between the U.S. and Canada. Such a tax would act as a disincentive for Canadian savers seeking higher rates of return in the U.S. It need not necessarily be resorted to in following a more independent interest rate policy. This would be so, for example, if lower interest rates and a more sensible policy of debt management, along with a programme of major government expenditure directed at social and physical infrastructure, led to a major reduction in unemployment rates. Such a significant recovery would counter the tendency toward exchange-rate depreciation. Finally, it is important to understand that the crowding out argument assumes that the fund of savings is static, in other words, a fixed mass that does not alter in size over time. In fact, this is simply not so. If the Bank of Canada were to change its policy, and, in particular, the timing of its entry into the money markets, government deficits would stimulate more economic expansion than is currently the case. This expansion, in turn, would enlarge the pool of savings thereby reducing the pressure on the rate of interest. Crowding out, at first glance, appears to be a convincing explanation of the risks of "excessive deficits." However, when it is examined critically it loses much, if not all, of its explanatory power. In the end, it is not much more than a reassertion of the old laissez-faire dogma in favour of sound finance and less government intervention in the economy.

Theoretically, it can be shown that the crowding out argument is a static one that misunderstands that the supply of total savings available, looking back at any given time, must always have met the total financing demands placed upon it. This misunderstanding occurs because the crowding out model confuses stocks and flows.[7] The supply of available savings is the outcome of the flow in investment, savings and consumption decisions by both the private and public sector. The pool of savings upon which the private sector has drawn in making its investment decisions that have resulted in less than full employment would have been reduced, if, in the preceding time period, government activities had been reduced.

Hence, attempting to avoid crowding out by cutting government expenditure plans in times of less than full employment can only shrink economic activity in the next round.

The real thrust of the crowding out argument is once again the deep-seated hostility to government involvement in the economy in the first place. It is in this sense that it can be recognized as simply a restatement of the canons of laissez-faire faith. In the present economic circumstances it constitutes a tragic and misleading policy confusion. If it is allowed to influence government policy it can only lead to sustained high rates of unemployment.

DOES THE SIZE OF THE DEFICIT MEAN THAT EVEN IF WE WERE TO RESTORE FULL EMPLOYMENT THE STATE OF GOVERNMENT EXPENDITURE AND REVENUES WOULD BE STRUCTURALLY UNSOUND?

According to economists, a *structural deficit* occurs whenever the expenditure and taxation policies of the governments are such that even at full employment and minimal inflation, the government's expenditures would exceed their revenues. This notion of the structural deficit raises a number of complications. Nevertheless, it is worth considering the concept briefly in order to make better sense out of the current debate. Because of the long period of inflation that Canada experienced from 1973 until 1982, new accounting techniques were developed to adjust economic data to the distorting impact of rising prices. This kind of adjustment was also developed for the treatment of the deficit and accumulated debt. It is generally accepted[8] that one should reduce the value of the outstanding debt and the annual deficit by the impact of inflation upon the interest rate burden of the debt. Since the portion of the interest rate that compensates for inflation simply guarantees the replacement value of the savings borrowed to finance the debt, it seems reasonable to deduct this amount when calculating the real burden of the debt.

The second adjustment concerns the normal swings in the business cycle. Clearly a very substantial portion of the annual deficit in recent years is the result of the high rates of unemployment.

If unemployment were to return to a more normal rate of about 4 percent, the government's revenue picture would change considerably for the better. It is argued by many economists that the deficit should be adjusted by the amount of additional revenue a normal full employment national income level would generate.

The inflation and cyclical unemployment adjusted budget balance would then look like this:

> Budget balance = taxes (less transfers) minus government expenditure on goods and services minus interest paid on the public debt less inflation portion minus business cycle adjustment.[9]

The resulting budget balance is very dependent upon whatever value is chosen for both the inflation component, and more importantly, the rate of full employment. Many economists would not accept 4 percent unemployment as normal full employment. Indeed, one prominent conservative economist, Michael Parkin, argues that full employment is closer to 10 percent unemployment![10] But clearly, choosing such a high rate for the acceptable natural rate of unemployment would tend to increase the occurrence of a structural deficit.

The question of whether we have, now, a structural deficit depends upon the assumptions one makes in calculating the adjusted budgetary balance. A number of important Keynesian and neo-Keynesian economists[11] argue that as recently as 1982, Canada, in fact, had an adjusted budgetary balance at the federal level that was a *surplus,* rather than a deficit.

Thus, attempts to cut federal government expenditure further and raise taxes in an effort to "lower the deficit" would be incredibly perverse policy. It would increase unemployment rather than decrease it. This increased unemployment would result in a larger actual debt ratio.

WHAT ALTERNATIVES DO WE HAVE TO THE PRESENT POLICIES?

The present economic and political circumstances are eerily reminiscent of the 1930s. The principal difference, of course, is the fortunate fact that Canada has a relatively well-developed "safety net" of income support programmes in place which have acted to prevent the very severe economic downturn of 1981 through 1983 from raising unemployment levels to those that prevailed in the years 1932 and 1933.

Nevertheless Table 5 (below) suggests that unemployment rates of above 11 percent are within the lower range of the high rates which prevailed during the 1930s.

These rates are unacceptable. They involve considerable hardship that is simply unnecessary. As well, they are associated with unemployment rates for younger people which approach 18 percent to 19 percent. Furthermore these rates have persisted now for three years. There is absolutely no historical evidence that simply allowing the "market

Table 5
Unemployment Rates

1930 - 1945		1975 - 1984	
1930	9.1	1975	6.9
1931	11.6	1976	7.1
1932	17.6	1977	8.1
1933	19.3	1978	8.5
1934	14.5	1979	7.4
1935	14.2	1980	7.5
1936	12.8	1981	7.5
1937	9.1	1982	11.0
1938	11.4	1983	11.9
1939	11.4	1984	11.3
1940	9.2		
1941	4.4		
1942	3.0		
1943	1.7		
1944	1.4		
1945	1.6		

Source: Statistics Canada

economy" to return the unemployment rate to its "normal" level will solve the problem. Despite many of the critiques of the practical relevance of the work of Keynes there is still considerable evidence that his fundamental assessment remains correct. The private sector left on its own cannot restore full employment. Keynes pointed the way toward solving the last Great Depression through greatly increased government social regulation of the investment process, the reduction of income and wealth disparities and the weakening of the power of rentier interests (that is, those who control great pools of wealth).

The current attitude that prevails in the business community and among a number of academic economists that government deficits are excessive and crowd out private sector investment is demonstrably wrong. But it is more than simply wrong. It is a cruel and ultimately dangerous counsel. Should these rates of unemployment continue we can expect growing numbers of disillusioned and embittered young people who will be the principal victims of these policies. In the 1930s such prolonged unemployment caused extremely serious destabilizing political and social pressures. In addition to the fundamental immorality of tolerating such high unemployment, there can be no doubt that politically and socially it is a time bomb. Surely we would not permit such a problem to persist in our own family if we had alternatives available. Why should we permit it to persist in our own society?

It is beyond the scope of this essay to spell out in detail alternative policies. The general direction is clear. Rather than attempting to slash government expenditure, we should be using government to stimulate the economy. We should do this by direct expenditures in labour-intensive activities such as housing, public works, educational and social expenditures. We should reinforce this stimulative impact by implementing reductions in regressive taxes, (for example, sales taxes) and in the income tax burden on the middle and lower income classes. We should ensure that government employment expenditures are financed both by borrowings in the money markets *and* by monetizing more of the government debt than the Bank of Canada has done to date. Once the economy recovers the Bank can turn to the money markets to refinance that portion of the debt it has monetized. Finally, the Bank of Canada should pursue a lower interest rate policy, independent of the U.S.

The combination of these policies would stimulate employment growth, reduce interest rates and restore a critical sense of optimism to the economy. The problem of inflation which has currently disappeared could then be anticipated and planned for through consultation with government, the unions and the corporate sector. But such consultation ought to be a part of an agenda for discussion once a situation of full employment has returned.

The current economic circumstances once again provide us with a critical test of both our courage and our intelligence. History, as the philosophers tell us may well repeat itself, the first time as tragedy, the second as farce. But there is nothing inevitable about such a repetition. Let us commit ourselves to proving the philosophers wrong. We can avoid repeating the tragedy of the 1930s. the technical intelligence is available. All that is lacking is the political courage.

If our elected leaders fail us they will have this burden of failure to carry with them for a long time to come.

NOTES

1. See the discussion in D.W. Conklin and Adil Sayeed, "Overview of the deficit debate" in D.W. Conklin and T.J. Courchene, *Deficits: How Big and How Bad?* (Ontario Economic Council: Toronto, 1983), p. 13ff., and the Honorable Marc Lalonde, Minister of Finance, The Federal Deficit in Perspective, April 1983, pp. 23ff.
2. *The Globe and Mail*, Nov. 3, 1984, B5.
3. See, for example Ruben Bellan, "The National Blessing", *Policy Options* Vol.5 #5 Sept. 1984.
4. See R. Barro, "Are government bonds net wealth?" *Journal of Political Economy* 82, 1974, 1095-1117 and Franco Modigliani, "Government Deficits, Inflation, and Future Generations" in Conklin & Courchene, *Deficits.* See also P. Paquette and M. Seccareccia "Les Illusions de l'austerité" *Policy Options* Vol. 5, 1984. For more recent discussion of these issues see my 1989 monograph, *The Deficit and Debt Management: An Alternative to Monetarism;* H.Chorney, "Deficits: Fact or Fiction? Ontario's Public

Finances and the Challenges of Full Employment" in D. Drache, *Getting on Track: Social Democratic Strategies for Ontario*, Montréal: McGill-Queen's University press, 1992; J. Rock, ed. *Debt and the Twin Deficits Debate*, Toronto: Mayfield Publishing, 1991; R.Eisner, *How Real is the Federal Deficit*, New York: W.W.Norton, 1989; R. Heilbroner & P. Bernstein, *The Debt and the Deficit: False Alarms/Real Possibilities*, New York: W.W. Norton, 1989.
5. See chart 2 in Lalonde, *The Federal Deficit*, p. 2.
6. See OECD Occasional Studies June, 1983 p. 22 Table 7., Lalonde, *The Federal Deficit*, pp. 37-38.
7. See, Edward Nell and Alex Azarchs, "Monetarism: Conservative Policy and Monetary Theory" in Edward Nell, ed., *Free Market Conservatism: A Critique of Theory and Practice*, (London: George Allen & Unwin, 1984).
8. See Lalonde, *The Federal Deficit;* Conklin & Courchene, Deficits, in particular J.C. McCallum, "Government Deficits: Historical Analysis and Present Policy Alternatives," pp. 254ff.
9. Ibid, McCallum, "Government Deficit."
10. M. Parkin, "What Can Macroeconomic Theory Tell Us About the Way Deficits Should be Measured" in Concklin & Courchene, Deficits.
11. See, for example, McCallum, "Government Deficits."

PART THREE

PUBLIC LIFE AND POLITICAL ECONOMY

6

Hannah Arendt:
Speech and the Public Space of Appearance

Phillip Hansen

Originally written in 1978 for the annual meeting of the Canadian Political Science Association, this essay represented my first systematic attempt to analyze the political thought of Hannah Arendt. At the time, Arendt's work was not widely known, at least not on the left. Since then, however, there has been a veritable explosion of interest in Arendt's ideas, particularly among current and former leftists searching for an alternative to a Marxism that no longer seems relevant or meaningful for contemporary concerns.

This essay sought to make the case that Arendt had an important contribution to make to a contemporary left analysis. At the heart of this contribution were the distinctions she drew between "public" and "private" realms, and the importance of what she called the "space of appearance" for the expression of certain important human qualities which could not otherwise find an outlet. Put otherwise, Arendt provides important sources for an account of public life, a theme that has also in recent years been given much attention. Without being fully aware of it at the time, I essentially sought in this essay to give voice to a growing sense of unease about the way that politics had been understood by both the defenders of the status quo and by its left critics, at a time when the critical analysis of the capitalist State was much in vogue. (This unease emerges much more clearly in "The Falling Rate of Legitimation," originally published two years later.) Events have justified the rise of neo-conservatism and the collapse of "actually existing" socialist states has shown the Marxist critique of the capitalist State, for all its intellectual elegance and theoretical sophistication, to be ineffectual indeed.

To be sure, this essay reflected the considerable influence this new Marxism had on my outlook at the time. In particular it expressed my enthusiastic response to the ideas of the Frankfurt School, which I had only recently discovered. This accounts for the general framework of analysis in the paper, as well as the occasional, and embarrassing, apocalyptic overtones in the argument. The picture of Arendt that emerges from this essay is in part that of a Marcuse-like critic of one-dimensional society.

This is a very misleading perspective on Arendt's work as a whole and were I rewriting this essay today, I would certainly de-emphasize the parallels between Arendt and the Frankfurt School. (This should be evident in my forthcoming book, Hannah Arendt: Politics, History and Citizenship.) In fact I have pretty much reversed my conception of the relation of Arendt to Marx. Whereas in this essay I essentially claimed that Arendt's analysis would have been improved had she been something of a Marxist, I now believe that Marxism itself has suffered grievously from its failure and perhaps inability to incorporate Arendt's concerns.

Yet there may still be merit in leaving the essay as it was written. In part this is because it still contains useful observations about certain of Arendt's fundamental concepts. But more importantly, it identifies concerns I still believe to be important. In this regard it is, in my view, highly ironic, and also unfortunate, that Arendt has been discovered by many on the left precisely as they have turned away, frequently in disillusionment, from Marx and have embraced what have ultimately proven to be more conformist, if not frankly conservative, alternatives. In these circumstances Arendt has been pressed into service on behalf of a more cautious and moderate politics which eschews radical change as potentially threatening to humane values. For a left in the process of rediscovering the supposedly long since dismissed values of liberalism, Arendt seems to be the epitome of the non-bourgeois liberal.

But in my opinion this seriously misrepresents Arendt's position and indicates the perils of using her ideas as a weapon with which to wage war against a now undesirable Marxist or radical past. For while Arendt was no Marxist, she was no anti-Marxist either. Indeed to be "pro" or "anti" any reasonable position in this sense is to express a dogmatic or ideological caste of mind of the sort Arendt frequently criticized. Thus while much in this essay may be obsolete or may no longer reflect fully my views, I still think the idea of a dialogue between two powerful thinkers, Marx and Arendt, one which respects the contributions of each, is worthwhile. In fact it accords with the demands of Arendt's position, shaped as it was by her own encounter with Marx's thought.

This paper is not intended to be a comprehensive examination of Hannah Arendt's political thought. It is, however, designed to suggest an important and largely unexplored dimension of Arendt's work that provides a crucial hint of its general significance for the study of modern politics. What I want to argue is that for Arendt the fate of politics in modernity is inextricably tied to the fate of speech, the ability of men and women to establish links of genuine intersubjective communication. Echoing the classical view that to "be political, to live in a polis, meant that everything was decided through words and persuasion and not through force and violence,"[1] Arendt sees in speech, not simply the human ability to answer and talk back, to respond to a given situation, but also the capacity to articulate and act upon alternative visions of reality. In so doing, and as a consequence of their efforts, people literally appear: they reveal who they are through word and deed. Political speech, in short, is inextricable from freedom. But it is precisely speech in this singularly creative sense that has come under serious threat in the modern age.

In discussing the nature of this threat as Arendt sees it, I want to suggest that, contrary to common assumptions about Arendt's theoretic stance, she is not a conservative apologist for a classical paradise lost but rather a variant of critical theorist, although certainly not without qualification. To see Arendt in this way admittedly requires an exposition of what at various points is only implicit in her work. Nevertheless there is a textual basis for this position and it seems to me to possess the added virtue of helping to clarify several key concepts in Arendt's work that have not received adequate analysis in most commentaries on her thought. Central to the argument is Arendt's distinction between the private and public realms or space of appearance. The bulk of the paper is given over to a detailed account of each of the two spheres because the uniqueness of Arendt's position is rooted in a precise understanding of the distinction between private and public. It is first of all essential, however, to explicate Arendt's understanding of politics as a human activity in order to see clearly why a genuinely public realm must possess, and is the only mode of human intercourse that can possess, the characteristics Arendt attributes to it.

For Arendt, politics properly understood is *sui generis*, an expression of and the necessary basis for the uniquely human capacity to act. To Arendt, indeed the central element in politics is action, which allows people to begin something new, to intervene in social and natural processes that would otherwise proceed in uninterrupted silence. Action, rooted in power understood always as a "potential," is the only human capacity that can incorporate the miraculous, for it is precisely in the always-surprising human ability to begin something new that miracles reside.

Through action individuals affirm themselves. By so doing they reveal what it means to be fully human. The key to understanding Arendt's entire enterprise, lies in recognizing the importance she attaches to human self-affirmation. And such self-affirmation is necessarily political because an individual reveals herself only in the context of human plurality, as one among the many who live on earth and inhabit the world.

Arendt's understanding of action suggests a dialectic of creativity as the centrepiece of political life. Politics is the search for and the realization of the human possibility of establishing consciously a multiplicity of mediated relations between human and human, and human and nature.[2] As such, genuine political life provides the forum in which we can bring something new, an addition to the edifice of human society. Or, more correctly, in the context of modern administered societies, a genuine politics cries out on behalf of suppressed and repressed creative possibilities for a fully human life; it asks us to imagine the unimaginable.[3] This role for the political — at least in terms of a critical perspective on contemporary social reality — is, in our current situation, especially crucial. We now face, as

Arendt seems to have understood, the apparent withering away of any genuine possibility for political and social transformation (at least as that possibility was understood by traditional radical theory), as social forces of domination, not satisfied with the conquest of earthly space, have invaded psychic space as well.[4]

It is with these developments as a backdrop that Arendt's political theory may be seen as a form of critical philosophic inquiry which attempts to keep alive the possibilities for breaking out of the reified logic and discourse — the tyranny of the given — of advanced industrial (i.e., capitalist or "socialist") society. Arendt wants to indicate concretely the essence of a genuine and genuinely human politics. That task involves the attempt to uncover politics where we have been conditioned least to expect it, but it also means de-politicizing those things that are not properly of the political realm although we are used to seeing them there. In this way, the ability to penetrate the veil of appearances thrown up by forces of domination and legitimized as "the facts," I take to be at the core of critical political thought. And such thought has as its aim not the abolition of politics, as orthodox Marxism, for example, has been wont to argue, but its vindication as a potentially, if not currently actual, humanizing force.

Critical thought thus wants to probe and so undermine alienated politics — politics as domination, as power over others — while attempting to outline a politics given over to the realization of the currently suppressed capacity for a life of common involvements: a life based on and in turn generating the rational regulation by individuals of their social and political relations.[5] Arendt's work seeks to expose the conditions under which alienated politics can thrive (the conditions produced by what she calls "world alienation"[6]) and suggests how through a reconstitution of genuine political experience, the human world as a multiplicity of mediated relations might be restored. For Arendt's insight is that the modern political being is homeless: she lacks a world in common with others. To build new lodgings, or at least to lay the foundation, is her theoretical task.

Basic to Arendt's attempt to restore genuine political experience is the Greek polis. It is in the polis that Arendt finds an historical and analytic model for those human relations whose sole reason to exist is to make possible, and in turn to be constituted by, the human capacity to act. However, if Arendt's polis is to be understood correctly it must be viewed from an essentially metaphorical standpoint. This is not to suggest that the empirical and historical determinants of the Greek experience are irrelevant to the problem of a genuine politics. The polis is not only a historical phenomenon but in an important sense is itself the source of human history — at least in political terms.[7]

However, the facts of history do not speak for themselves, as it were. Not only do they require an analytic framework which is shaped by, and in turn establishes a basis for, a sedimented conception of human wants, needs and purposes such that there arise "depth connections among the assumptions, conceptual contours and test procedures in a theory of politics or society;"[8] they are also themselves constituted in part by the very intentions of individuals, captured in language and action (praxis), that serve as the "objective" data of historical understanding. History cannot be appropriated neutrally. People are not indifferent to the world's outcomes and hence history must be seen as a forum for the creation, articulation and appreciation of meaning: the attempt by sensuous, living individuals to endow their actions with a sense of purpose that allows them to say both who they are and might yet become. Humans are the only beings who can literally "make" history. Our intentions, mediated by and thus given expression through socially determined, intersubjectively constituted patterns of symbolic interaction are a moment of history's objective process. To be sure that process is not exhausted by such intentions. They do not appear ex nihilo but are themselves historically circumscribed. As Marx said in the Eighteenth Brumaire people do not make history simply as they choose; they act within a given range of determinate historical possibilities.[9] But those possibilities are realized by and through conscious human activity. Hence history to be humanly meaningful, cannot simply be recounted, it must be interpreted. It does not exist "out there." Positivist accounts that view history in this way veil it with a false "naturalism" which gives it a scientistic inevitability. Human activity is understood objectivistically, as real (and thus rational) necessity. That individuals in advanced industrial societies in fact do "function" as appendages of a process, as objects and not subjects of history such that it operates as a blind naturelike force beyond human control, must itself be understood objectively, i.e., as a human creation, if a deformed one.

To say that history cannot be understood as something merely "in-itself" and thus capable of being grasped without reference to human intentions and concerns that are ontological in nature, is to point out that the process of history (and indeed history understood as process) must be apprehended in terms of both the realization and denial of human capacities. History celebrates but it also laments; it has its victors but more importantly its suffering victims. It cannot be seen as an all-inclusive net which merely by virtue of catching everything that happens, gives sense, and hence justification, to the entire process. History must be understood as a dialectical process of inclusion and exclusion of possibilities for realizing genuine human capacities. Not all historical change is "progressive." Valuable things can be and have been lost along the way.[10] Arendt's concept of the polis is an attempt to disclose and account for the loss, or at least sublimation,[11] of something humanly important: the capacity for genuine political action. When in Arendt we read the polis as history, we must also read history through the mediating power of the polis.

The Greek experience that gave rise to the polis as both an historical phenomenon and philosophical concept is predicated on a distinction whose significance has been overlooked in the modern world: the distinction between the private and the public. To be sure, the terms "private" and "public" continue to survive and prosper in contemporary political discourse. Our speech is replete with references to "private" enterprise, or the "public" interest. But the real significance of the dichotomy is lost, for as Arendt sees it, what now passes for "public" or "private" is not truly either. Instead, a hybrid mixture of public and private, the social realm has emerged over the course of modernity as the communally generated locus for the establishment and consecration of both individual identity and collective good. Indeed we have become so accustomed to defining our situation in what Arendt understands to be social terms that our universe of discourse is shot through and through by the spectre of (bourgeois) society. And not merely our theoretical apprehension of the world is so determined. Hobbes' atomized individual competitor for power over others needs those very others in order to realize his individuality. Hobbes' private man is not so much private as he is alone;[12] and his loneliness is the socially produced anxiety of men in a market order. Market man's privacy is the pseudo-privacy of he who must stand naked before others to ensure in his own mind and theirs his very existence as a self-interested competitor. As Hobbes puts it, the "Value, or Worth of a man is as of all other things, his Price; that is to say, so much as would be given for the use of his Power: and therefore is not absolute; but a thing dependent on the need and judgment of another."[13] And the public sphere in a market social order exists largely to protect and preserve the self-interested pursuits of "private men, in the process rendering opaque, the class domination those pursuits spawn.[14] In Arendt's terms, what passes for the public realm in modernity is social, not political, in character.

In this as in other respects a good Kantian, Arendt sees the distinction between a genuine public and private sphere as parallel to the split between the realm of necessity and the realm of freedom.[15] In Arendt's works the relation between the two realms is complex and subtle. It is thus essential to specify quite precisely yet extensively, those characteristics of each sphere that make the question of speech such a crucial, if only for the most part, implicit, aspect of her work.

The private sphere incorporates the relations of the household, those conditions guaranteeing the reproduction of the material basis of life. While clearly an essential and natural form of human association, the household must also be viewed as an extremely limited kind of human organization, a concession to "the needs of biological life, which are the same for the human animal as for other forms of animal life."[16] In the household the "driving force was life itself...which for its individual maintenance and its survival as the life of the species needs the company of others...Natural community in the household therefore was born of necessity, and necessity ruled over all activities performed in it."[17]

Because of its roots in the requirements of biological existence, the private realm is for Arendt the seat of the labour process, the cyclical human activity concerned with the production and consumption of things necessary for mere physical survival. While bearing obvious relation to the specifically modern mode through which human production is organized in an exchange economy, Arendt's concept of labour has more general ontological significance: the "human condition" of labour is life itself. It is interesting at this point to note the distinction that Arendt draws between labour and work. What makes labour as opposed to work especially important from the point of view of political life, is its inherently "unworldly" quality, the fact that its products assume none of the permanence or durability of those "use objects" of work which provide "an 'artificial' world of things distinctly different from all natural surroundings,"[18] and give "the human artifice the stability and solidity without which it could not be relied upon to house the unstable and mortal creature which is man."[19]

The labour process expresses and recreates the cyclical character of biological life in which the production and consumption of the means of life, each undertaken for the sake of the other, is the central feature. Animal laborans produces to consume and consumes to produce. Dominated by the rhythms of "the natural metabolism of the living body,"[20] labour possesses a certain futility. Given that its products perish through consumption almost immediately following their production, labour as an activity simply cannot guarantee the existence of that stable, permanent world of useful objects — literally an "objective" reality — which serves as man's permanent habitation on earth.[21] In this sense labour is "natural," work "unnatural." As natural beings, we must humanize nature and in a sense de-naturalize ourselves to become fully human.

Traditionally labour was the most despised of human activities precisely because it served the "slavish" demands of necessity.[22] Insofar as it was bound to the endlessly repetitive natural process of growth and decay, labour was seen as essentially purposeless, with no definable beginning or end. As such it was above all, silent. It lacked the revelatory qualities of both work and action, the other components of what Arendt calls the *vita activa*. Both work and action, each in its own way, require speech to exist at all: speech embodied either in the imagined vision of the end product guiding the worker; or in those direct encounters between individuals who attempt to distinguish themselves before others and so insert themselves through "word and deed" into the human world — what Arendt calls action. The silence of the labour process means that labour is always and in every case a solitary activity, nonetheless so for its being carried out by organized groups of people, be they the slaves of antiquity or the labourers of modernity.[23] This most important of labour's characteristics accounted for its location in the private realm. The needs of the household which labour addressed were literally a source of genuine privation. Those who lived exclusively private lives were "deprived of things essential to truly human life...the reality that comes from being seen and heard by others...an 'objective' relationship with them that comes from being related to and separated from them through the intermediary of a common world of things."[24] Labour thus had to be "hidden": because of its futility it could not be seen, heard or remembered. Taking a cue from Freud, Arendt links the futile worldlessness of labour with the human sense of shame over our bodily functions, functions which must be discharged for human life to be maintained at all but which nevertheless seem to make us less than human. For the ancients, and for Arendt, "man's" labour is literally the "labour of his body."[25]

As Arendt sees it, the key to modern politics lies in the elevation of the labouring process to public status, to a position of primacy over work and action. The transformation of labour from the most despised and hence hidden to the most honoured and thus visible of human activities parallels the growth of market society, or in Arendt's terms, the social realm. With an explicit debt to Marx, Arendt argues that labour's rise to prominence is traceable to its enormous productivity, its ability, particularly under modern conditions, to produce as human labour "power" not merely the means of its own subsistence but a "surplus" as well. Such a surplus secures not only the reproduction of labour power per se but also the life processes of those not directly involved in the activity of labour itself — "the labour of some suffices for the life of all."[26] The dramatic ascension of the labour process promises the realization of the age-old dream of abundance and liberation from the bodily pain of toil in the service of necessity.

Yet labour's "silence" means that however fertile or productive the labour process might be under the impact of an increasingly sophisticated division of labour and machine technology, it cannot ensure, and in fact threatens, those conditions which make a genuine politics possible. Of particular significance here are two issues growing out of an analysis of the central elements of the private realm and the nature of labour: the role of force and violence and the character and function of private property.

That force and violence are to Arendt implicit in the performance of the household function reflects the fact that it is impossible for people to escape completely the pull of necessity. The slave in antiquity and the worker under capitalism, whose association with labour as a process was (and is) most intimate, were (and are) obviously subjected, at least potentially, to the exercise of force, by the master or the market. But more importantly, as Arendt sees it, violence and force inhere in the very core of the master-slave or capitalist-worker relationship because the condition of ruling and being ruled that defines those relations is necessarily coercive; historically, household rule was despotic. Given the demands of necessity and the private realm,

> force and violence are justified in this sphere because they are the only means to master necessity — for instance by ruling over slaves — and to become free. Because all human

> beings are subject to necessity, they are entitled to violence toward others; violence is the prepolitical art of liberating oneself from the necessity of life for the freedom of the world...To be poor or to be in ill-health meant to be subject, in addition, to man-made violence. This twofold and doubled 'unhappiness' of slavery is quite independent of the actual subjective well-being of the slave.[27]

In raising the significance of force and violence as central aspects of the realm of necessity, Arendt wishes not merely to specify their role strictly in the context of man-made social relations, rather, the point seems much more profound: from the standpoint of human biological life and its maintenance, our relation to physical nature is necessarily antagonistic. This antagonism is not eliminated by the enormous productivity generated by the modern animal laborans, although it may be well disguised.[28] To give in to the cyclical rhythms of biological life that define "man's metabolism with nature" the way a "labouring," or "consumer" society does, is to capitulate to the futility of labour and hence a life of "productive slavery."[29] That is, our apparent triumph over necessity has intensified necessity's hold on us and (although Arendt is somewhat ambiguous on this point) at the same time created the possibility of greater social and political conflict as well.[30] Rooted as she is in the German speculative tradition, Arendt sees the key to human freedom not in the elimination of necessity but in its rational mastery. As she puts it, man "cannot be free if he does not know that he is subject to necessity, because his freedom is always won in his never wholly successful attempts to liberate himself from necessity."[31]

This attempt to liberate ourselves from necessity, and the antagonistic relation with nature that is their basis, must not, argues Arendt, be confused with the chaotic "state of nature" of seventeenth century political thought. The difference is important. The rational attempt to master nature in the interest of constructing a genuine political realm is in Arendt's terms a meaningful political project, perhaps the most meaningful of all given the fragility of the stable world that the political realm requires. It is politically meaningful, in other words, to master necessity for the sake of politics. However, the state of nature is the product of the politicization of the household realm; the politics growing out of it is designed to serve the domination of nature, human and non-human, in the interest of abundance. The state of nature thus represents the elevation of violence to that sphere of human existence which is supposed to be immune to it: the public realm.

The politicization of this violence, which necessarily attends the project of dominating nature, finds its institutional expression in the modern notion of government as that agency which through its monopoly of the means of force and power, regulates the conflict-laden affairs of competitive individuals. Government (and politics) in this context are seen "as at best...a 'necessary evil' and 'a reflection on human nature', at worse a parasite on the otherwise healthy life of society."[32] The "human nature" requiring repression is that of animal laborans. Hence the relation of ruling and being ruled which defines the subservience of man to that "power able to over-awe them all,"[33] and which as we've seen characterizes the household, is essentially prepolitical and, to the Greeks at least, not worthy of inclusion in the public realm at all. Once again the silence of the labour process looms as crucial in pinpointing the private character of bourgeois public life.

> To be political, to live in a polis, meant that everything was decided through words and persuasion and not through force and violence. In Greek self-understanding, to force people by violence, to command rather than persuade, were prepolitical ways to deal with people characteristic of life outside the polis, of home and family life...[34]

Labour, violence, silence: an unholy triumvirate whose usurpation of the political sphere threatens that sphere and the speech and action it both requires and makes possible.[35]

* * *

In guarding the labour process, modern politics simultaneously protects and preserves the social institution in which that process is given its most specific form: private property. Property is of course of utmost importance for Arendt's analysis of the private realm. In fact she believes that a form of private property is absolutely required if there is to be a meaningful political realm at all. She is also aware that if modern government is about anything at all it is about property. Economics, à la Smith, Ricardo, Marx, et al, " — until the modern age a not too important part of ethics and politics and based on the assumption that men act with respect to their economic [i.e., household] activities as they act in every other respect — "[36] has become the science of such a government, literally political economy.

Yet Arendt also wants us to see that the private property essential for entrance into the political realm differs from the private property that modern civil government seeks to maintain. Specifically, what is now commonly called private property is in reality wealth — and the two are not identical although we tend to see them as such. They may in fact even be antithetical to each other: Arendt argues that our potentially wealthy societies are ironically becoming increasingly propertyless. What might that mean?

Historically, of all private concerns, private property had the greatest relevance for the public realm because it served as the chief condition for admission to political life. From this standpoint it had a very specific, tangible, objective content: "Originally, property meant no more or less than to have one's location in a particular part of the world and therefore to belong to the body politic, that is to be head of one of the families which together constituted the public realm."[37] Property carefully demarcated and kept in check the silent process of meeting physical necessity. At the same time, it offered "the only reliable hiding place" from common affairs, a refuge required because a "life spent entirely in public, in the presence of others becomes, as we would say, shallow...[It] loses the quality of rising into sight from some darker ground which must remain hidden if it is to lose its depth in a very real, non-subjective sense."[38]

Private property was thus the *sine qua non* of privacy. Its necessity points to the tension inherent in the very existence of the private realm. While its major activities (which meet needs that require fulfilment for us to be fully human but do not themselves constitute fully what it means to be human) perform a kind of negative role in human affairs, a genuine private realm also secures the conditions which alone make possible the flowering of certain distinctively human attributes—"the passions of the heart, the thoughts of the mind, the delights of the senses"[39] — that comprise the sphere of intimacy. It is privacy in this sense, however, that is most under seige in the modern world, even as the private household has become the public one. The modern assault on privacy parallels the loss by property of its worldly character, its content as a tangible place of one's own.

Wealth, on the other hand concerned specifically the means by which one draws a livelihood, those objects of use and consumption required for biological existence. Since public life is possible "only after the much more urgent needs of life itself" are met, to possess wealth means "to be master over one's own necessities of life and therefore potentially to be a free person, free to transcend his own life and enter the world all have in common."[40] Thus wealth, like property, had political significance not, to be sure, for its own sake but for the sake of the freedom it could make possible. As private property provided the institutionalized boundaries which marked off the private from the public sphere and thus preserved the integrity of both, so private wealth organized the realm of necessity within the walls of the household such that one could leave it and enter political life.[41]

But wealth lacks the durability and stability of property. It is literally "in-come," what liberal theory might call that continuous flow of material utilities designed to reproduce one's physical (and for the liberal, saleable) capacities. It is in the nature of wealth that it is capable of expansion, that it can, in other words, be accumulated. Thus while the ancients considered property sacred, they never viewed wealth in the same way because the property owner who "chose to enlarge his property [wealth] instead of using it up in leading a political life...willingly sacrificed his freedom and became voluntarily what the slave was against his own will, a servant of necessity."[42] Wealth only became "sacred" with the rise of modern society and its equation of wealth with property, such that the political community became the commonwealth.

Given the ephemeral quality of wealth (whose roots in the labour process are given an explicitly modern formulation in Locke's labour theory of value), its existence can never be guaranteed as fully as can one's private share of a stable common world. But if any specific object of wealth is perishable, the process of wealth generation itself might at least bear some of the marks of the permanence of property. In this context the difference between property and wealth is obscured. Here are to be found the roots of accumulation which itself is based on appropriation.

For appropriation to operate effectively, to ensure the continued generation of wealth, everything must be capable of being appropriated. For Arendt, this has grave significance for the stability of the common world. Continuous appropriation, or accumulation, destroys property in the older sense. Arendt understands this, literally, as the actual destruction of tangible use objects as they are dissolved in the process of production and consumption that gives the accumulative drive its phenomenal form. But she also sees the basis of accumulation in the political, historical and institutional process of expropriation "the expropriation of the peasant classes which in turn was the almost accidental consequence of the expropriation of Church and monastic property after the Reformation..."[43] Thus, "Proudhon's dictum that property is theft has a solid basis of truth in the origins of modern capitalism..."[44] In the end private property is sacrificed to the demands of accumulation when the two come into conflict. What modernity defends is not "property as such but the unhampered pursuit of more property..."[45]

In effect what Arendt undertakes in her analysis of wealth and property is a distinction between property as a stable basis for free activity and property as capital. In a lucid account of the key element in the transformation of property into its modern form — the substitution of exchange for use value as the governing criterion for the production of things — Arendt provides a unique assessment of the political consequences of that shift in terms of her distinction between private and public and the fate of the private realm in modernity:

> The dissolution of this [private] realm may most conveniently be watched in the progressing transformation of immobile into mobile property until eventually the distinction between property and wealth, between the fungibles and the consumptibiles of Roman law, loses all significance because every tangible "fungible" thing has become an object of "consumption"; it lost its private use value which was determined by its location and acquired an exclusively social value determined through its ever changing exchangeability whose fluctuation could itself

be fixed only temporarily by relating it to the common denominator of money.[46]

Denied a place in a stable, common, external world, people have taken flight into a world of "inner subjectivity" which because it is mediated socially (in Arendt's terms) cannot serve as an adequate substitute for the "objective" subjectivity growing out of involvement in a common world. One literally ends up talking to oneself, discussion with others becomes "mere talk."[47] The social sciences tell us the truth: our "value judgments" are merely expressions of "subjective preference" because the most important qualities of private beings are by the nature of the case uncommunicable and unshareable.

The problem is intensified by the character of modern private property whose impermanence and exchangeability in terms of the abstract commodity, money, threatens the very basis of that remembrance which makes possible a life of genuine common pursuits.[48] But that may be all we might reasonably expect when "both the public and private sphere of life are gone, the public because it has become a function of the private and the private because it has become the only common concern left..."[49]

* * *

My discussion of the private realm necessarily required that I raise, at least by implication, some of the important features of the realm of freedom. Indeed, as Arendt sees it, each must be understood in terms of the other: each "conditions" the other. As Arendt's discussion of private property makes clear, the nature of the polis can only be grasped by differentiating it from the household. More specifically, however, the public realm is given substance by, and in turn provides the basis for, the twin capacities of lexis and praxis — speech and action — that are at the very core of politics.

The public realm is the scene of an existential drama that in its political form has as its stage the "interest," the "worldly space" that unites individuals while simultaneously separating them, and is the basic condition of plurality that makes politics possible. The public realm provides the means through which people reveal "who" they are, an expression of "the living essence of the person as it shows itself in the flux of action and speech..." It is the forum in which it is possible "to think what we are doing."

The forum of politics provides as a specific vehicle for self-revelation what Arendt understands to be "the space of appearances," or simply "public space." For Arendt, this notion involves the existence of a common world, a common point of reference which allows us, literally, to be "seen and heard by others as well as by ourselves...,"[50] for it is the "presence of others who see what we see and hear what we hear (that) assures us of the reality of the world and ourselves..."[51] Not identical with the earth or with nature, this common world is a product of human artifice and is related "to affairs which go on among those who inhabit the man-made world together. To live together in the world means essentially that a world of things is between those who have it in common, as a table is located between those who sit around it ..."[52] Only through living together in this way can we appear and act. And on the other hand, to be human, and more precisely to be politically so, is to be able to create communally a common object that will stand simultaneously as the basis and expression of our capacity to establish through action monuments to human virtue and aspiration — monuments that suggest permanence for humanity even as individual humans are mortal.

The common world and the space of appearances, or the public realm as Arendt also calls it, are not reducible one to the other because not all "worldly" activities are or should be political or public. And neither can the common world of itself give expression to the revelatory dimension of human action, which can only be brought forward in, while simultaneously bringing forth, public space. Nevertheless we require a common world to erect a space of appearances. That is why for Arendt modern challenges to "worldliness" are so destructive of political life, and also that private life with which the public realm exists in symbiotic relation.

While the concept of the space of appearances has from an institutional perspective clear spatial and temporal implications[53] — by suggesting the necessity of political culture in the broadest sense — its main significance is that it points to those aspects of the individual human character that can only be realized in the presence of others, as opposed to those capacities that require a private sphere of existence. To deprive people of the possibility of acting together through word and deed in a common world is to imprison them "in the subjectivity of their singular experience, which does not cease to be singular if the same experience is multiplied innumerable times."[54] It is the nature and end of the activity, and not merely its spatial or temporal characteristics, that determine whether it partakes of the character of action. Wherever I come together to establish a common ground, and seek to take the initiative and inject themselves by word and deed into the events going on around them, they have created a public space of appearances, a forum for action that is itself the outcome of action. Thus Arendt's deep interest in the fighters of the French Resistance in World War II.[55] The importance of the space of appearances for the prospect of a genuine politics is clear. The Marxian enterprise, for example, may reasonably be seen as an attempt to state the necessary conditions for the development of our social nature, and to demonstrate that foremost among those conditions is something like the ability to appear — as a genuine subject or actor on the stage of history. Arendt's most perceptive comment on Marx's work suggests that she sees this as an important element in his revolutionary theory. In discussing the importance of what she calls "the social question" — poverty — for modern revolutionary movements, Arendt suggests that "the conviction that darkness rather than want is the curse of poverty is extremely rare in the literature of the modern age, although one may suspect that Marx's efforts to rewrite history in terms of class struggle was partially at least inspired by the desire to rehabilitate posthumously those to whose injured lives history has added the insult of oblivion."[56] The oblivion of those denied the private property essential as a basis for action in bourgeois society gives telling evidence of the inability of that society to provide for the realization of humans in their universal wholeness. It expresses eloquently the outraged silence of those who from the outset of the modern age have been denied a voice with which to speak into history. This denial, which in Arendtian terms corresponds to the progressive withering away of the space of appearances, is at once the central and most threatening political fact of the modern era.

It is at this point that the issue of remembrance becomes crucial. The withering away of the space of appearances precludes the possibility of visualizing and articulating alternatives to what is: it fosters what might be called an uncritical, uncontemplative, non-consciousness. The consequence of this narcotizing process is that various nuances of meaning and conceptions of politics have in the course of the modern age been lost or overlooked. Arendt's task may be seen as an attempt to restore lost meaning and hence one of her prominent concerns lies with the major human vehicle for meaning: speech, most especially political speech.

Her concern in this respect, however, suggests no mere narrow exercise in linguistics (which is why she discusses speech and not language). The nuances of meaning that engage Arendt underlie what we do in a practical political sense. This is so because political speech and the terms that comprise it articulate various subtle, complex and differentiated, though related, usages which have developed over time as men have brought forward additions to the human artifice. For Arendt meaninglessness lies at the root of our inability to say what it is we are doing. It is a malaise affecting all speech in general and political speech in particular.

It is in the context of this problem that Arendt, who was deeply influenced by Heidegger and Jaspers, repeatedly makes clear that the issues that concern her derive from the kind of experiences familiar to all of us within the concrete human reality of interpersonal relations and inter-subjective truth. Political speech is problematic because both interpersonal relations and inter-subjective truth have been undermined where not directly threatened; the one by the withering away of the public space of appearances,[57] the other by the organized and systematic attempts to occlude social facts.[58]

That political speech is problematic indicates the extent to which we have difficulty in what John O'Neill understands as "unveiling the world," or describing situations in order to transcend them.[59] A failure of speech, or more precisely the inability of speech to triumph over language (save in what Arendt sees as the dangerous context of lying), expresses the shrivelling up of the imaginative faculty for creating alternatives and fashioning an image of the human as a creative being affirming herself in her life and work. That failure is a threat to, or more accurately in our society the commodification of, what Malraux and Merleau-Ponty understand as the "creative deformation" of available linguistic significations which allows us to situate them in a speech apparatus in a way not earlier foreseen, and in a manner which enables us to make coherent claims about the world and our place in it.[60] In short, speech denuded of the capacity to create new meanings bespeaks our inability to evolve new understandings of political reality and the political strategies necessary to bring that reality into being — or more simply, the absence of political consciousness. If we cannot say what we are doing, we will not be able to say what we should be doing.

Arendt's historical sensibility is thus conditioned by her concern with the fate in our time of the things of the world that for us make the earth a habitable place. Such things are not merely physical objects, although they are that, but, as the notion of the space of appearances indicates, they also suggest the capacity to transform nature creatively in accordance with a pre-conceived plan. In a sense the vehicles, both symbolic and natural, for this transformation constitute what Arendt understands by "tradition."[61] The threat posed by a modern labouring society is a threat to tradition in this broad sense; to those things that are "the work of our hands, as distinguished from the labour of our bodies — homo faber who makes and literally 'works upon' as distinguished from the animal laborans which labours and 'mixes with'..."[62] The human world, composed as it is of those things that are the work of our hands, is the essential condition for the presentation and preservation of the individual in both his or her unique particularity and what we might call, following Marx, his or her "species being" character. The existence of the world allows us to give representation to our intentions in both an individual and collective sense. Worldliness, then, is an expression of human plurality and the basis for its political articulation in the space of appearances through its unique ability to separate people, while simultaneously uniting them.

It is Arendt's view that the modern condition is characterized by a pervasive challenge to worldliness. In a peculiar way Arendt agrees with Hegel that all history is truly world history — with "world" understood in a critical sense.[63] Hence her famous claim that "World alienation, and not self-alienation...has been the hallmark of the modern age."[64] The threat to the ability of humans to maintain a world is at the same time the threat to destroy their capacity to give rein to the imaginative transformation of the human situation. You cannot change the world if it is no longer, in some elemental and critical sense, yours to change. Thus Arendt: "With the disappearance of the sensually given world, the transcendent world disappears as well, and with it the possibility of transcending the material world in concept and thought."[65]

* * *

As I've suggested it is Arendt's view that in fact both the public and private realms have been virtually destroyed in modernity by the rise of the social realm: the elevation of the economic concerns of the household to the public sphere. The contemporary form assumed by this privatized public realm is the administrative State. Arendt's critique of administration and the bureaucratic apparatus that sustains it is extensive and wide-ranging. It lies at the core of her massive study of Nazism, *The Origins of Totalitarianism*, as well as her controversial account of the Eichmann trial in Jerusalem. For our purposes here, the major significance of the bureaucratic form is that it moulds and enforces a specific kind of human response to the social and political world: what we call "behaviour."

Critiques of behaviouralism in the social sciences have of course proliferated in recent years. While many are extremely pungent and lucid, they generally assume, implicitly or otherwise, either that behaviourism is descriptively inaccurate, ideological in its moral defence of the way political and social institutions function now, as opposed to how they might function if placed in the right hands and deployed for the right purposes. It is to Arendt's credit that in her view, the institutions of the administrative State in advanced industrial society both require and make possible only the kind of human response that the social scientist, armed with his quantitative methods, is able microscopically to study and dissect. If politics served necessity, then we will surely be "free" only to do what we must.

As Arendt puts it, once, with the rise of the social realm, "we see the body of peoples and political communities in the image of a family whose everyday affairs have to be taken care of by a gigantic, nation wide administration of housekeeping," the "scientific" thought most appropriate to the new situation is "no longer political science but 'national economy' or 'social economy'...a kind of 'collective housekeeping'..."[66] As with the "housekeeping" of the private realm, public housekeepers find action, with its unpredictability and its unmanageability, to be anathema. As commitment to the dictates of necessity in the private sphere requires subservience to the rhythmic order of the life process, so the same commitment in the public realm requires, as Weber cogently demonstrated, submission to the rational, calculable, ordered processes of the public household.[67] Deviance from such an ordered process is "irrational." Thus society (and of course bureaucracy in particular) "excludes the possibility of action, which formerly was excluded from household. Instead, society expects from each of its members a certain kind of behaviour, imposing innumerable and various rules, all of which tend to 'normalize' its members, to make them behave, to exclude spontaneous action or outstanding achievement."[68]

Under the process of administration, the "normalized" citizens of advanced industrial societies are subjected to the conformist pressures of the bureaucratic machinery. As Arendt understands it, this is the essence of the "equality" promoted by those societies; such equality becomes possible "only because behaviour has replaced action as the foremost mode of human relationships..."[69]

To the extent that such conformist tendencies can and do operate effectively, and human beings almost universally behave to satisfy specified role requirements, their activities can be handled scientifically. The laws of statistics can be applied to human behaviour because action and speech, with their inherent unpredictability, could be viewed simply as rare deviations from the norm of everyday life. That statistical laws can be so applied to politics or history "signifies nothing less than the wilful obliteration of their very subject matter, and it is a hopeless enterprise to search for meaning in politics or significance in history when everything that is not everyday behaviour or automatic trends has been ruled out as immaterial."[70]

Arendt somewhat uncritically appropriates the Greek notion that the major threat to the political realm lies in the existence of a large population. With no attempt to explore what that might mean in a modern context, Arendt articulates the rise of the social realm, the growth of bureaucracy and its associated characteristics — "conformism, behaviourism and automatism in human affairs" — to the presence of large populations. Nevertheless her general overview of behaviourism is quite incisive.

> The unfortunate truth about behaviourism and the validity of its "laws" is that the more people there are, the more likely they are to behave and the less likely to tolerate nonbehaviour. Statistically, this will be shown in the levelling out function. In reality, deeds will have less and less chance to stem the tide of behaviour, and events will more and more lose their time. Statistical uniformity is by no means a harmless scientific ideal; it is the no longer secret political ideal of a society which, entirely submerged in the routine of every day living, is at peace with the scientific outlook inherent in its very existence.[71]

Under the circumstances, the Benthamite utilitarian claim that for the purposes of calculating aggregate utility, each is to count as one and no more than one takes on a frightening literalness. In the overall process of administration, each can in fact be counted while no one counts. And this calculability, linked with the worldless subjectivism that results from the increasing propertylessness of the "job holders" society, is at the heart of the basic utilitarian formula.

> Bentham's invention of the "pain and pleasure calculus" combined the advantage of seemingly introducing the mathematical method into the moral sciences with the even greater attraction of having found a principle which resided entirely on introspection...Benthan's basic assumption [is] that what all men have in common is not the world but the sameness of their own nature, which manifests itself in the sameness of being affected by pain and pleasure...[and] ...Pain is the only inner sense found by introspection which can rival in independence from experienced objects the self-evident certainty of logical and arithmetical reasoning.[72]

The point is that the Utilitarian view of human nature is "correct" given the character of the modern public realm.[73] What's more, with the growth of (bureaucratic) scientific innovation, the last real bastion of action in any meaningful sense, modern society is capable of launching self-validating 'natural' processes that create and in turn require increasingly more and more explicitly defined forms of behaviour. Such processes have the compelling urgency of the necessity in which they are routed. While a totalitarian system clearly exhibits this tendency in its most highly-developed and frightening form, all bureaucratic regimes

> demonstrate that action can be based on any hypothesis and that, in the course of consistently guided action, the particular hypothesis will become true, will become actual, factual reality. The assumption which underlies consistent action can be as mad as it pleases; it will always end in producing facts which are then "objectively" true. What was originally nothing but a hypothesis, to be proved or disproved by actual facts, will in the course of consistent action always turn into a fact, never to be disproved.[74]

Such is the character of the ubiquitous functionalization of modern society that in Arendt's eyes erodes almost totally the capacity for rational, meaningful speech and action in that society's severely impoverished public sphere. For the scientist there is an anti-action kind of action. For most of the rest of us, "routinized, habitual life, with its premeditated, bureaucratized spontaneity — spasms of unreflective inadequacy..."[75]

To be sure, Arendt does not yield to nihilistic despair in her evaluation of our current situation. History is not a closed book; counter tendencies have emerged and will likely continue to do so. There remains the possibility of a radical reconstitution of speech, of symbolic interaction, of public space and certainly the most significant phenomenon embodying these possibilities has been revolution.

I cannot undertake here a full-scale critique of Arendt's extremely complex account of revolution as a political force. More specifically I cannot consider in detail her well-known, frequently criticized view that modern revolutionary movements have been undermined by the intrusion of the social question (i.e., poverty) onto the public scene as a mass phenomenon, other than to suggest that the elimination of poverty, as that has come to be understood, is not of itself a revolutionary phenomenon. At best, it is likely to generate what Marx denounced as crude communism: "...only an apparent form of the vileness of private property trying to set itself up as the positive community."[76]

However, it is important to point out that for Arendt there cannot be revolution in a meaningful sense without a commitment to reconstituted political space. All authentically revolutionary movements have been animated by that pursuit. A revolution to the extent that it is authentically political must be concerned first and foremost with the establishment of freedom in the context of the construction of a public space of appearances. The political institutional form most commonly established to create a new public realm — in Europe of 1848, in Paris of 1871, in Russia of 1918, and in Hungary of 1956 — is the self-governing council. Created spontaneously by acting individuals, this new form of political space, a soviet in the truest sense, is a product of freedom's quest and in turn gives that quest further impetus.

Despite the failures of those revolutionary movements under which the councillor form emerged, Arendt remained always enthusiastic about its qualities and its potential for providing people with the taste of "public happiness": The sheer joy of the pursuit of public things by people who simply come together and act, who "have been permitted for a few days, or a few weeks or months, to follow their own political devices without a government (or a party program) imposed from above.[77]

But sadly we appear no longer to have that taste for public happiness. Indeed the very terms "public" and "happiness," as Arendt understands them, seem to have become virtually meaningless in the lobotonized consumerist universe of advanced industrial society. We are in danger of automating our activities to such an extent that we no longer act but instead behave. Even as the institution of the free market dies out, it takes its revenge and realizes its dream through the steadily advancing process by means of which the government of people becomes the administration of things — including humans considered as things. The process may be thought equivalent to Weber's "disenchantment of the world." But for Arendt we may no longer have a real world to disenchant. Yet there remains still the "miracle" of natality. With the continuous and always surprising entrance of the newly born into the world, we face always the possibility of a new beginning and a renewed faculty to act which may interrupt "the inexorable automatic course of daily life."[78]

NOTES

1. H. Arendt, *The Human Condition* (New York, 1958), p.26.
2. Cf. A. Sanchez Vasquez, *Art and Society* (New York, 1973), ch.3.
3. And there are forces greater than one might imagine lined up against the possibility of such an articulation. The Tri-Lateral Commission, a multinational study group manned by important members of the political and economic elites of North America and Western Europe has gloomily suggested the possible incompatibility of liberal democratic institutions with the continued stability of Western economies. As a result, the Commission has argued the increasing need to preserve Western governments from 'excessive' popular pressures that could threaten the "governability of democracies." See the Commission's report, *The Crisis of Democracy* (New York, 1975). For an analysis of what has been called the new authoritarianism, see S. Bowles, "The Trilateral Commission: Have Capitalism and Democracy Come to a Parting of the Ways?," *The Progressive* (June, 1977).
4. Arendt considers the conquest of external space a critical problem in terms of the possibilities of a genuine politics. See "The Conquest of Space and the Stature of Man," in *Between Past and Future*, 2nd edition (New York, 1968), pp. 265-80. For a cogent analysis of the invasion of inner space — by the advertising industry — see S. Ewan, *Captains of Consciousness* (New York, 1976).
5. Cf. A. MacIntyre, "On Democratic Theory: Essays in Retrieval by C.B. Macpherson," *Canadian Journal of Philosophy*, vol.6, no.2 (June, 1976), pp. 177-181.
6. Arendt, *The Human Condition*, ch.6.
7. See Arendt, "The Concept of History," in *Between Past and Future*, pp. 44 ff.
8. W. Connelly, "Theoretical Self-Consciousness," in W. Connelly and G. Gordon (eds.), *Social Structure and Political Theory* (Lexington, Mass., 1974), p.41.
9. Cf. T.W. Adorno, "The Actuality of Philosophy," *Telos*, no.31 (Spring, 1977), pp. 126-129.
10. Cf. M. Horkheimer, "The Authoritarian State," *Telos*, no.15 (Spring, 1973), p.8: "Only the bad in history is irrevocable: the unrealized possibilities, missed opportunities, muder [sic] with and without legal procedures, and that which those in power inflict upon humanity. The other is always in danger."
11. See S. Wolin, *Politics and Vision* (Boston, 1960), ch. 10. Cf. C. Pateman, "Sublimation and Reification: Locke, Wolin and Liberal Democratic Conception of the Political," *Politics and Society*, 15 (1975), pp. 441-467.
12. The distinction between privacy and loneliness as I think Arendt might understand them is most cogently expressed by the final sentence of *The Human Condition* (p.297), in which she cites Cato: "Never is he more active than when he does nothing, never is he less alone than when he is by himself." Arendt of course is referring here to the question of thinking, a question to which she devoted most of her attention during the last year of her life. But the nature of thinking is never divorced by Arendt from the political context in which it is embedded: it is significant that in her recently published work on the subject she asks above all of the worldliness of the enterprise. That for Arendt genuine thought is possible only in the context of a common world, or what she calls the "space of appearances" can I think be deduced from her notion of world alienation. In terms of the status of man in market society, note, too, the Hobbesian view that truth will be considered inviolable by most men only when seen "as a thing that crosses no man's ambition, profit, or lust." [*Leviathan* ed. C.B. Macpherson (London, 1968), XI (pp.166).]
13. *Leviathan*, X (pp. 151-152).
14. Cf. J. Keane, "The Legacy of Political Economy: Thinking With and Against Claus Offe," *The Canadian Journal of Political and Social Theory* (forthcoming).
15. There is also in Arendt's division of the two realms an analogue to Kant's dualistic separation of the noumena and the phenomena — the "in-itself" and the "for- itself." Arendt's private realm possesses the qualities of the unknowable "in-itself": "The non-privative trait of the household realm originally lay in its being the realm of life and death which must be hidden from the public realm because it harbors the things hidden from human eyes and impenetrable to human knowledge. It is hidden be-

cause man does not know where he comes from when he is born and where he goes when he dies." (*The Human Condition*, pp. 57).
16. Ibid., p.24.
17. Ibid., p.29.
18. Ibid., p.9.
19. Ibid., p.119.
20. Ibid., p.87.
21. Ibid., p.120.
22. Ibid., p.74.
23. Arendt uses this point to make an interesting comment on the source of the division of labour in modern industrial societies. Distinguishing between division of labour and "specialization of work" which "have in common only the general principle of organization, which itself has nothing to do with either work or labour but owes its origins to the strictly political sphere of life, to the fact of man's capacity to act and act together and in concert," she suggests that division of labour "presupposes the qualitative equivalence of all single activities for which no special skill is required, and these activities have no end in themselves, but together in a purely quantitative way. Division of labour is based on the fact that two men can put their labour power together and 'behave toward each other as though they were one.' This oneness is the exact opposite of co-operation, it indicates the unity of the species with regard to which every single member is the same and exchangeable." (*The Human Condition*, p.107). Prefiguring the work of analysts such as Harry Braverman, Arendt attributes the degradation of work to the application of the division of labour to the processes of work such that the production of use objects assumes the character of the perishable, consumable products of labour. The result: "the objective difference between use and consumption, between the relative durability of the use objects and the swift coming and going of consumer goods dwindles to insignificance." (The Human Condition, p.109). Again it should be noted that Arendt sees labour as a natural phenomenon of human existence. Its modern manifestation as wage labour simply intensifies the impact of its "permanent" features. However questionable her assumption of labour's ahistorical character might be, Arendt nevertheless provides important insights into how a specific kind of human production process moulds the human material comprising it. As we shall see below, these insights are particularly important as a basis for Arendt's distinction between "behaviour" and "action."
24. Ibid., p.53-54.
25. J. Locke, *The Second Treatise of Government*, Sec. 27.
26. Arendt, *The Human Condition*, p.77.
27. Ibid., pp. 29-30.
28. In an ironic fashion Arendt links the question of force in social relations with the violence imposed by necessity in the context of the tendency of modernity to downgrade "all activities which either spring directly from violence, as the use of force in human relations, or harbor an element of violence within themselves...It is as though the growing elimination of violence throughout the modern age almost automatically opened the doors for the re-entry of necessity on its most elementary level." (The Human Condition, p.112). While there is a serious ambiguity in Arendt's position here — on the one hand she unfavourably contrasts violence with speech and action and argues that those bound to relations of violence can never be fully human; on the other she hints that the elimination of political and social or "man-exerted," violence has had a deleterious impact on modern political life — her basic point is of crucial importance. As she puts it the "emancipation of labor and the concomitant emancipation of the laboring classes from oppression and exploitation certainly meant progress in the direction of non-violence. It is much less certain that it was also progress in the direction of freedom." (ibid.) Whatever the historical validity of her claim about the emancipation of the "laboring classes," Arendt has fingered a key issue of the modern age: the relation of scientific to moral progress, or, as Habermas puts it, technical progress to the social life-world (*Toward a Rational*

Society, ch.4). That there is no easy coincidence of the two forms of progress is I think the necessary starting point for any meaningful critical philosophy. As a critical thinker Arendt is acutely aware of the dimension of this problem. She wonders if the elimination of violence through technical expansion (i.e. the classical liberal dream) will not produce something far worse. Her position seems to be that we should recognize the existence of an ineradicable element of force and violence, while in a sense re-privatizing the labour process that is their home and by so doing domesticate their impact. A critique of Arendt's stance can only be suggested here. It seems to me that unlike Merleau-Ponty, for example, Arendt does not attempt to distinguish eradicable from ineradicable violence, either humanly-made or naturally generated. This in turn follows from her failure to carry through with her distinction between the violence of necessity and the violence of individuals to a point where the possible interrelation of the two can be specified and analyzed. In the end she seems to suggest that humanly-made violence is not simply a socially and historically mediated expression of natural violence (a defensible position), but that it is itself natural i.e. a kind of "second" nature. Arendt's failure here is ontological: she denies the existence of human nature, at least in terms of any positive content, as a standard of judgment and so lacks a real basis for distinguishing between eradicable and ineradicable violence, although her argument requires it. On the other hand, that same argument appears to suggest elements of a "negative" human nature which even given its importance for her analysis cannot in Arendt's terms be recognized as such and hence criticized. On the question of eradicable versus ineradicable violence, see M. Merleau-Ponty, Humanism and Terror, (Boston, 1969); and M. Langer, "Merleau-Ponty: The Ontological Limits of Politics," in A. Kontos (ed.), *Domination*, (Toronto, 1975), pp. 102-113.
29. Arendt, *The Human Condition*, p.91.
30. "...the spare time of animal laborans is never spent in anything but consumption, and the more time left to him, the greedier and more craving his appetites. That these appetites become more sophisticated, so that consumption is no longer restricted to the necessities but, on the contrary, mainly concentrates on the superfluities of life, does not change the character of this society, but harbors the grave danger that eventually no object of the world will be safe from consumption and annihilation through consumption." (ibid., p.115).
31. Ibid., p.105.
32. Ibid., p.95.
33. Hobbes, *Leviathan*, XIII (p.185).
34. Arendt, *The Human Condition*, p.26.
35. As we shall see below, Arendt argues that modern bourgeois institutions of government, and bourgeois public spheres (such as it is) they maintain, have in turn given way to administration and bureaucracy: the rule of nobody. The bureaucratic form conceals human relations of sub and super-ordination under a veil of technical rationality: it transforms the natural violence given human form by the antagonistic relations of the market and the bourgeois public sphere back into natural terms. As Arendt writes, "the growing elimination of [man-exerted] violence throughout the modern age almost automatically opened the doors for the re-entry of necessity in its most elementary form." For Arendt, of course, the natural character of violence under administration — the *sine qua non* of labouring society — is literal. And so it is. Yet there is a dialetic here that, although implicit in Arendt's position, again is not made clear or followed through. The re-naturalization of the violence of necessity is a mediated one. The social conflict of industrial society provides both the context and content for the exploitation of the labour process. The antagonistic relation to nature is not purely natural: if animal laborans in his modern guise becomes "greedier and more craving [in] his appetites" the more he consumes, that is because as Marcuse and others have suggested, he is moulded by social relations which foster and express outmoded forms of the struggle for existence a backdrop of contrived scarcity. These limits dictate that rationalization of man's metabolism with nature serves the irrational purposes of the social and political organization within

which it takes place. That the dialectic of reason and unreason produces a situation in which man's apparent greater control over nature is matched by an increasing inability to control his own affairs has been a central theme of much recent critical social and political theory. Arendt herself provides tantalizing evidence of such an analysis — notably in her view, basic to the very notion of "the human condition" that men "are conditioned beings because everything they come in contact with turns immediately into a condition of their existence." (*The Human Condition*, p.11). It is in the light of these hints that the strength and weakenesses of her notion of administration, bureaucracy and indeed her whole position on the privatization of public life, must be understood.

36. Arendt, *The Human Condition*, p.39.
37. Ibid., p.56 Cf. Arendt, *On Revolution*, p.180.
38. Ibid., p.63.
39. Ibid., p.46. Cf. C.B. Macpherson, "The Maximization of Democracy," in Democratic Theory: Essays in Retrieval (Oxford, 1973), p.4.
40. Ibid., p.58.
41. Arendt is well aware that private wealth of the kind sufficiently large to allow escape to the public realm has historically been gained through oppression and exploitation, either of slaves [in antiquity, "the wealth of a person...was frequently counted in terms of the number of laborers, that is, slaves he owned" (*The Human Condition*, p.58)]; or of "free" labour whose "expropriation" ushered in the age of modern (capitalist) politics. I question whether Arendt believes, as critics of her "elitism" suggest, that a genuine politics requires an exploited class denied access to the political realm. She has in fact argued quite the opposite. [See, for example, her "Thoughts on Politics and Revolution," in *Crises of the Republic* (New York, 1972), p.233.] Nevertheless there is ambiguity in her position, especially given her criticism of both the rise of the labour process to public prominence and the importance of the "social" question i.e. the issue of poverty for modern revolutionary movements. But see *On Revolution*, pp.279ff.
42. Arendt, *The Human Condition*, p.59.
43. Ibid.
44. Ibid.
45. Ibid., p.95.
46. Ibid., p.61.
47. Arendt, *Men in Dark Times* (New York, 1968), p.ix.
48. Cf. R. Jacoby, "A Falling Rate of Intelligence?," *Telos* No.27 (Spring, 1976), pp.141-146; and *Social Amnesia* (Boston, 1975). Note, too, Marx's position on the limits on the development and exercise of human capacities imposed by the institution of (bourgeois) private property: "Private property has made us so stupid and one-sided that an object is ours only if we have it, if it exists for us as a capital or is immediately possessed by us, eaten, drunk, worn, lived in, etc., in short used; but private property grasps all these immediate forms of possession only as means of living..." ["Private Property and Communism," in L.D. Easton and K.H. Guddat (eds.), *Writings of the Young Marx on Philosophy and Society* (New York, 1967), pp.307-308. Needless to say, Arendt would concur with Marx on this point.]
49. Arendt, *The Human Condition*, p.61.
50. Ibid., p.45.
51. Ibid., p.46.
52. Ibid., p.48.
53. Cf. Wolin, op. cit., ch.1, especially with respect to the concepts of "political time" and "political space."
54. Arendt, *The Human Condition*, p.53.
55. Of whom Arendt writes: "they had discovered that he who 'joined the Resistance found himself, that he ceased to be "in quest of [himself] without mastery, in naked unsatisfaction, "that he no longer suspected himself of "insincerity," of being "a carping suspicious actor of life, "that he could afford "to go naked. "In this nakedness, stripped of all masks — of those whose society assigns to its members as well as

those which the individual fabricates for himself in his psychological reactions against society-they had been visited for the first time in their lives by an apparition of freedom, not, to be sure because they acted against tyranny and things worse than tyranny...but because they had become "challengers" had taken the initiative upon themselves and therefore, without knowing or even noticing it, had begun to create that public space between themselves where freedom could appear. Arendt, *Between Past and Future*, p.4.
56. Arendt, *On Revolution*, p.64.
57. See Arendt, *The Origins of Totalitarianism*, ch.13, for an exposition of how totalitarianism's main concern is precisely the destruction of public space.
58. See Arendt, "Truth and Politics," in *Between Past and Future*, ch.7; and "Lying and Politics," in *Crises of the Republic*, pp.3-47.
59. J. O'Neill, "Situation and Action," in *Sociology as a Skin Trade* (London, 1972), p.91.
60. Merleau-Ponty, "On the Phenomenology of Language," in *Signs* (Evanston, Ill., 1964), p.91.
61. See Arendt, "Tradition and the Modern Age," in *Between Past and Future*, pp.17-40.
62. Arendt, *The Human Condition*, p.119.
63. Of course the similarities between Arendt's thought and Hegel's do not end here. Note Hegel's claim in the Philosophy of Right that "the System of Needs of Civil Society" articulates "that specifically modern reality in which for the first time the process of production is freed from the household and natural conditions, to emerge as an independent sphere of social interaction in which the private self-seeking individual as such becomes." [R. Winfield, "The Dilemma of Labor," Telos No.24 (Summer, 1975), p.117].
64. Arendt, *The Human Condition*, p.231.
65. Ibid., p.262.
66. Ibid., p.28.
67. It is no accident that Arendt explicitly links Weber to her pivotal notion of world alienation, that loss of a stable, humanly-made habitation occasioned by the expropriation of large masses of people in the dawn of capitalism and the consequent growing significance of wealth accumulation: "The greatness of Max Weber's discovery about the origins of capitalism lay precisely in his demonstration that an enormous, strictly mundane activity is possible without any care for or enjoyment of the world whatever, an activity whose deepest motivation, on the contrary, is worry and care about the self." (*The Human Condition*, p.230-231).
68. Ibid., p.38.
69. Ibid.
70. Ibid., p.39.
71. Ibid., p.40.
72. Ibid., pp.282-283.
73. See note 43, above.
74. Arendt, "The Concept of History," pp.87-88.
75. Kontos, "Domination: Metaphor and Political Reality," in Kontos (ed.), op. cit., p.226.
76. Marx, "Private Property and Communism," p.303.
77. Arendt, *The Origins of Totalitarianism*, p.497.
78. Arendt, *The Human Condition*.

7

"When men [sic] are different from one another and do not live alone":
ORWELL AND ARENDT ON TOTAL CONTROL AND ONTOLOGY

Phillip Hansen

This essay, which was also originally written in 1987, seeks to link the ideas of Hannah Arendt and George Orwell about new and unprecedented forms of domination in the twentieth century. Surprisingly there is little analysis of the relation of these two thinkers, even though there are, to me at lest, striking similarities between them. Not the least of these similarities is the fact that both have been used, by partisans on the left and the right, to inveigh against the evils of the Soviet Union and Communism and thus to justify the Cold War. But the use of their ideas in this way has profoundly distorted them, as well as the intentions of both thinkers. It was for this reason that I elected to use "total control" instead of "totalitarianism": this latter term carries ideological connotations which can preclude a sensible analysis of both the ideas of Arendt and Orwell and of the phenomenon itself. (In my forthcoming book on Arendt, however, I have resorted to "totalitarianism," for reasons which I try to make clear in that study.)

Both Arendt and Orwell were highly critical of the very ideological thinking to which their own ideas have been assimilated. Such thinking substitutes dogmatic preconceptions about the world for careful reflections and a willingness to judge, to let the phenomena present themselves to our critical intelligence. Such dogma has by no means been restricted to communists or fascists, but can be found in the self-congratulatory bromides of liberals and democrats. Both Arendt and Orwell would have stoutly resisted the current tendency to trumpet the "triumph" of capitalism in the wake of the collapse of communism because it reflects the same mode of thinking as that of an erstwhile adversary. The lesson which Arendt and Orwell ultimately teach us is that if we are not only to get a clear picture of their ideas and the uses to which they could be put in fostering a vibrant public life, but also to develop a sensible understanding of the world that needs to be changed, we must self-consciously strive to leave ideology behind — to begin, to use Arendt's striking metaphor, to "think without a bannister."

"When Men [sic] are different from one another and do not live alone: Orwell and Arendt on Total Control and Ontology"

Like all concepts which can be used ideologically, "totalitarianism" can celebrate and condemn; mobilize and paralyse; ultimately reveal and conceal. while George Orwell and Hannah Arendt would have acknowledged a distinction between totalitarian and non-totalitarian States, they would not have believed that this was the end of the story. For them, totalitarianism necessarily included political, economic and cultural questions which transcended the merely institutional, and thus involved forces not restricted to Hitler's Germany or Stalin's Soviet Union alone.

Nineteen Eighty-Four says little about institutions beyond the fact of pervasive bureaucratic authority. Arendt's account of the total State, crystallized in the metaphor of the onion, explores the "false" institutionalism of a new and peculiar from of State which, to survive, must constantly expand and which therefore can know no settled arrangements. In both cases the emphasis is on patterns of thought and action which display a certain kind of obsessiveness and which thus suggest more than anything else a world out of joint. The very comprehensiveness of this situation precludes easy categorization. As a concept, "totalitarianism" can be a facile label which promises insight, but more often leads us away from a critical encounter with our liberal democratic political universe.

What Orwell and Arendt really attempt to explore is not simply totalitarianism, but rather total control. It is only from this vantage point that the socio-historical tendencies at work in Nazi Germany and Oceania reveal their true uniqueness. Not just the concentration and ruthless application of power without accountability, nor even the full-scale assault on all domains of social and personal existence by an all-pervasive State apparatus, is at stake. The emergence of new human possibilities is at the centre of this project; total control and the search for it reveal a real human potency.

Of course the quest for total control signals the serving of power and ethics. But there is more. What it ultimately threatens/promises, as O'Brien, the Grand Inquisitor, makes clear, is the severance of *reason* from ethics. Reason, which was to check total power, threatens to become its compliant servant. This is not simply a case of the ascension to power of a new class of scientists and technocrats, as Goldstein claimed. It is a collective process of spontaneous reproduction of servitude as (erotic) gratification, as real and as false as the song of the woman hanging laundry outside Winston and Julia's "secret" retreat. The pursuit of total control holds the terrible possibility that it might "work": that it might successfully establish a political order within which a blighted humanity could be "realized." "In this light, we might describe fascism as a satanic synthesis of reason and nature

— the very opposite to that reconciliation of the two poles that philosophy has always dreamed of."[1]

The universe of total control incorporates perverted forms of genuinely human drives and aspirations. This is the insight upon which Orwell and Arendt, if somewhat differently in each case, build their accounts of the main challenge to the possibility of a truly human politics in the contemporary era. Both are aware that something radically new has occurred to subvert our traditional understanding about human institutions, and indeed human nature itself. There is in the work of each writer the sense that old standards of conduct, thought and judgement no longer hold, that one must now, in Arendt's expression, think without a bannister.[2] In other words, each recognizes that modernity itself may be in crisis, that modern experience as such has become problematic in new and unforeseen ways. This crisis, which is a general human predicament for both Orwell and Arendt, is best captured metaphorically by the powerful image of a humanity suspended "between past and future": "The past was dead, the future was unimaginable."[3]

Although neither Orwell nor Arendt is explicit about it, the need to rethink human ontological possibilities is clear. But here a problem arises. The very concepts available for the task are not innocent in the crisis.

The language of politics has come to serve anti-political, or more correctly, *falsely* political goals. Although never in a totally transparent way, standards of political thought and judgement once bore an internal relation to social practices and institutions such that they simultaneously helped constitute and delimit possible forms of social structure and social behaviour. Now, they merely register desires and appetites, and the bureaucratic response to them. This response is at the same time the activity of (re)producing them — "interpellation" in the bureaucratic language of structuralism. Political categories are no longer determining but rather determined factors of public life, "the highly efficient talk and double-talk of nearly all official representatives…"[4]

For Arendt, the "key words" of political thought and speech have become "mere concepts," "empty shells with which to settle all accounts, regardless of their underlying phenomenal reality." Categories such as "freedom and justice, authority and reason, responsibility and virtue, power and glory" have lost all roots in "valid human experience."[5] Arendt's language here is suggestive. She argues that as human reason has been transformed into market rationality, that is, transformed "from being an inner light disclosing truth" into a mere "faculty of reckoning with consequences"[6] political categories have been drained of objective content. Lacking such content, they now tend to function as outward expressions of "subjective" preferences, as bearers of social exchange value deployed in the service of private, individual goals. As such, they appear utterly inadequate for illuminating the conditions under which modern human societies reproduce themselves.

Indeed the status of human community itself has been eclipsed as an explicit political question. The emergent properties of social orders anchored by the capitalist market, modern science and the bureaucratic State have increasingly assumed the visage of a "second nature," not only beyond change but also beyond comprehension *as changeable*. The capacity to question politically the character and limits of existing forms of social and political organization is threatened with suppression or even, as in the case of Orwell's Oceania, exclusion. in these circumstances, it becomes difficult to resist the institution of arrangements which transform human creative energies into a material, but in Arendt's sense "unworldly," reality. Such a "new reality" incorporates mechanisms that increasingly limit the exercise of autonomy, while at the same time defining and "meeting" new human "needs." If classical thought assumed that the possible must be assessed in light of the desirable, modern thought implies that the possible must also and necessarily *be* desirable.[7] It sacrifices the critical distance essential for a full interrogation of the existing order of things. Yet what is, for Arendt, a failed "tradition" is all we have.

For Orwell, too, the theoretical imagination appears stifled by the harnessing of language to the requirements of power. This is of course the meaning of his famous account of Newspeak and his sardonic dissection of the politics of the English language.[8] But it is almost tellingly and brilliantly revealed by Goldstein's "book." The searing indictment of "oligarchic collectivism" is itself an industrial product: the State managers articulate their own radical critique.

Rooted much more explicitly in the socialist tradition than Arendt, Orwell perceived the horrible suppression and distortion of the possibilities for a more fully human existence with a deeper sense of betrayal and loss. He saw the fitful race between ontology and technology, between the forces and relations of production, the culmination of which produced his own "satanic synthesis" of reason and nature in the total State. Orwell's recognition that human genius could foster ever more elaborate forms of servitude, and not freedom, underscores the sense of amazement that characterizes *Nineteen Eighty-Four*. This sense of amazement, much like Arendt's in the face of totalitarianism and its "origins," exhibits more than a tinge of sadness and regret.

For both Arendt and Orwell, however, there is always hope. The human essence can be battered and disfigured, but never totally suppressed or extirpated. In spite of their efforts to downplay or deny it, there remains for each an implicit ontological standard and the necessity and capacity to judge what is truly human and what is not.

And judge they do. Theirs is a virtual but withheld ontology.[9] In what follows, I wish to validate this claim by examining the ontological themes which emerge from Arendt's and Orwell's accounts of total control and total State, in light of the context which seemed to require them to obscure explicit ontological issues. I want also to suggest that what is most crucial in these accounts is that they illuminate the general failure of the left to fill the political vacuum created by the collapse of the nineteenth century radical vision — a political space filled all-too-willingly, and ominously, by the right.

What emerges from the dilemmas of their thought are precisely the unresolved ontological issues which must be addressed if human social and political relations are to be put on a more rational basis. While neither Orwell nor Arendt are unknown to the left, the inability/unwillingness of many on the left to confront the ontological dimension of their work restricts a proper appreciation of the critical power and significance of that work. In an important sense, this reflects the left's contemporary crisis. To begin to overcome this crisis, the left must think again about the relation of the individual to the community, of autonomy to social structure - of the possibility of a world in which, as Winston Smith puts it in his diary, "men [sic] are different from one another and do not live alone."[10]

I

As everyone knows, Winston Smith's struggle against Big Brother ends in failure. This failure is quite properly seen as confirmation of the awesome power of the total State and its ability to snuff out all opposition. But the justifiable concern for the instruments of domination should not obscure an equally important thread of Orwell's account. This thread treats Winston's demise as in large measure preordained, his fate a product of a ruthlessly inevitable dialectical logic which, ironically, Orwell himself had come to mistrust. Winston is doomed not simply because of the power of the bureaucratic apparatus, but also because in a fundamental sense he has from the beginning of the novel already been won over in an emotional/sensual way to the purposes of the total State.

Winston's defeat lay in his ambivalence. While at one moment he could loathe Big Brother and all he represented, at the next, "his secret loathing of Big Brother changed into adoration, and Big Brother seemed to tower up, an invincible, fearless protector, standing like a rock" against the enemies of the state.[11] This double-edged relation to total power is central to the dramatic dynamics of the novel.

Because Winston does not, and cannot, see his real plight, he has no basis for grasping the necessity of rebellion and he misunderstands the real political implications of his relationship with Julia. The question about total power that ultimately haunts Winston and provides the intellectual basis for his rebellion — "I understand *how*: I do not understand *why*"[12] — is the other side of his own lack of insight into the depth of his situation. There is much in Winston's actions that is foolish, and even comic.

Yet Winston is not a fool. Orwell neither presents him as totally pathetic, nor depicts his rebellion as ridiculous or futile. There is heroism in his stance and tragedy in his ultimate defeat. Certainly Winston knew that from the moment he had begun to harbour doubts about the purposes of the Party and the State, he had embarked on a path that would lead to the Ministry of Love. "'You knew this, Winston'," O'Brien, his intellectual and political antagonist, tells him. "'Don't deceive yourself. You did know it — you have always known'."[13] And indeed Winston had known. He could not even say or believe that O'Brien had truly betrayed him. In any case, at one level betrayal did not even matter. O'Brien was, after all, someone Winston could talk to.

But there is a betrayal, little noted by Winston, which may be equally decisive. It is that of Mr. Charrington, the kindly 'old' antique shop owner, in reality a member of the Thought Police who had set Winston and Julia up for their ultimate capture. To be sure, Orwell provides clues to alert Winston to Charrington's real identity — the different name on the shop front inscription; the fact that Charrington possessed an accent "less debased than that of the majority of proles." However, for Winston to have immediately suspected Charrington would have seemed paranoid. Yet Winston's failure to do precisely this was fatal.

What Orwell presents here is a world that is indeed the horrible realization of a paranoid vision. It is a world in which it is literally true that anyone could be an agent of the State, an enemy willing and able to bring about one's downfall. In the circumstances, not to be paranoid is a sign of social maladjustment.[14] The situation recalls Arendt's ironic depiction of everyday life in Nazi Germany where evil "had lost the quality by which most people recognize it — the quality of temptation. Many Germans and many Nazis, probably an overwhelming majority of them, must have been tempted not to murder, not to rob, not to let their neighbours go off to their doom...and not to become accomplices in all these crimes by benefitting from them."[15]

As the towering intellectual figure in *Nineteen Eighty-Four*, O'Brien represents for Orwell the arid abstractness of a universalist, totalist conception of the world. O'Brien's quest for total power is in this light understandable. He is the concrete realization of Hegel's Absolute Spirit. As Winston saw him, "O'Brien was a being in all ways larger than himself. There was no idea he had ever had, nor could have, that O'Brien had not known, examined, and rejected. His mind contained Winston's mind."[16] The realization of Absolute Spirit requires Absolute Power if the identity of mind and the world is to be established.

By contrast, Charrington represents something more intriguing, perhaps even more significant: the humanist intellectual's capitulation to, and complicity with, the power of the State. He upholds values which are not only those which Winston treasures, but also those of Orwell himself. Charrington's intellectual outlook is much more modest than that of O'-Brien. It is concerned with everyday matters rooted in a particular time and place, not with grand theory. Charrington seems to be the bearer of genuine historical memory, a memory not of historical 'trends', but of the lived experience of ordinary mortals loving, working, grieving and celebrating. He appears to remember what things were like "when there was still privacy, love, and friendship, and when members of a family stood by one another without needing to know the reason."[17] The conversation between he and Winston about "a lost London that still existed somewhere or other"[18] provides one of the most touching and affecting scenes in the novel. Although there is no evidence that Party heretics such as Winston could ever be 'rehabilitated', one wonders whether perhaps at an earlier time Charrington had not even been like Winston himself. (There can be no doubt about O'Brien: "They got me a long time ago."[19])

If indeed Charrington had once been like Winston, his transformation is sad, even tragic. If prefigures one possible form of Winston's own destruction.

Of course, Charrington may in fact be another O'Brien. At one level this might be comforting; at another it is ominously sinister, and even devastating. For it would mean that the values to which Winston holds fast in his revolt are not immune to the power of the total State to define reality in its own terms. These values can, in short, be turned into ideology. To the triumvirate of claims that "War is Peace"; "Freedom is Slavery"; and "Ignorance is Strength" might be added another: "Indecency is decency." Winston fears that he may have lost his bearings. In fact, he may not know how truly precarious his situation is. The State may be succeeding far more completely in its aims than even O'Brien argues or suspects; after all, O'Brien does not even pretend decency.

Whatever the basis of Charrington's betrayal, it illuminates an important point: simple experiences which could not possibly seem significant for those who wield total power in Oceania in fact come under their direct scrutiny. This state of affairs demonstrates both the depth to which domination had penetrated society, and the Party's recognition that social control could never be complete unless and until it incorporated the most intimate desires and longings of people into its fabric.

Hence while the total State is managed by people such as O'Brien, it requires for its successful functioning the active support of people such as Charrington — and Winston. Only they can fully transform those everyday bonds which tie people together into that web of associations which imparts order and predictability — for even the total State requires some order — to the affairs of life in Oceania.

In other words, Oceania requires its own 'normality' if it is successfully to reproduce itself. The condition of normality suggests those qualities of totalitarian organization which Hannah Arendt illuminates in her metaphor of the onion. For her, "the extraordinarily manifold parts" of the totalitarian movement are "related in such a way that each forms the facade in one direction and the center in the other, that is, plays the role of normal outside world for one layer and the role of radical extremism for another." Thus the movement provides for each of its layers "the fiction of a normal world along with a consciousness of being different from and more radical than it." Deluded, like O'Brien, into believing in the rationality and sanity of the totalitarian universe, members of the movement "need never be aware of the abyss which separates their own world from that which actually surrounds it. The onion structure makes the system organizationally shock-proof against the factuality of the real world."[20]

Life in Oceania has actually moved a step beyond this state of affairs. There is decreasingly a real world of factuality against which the fantasy world of the movement can be checked. The abyss begins to disappear. In essence the totalitarian fictions become reality.

Arendt had understood that such a process could occur. But she had restricted its presence, at least in a complete form, to the concentration camp, "a phantom world which, however, has materialized, as it were, into a world which is complete with all sensual data of reality but lacks the structure of consequences and responsibility without which reality remains for us a mass of incomprehensible data."[21] For Orwell, the logic of the concentration camp suffuses the world of the Party and thus, indirectly, the whole of society. A "structure of consequences and responsibilities" is after all another way of defining socialization. In Oceania, it is not so much the absence of such a structure but a reversal of the relation between action and outcome which is central to everyday experience. 'Self-evident' consequences, those which the Party wishes to affirm in the immediate here-and-now, breed their requisite appropriate 'actions'. The Party will tell you not 'what is to be done', but rather 'what must have been done' to achieve what is currently defined as the 'truth'.

This 'false' structure of consequences and responsibility is the foundation of the Party's efforts to shape the future by controlling the past. It manifests the 'spirit of the laws' — or more precisely, in true doublethink fashion, the spirit of the lawlessness — in Oceania. Its presence challenges what seems to both common sense and theoretical insight as beyond question: the fixed spatio-temporal character of human actions. Winston holds fast to his sense that what has happened is thus and so, and cannot be otherwise, that there is a reality external to the human mind. O'Brien seeks to undermine and destroy this sense because it points to domains of experience beyond power, and thus to sources of standards by means of which power might be judged.

O'Brien can plausibly hope to succeed in this aim because he recognizes what Winston does not and what Orwell himself appears to have difficulty accepting. He recognizes that truth and meaning, while related, are not identical. While truth concerns material outcomes, meaning involves the relation between intentions and outcomes. Since the world is characterized, as Arendt puts it, by the (apparently) irreducible fact of plurality, i.e. the existence of not merely one person but many people, these intentions are shaped by and through interpersonal interactions, and outcomes emerge from the intersection of intentionally-motivated individual activities. It any situation there are thus multiple sources of meaning; the process by which meaning is generated is inherently ambiguous.

Putting it another way, human relations have an opaque quality. This opacity results from both the obscure nature of inner motives, and from the peculiar double relation of nearness and farness through which people are associated. People are both "equal and distinct," that is, "human, in such a way that nobody is ever the same as anyone else who ever lived, lives, or will live."[22] The nature and significance of human action depends therefore upon the agreement of people to endow it with, literally, a 'common sense'. They consent to the shape of the world. This consent is the foundation of, and the manifestation of, what Arendt defines as the human faculty for making and keeping promises; it is the experiential content of a "structure of consequences and responsibility." Consent makes possible the temporal continuity of social life and hence a sense of personal and social identity. Without it, the realm of human affairs, which consists of a "web of human relationships...with its innumerable, conflicting wills and intentions...,"[23] would be unpredictable and chaotic, indeed hardly a public "realm" at all.

Winston is haunted by the fact that in a fundamental way reality is the product of consensus. He fears that a reality which relies for its human existence upon intersubjective agreement cannot possibly have the apparent stability of either what Arendt calls "rational" truth — that two plus two equals four — or "factual" truth — that something that exists in the material world is thus and so, and not otherwise. In questioning the infallibility of Big Brother, Winston "wondered...whether he himself was a lunatic. Perhaps a lunatic was simply a minority of one. At one time it had been a sign of madness to believe that the earth goes round the sun: to-day, to believe that the past is unalterable. He might be alone in holding that belief, and if alone, then a lunatic. But the thought of being a lunatic did not greatly trouble him: the horror was that he might also be wrong."[24] This dilemma masterfully expresses Winston's predicament. He wants to pursue truth, but what he is really after is meaning. His confusion is understandable. His confrontation with his own past, political and personal, had triggered, or at least accompanied, his increasingly strong desire to rebel. While for most people, most of the time (and this includes most Party members), 'what is' is less problematic that 'what should be', for Winston both dimensions are at issue. His sense that the experiential ground has been cut from under him is decisive for his effort to understand himself — to grasp, in Arendt's terms, "who" he is, what kind of agent he is when "he discloses himself in deed and word."[25]

Winston wants to know the truth about his relation to his family, for a long time repressed by his unconscious, and the real purposes for which power is exercised by the total State. He sets out to pursue a critique of ideology; he is a combination of Freud and Marx. When asked rhetorically by O'Brien why the Party wants power, Winston is certain that the 'correct', i.e. ideological, answer is that the exercise of power is essential for the good of the majority of people, who are incapable of governing themselves. Since Winston knows this to be false, he is confident that he possesses a critical basis for understanding the real situation in Oceania. He thinks the truth lies in the discrepancy between the Party's professed aims and the actuality of its brutal rule.

He is unprepared for the violent response his answer receives, unprepared for O'Brien's assertion that power is acquired and maintained purely for its own sake. For Winston this could not be true. Power must be exercised for an identifiable material interest, as the book had so cogently argued. As a representative of a classically socialist position, Winston fails to see that the move from the tyrannical determination of identity and behaviour by unmastered material interests to the conscious mastery of human powers, that is, the move from the realm of necessity to the realm of freedom, need not be the exclusive concern of a progressive politics. In other words, he does not see that the Party has created, and seeks constantly to recreate, a world in which the always problematic element of consent is an objective component of it. The Party wants to create a kind of meaning which, in its apparent solidity, resembles truth.

In the process, both meaning and truth are transformed. In the circumstances, it is, as O'Brien notes, irrelevant whether the stars exist or not, or whether the law of gravity operates independently of the will of the Party. The content of these scientific truths is determined by political power. To be sure, truth has its uses: "When we navigate the ocean, or predict an eclipse, we often find it convenient to assume that earth goes round the sun and the stars are millions and millions of kilometres away...," O'Brien notes.[26] Nevertheless, social bonds can be established just as readily on the basis of the denial of these truths.

The problem for O'Brien and the Party is that Winston has not yet accepted as true simultaneously both what has happened and what might have happened. He has not, in other words, yet mastered the art of doublethink. Doublethink can only occur when it is 'freely' undertaken, when it is unreflectively engendered by an inner compulsion. Winston must willingly embrace the Party and its purposes, must come to love power and its exercise, must do what power requires.

O'Brien is right to think that Winston can be brought over. At one level Winston already loves Big Brother and indeed O'Brien himself. However, before this transformation can be completed, Winston must be brought face to face with the reality of power. Until this occurs, power is only a word for him, as O'Brien clearly understands. In an apparent parody of traditional Christian doctrine, Winston can only reconcile himself to the God of power by undergoing suffering. From the heretic, "Obedience is not enough. Unless he is suffering, how can you be sure he is obeying your will and not his own?"[27] The infliction of pain strips people of dignity and makes them utterly vulnerable. But pain is an intrinsically private, not public, experience. The terrible genius of the Party lies in its ability to politicize pain.

Suffering is the sensuous basis for the reconciliation of theory and practice, the substitution of meaning for truth. Pain has a materiality, and above all a commonality, that seem to make it ideal as a basis of community. This insight is central to utilitarianism; as Arendt notes, Hobbes is both the true philosopher of the bourgeoisie and a philosophical precursor of totalitarianism.[28] But in a bourgeois society, and even as O'Brien suggests, in the totalitarian States of the mid-twentieth century, pain has functioned as an essentially negative, or passive, foundation for social order. What the Party strives to accomplish is the conversion of pain, or suffering, into a positive principle of a community for which the sole value is total power for its own sake. Instead of being a contingent fact of human life, pain is turned into an ontological necessity. "Do you begin to see, then, what kind of world we are creating?...A world of treachery and torment, a world of trampling and being trampled upon, a world which will grow not less but more merciless as it refines itself. Progress in our world will be progress towards more pain."[29] Pain must be an essential element in the constitution of personal identity, a way of being in the world. In this light, to be fully human is to inflict pain, upon others, but also upon oneself.

For pain and suffering to become the dominant content of the individual personality, other qualities must first be extirpated. However, this creates a problem. How can a sensuous bond be established between the Party/State and the individual in the absence of "love, or friendship, or joy of living, or laughter, or curiosity, or courage, or integrity..." — precisely the qualities "O'Brien promises to drain from Winston's personality?[30] Winston believes it impossible to found an enduring civilization on fear, hatred and cruelty. Even the bourgeois social order, in which the quest for power and the fear of violent death are so decisive, cannot subsist on these passions alone.[31]

In its success and horror, the solution of the Party is both elemental and profound. The infliction of pain, or the terror of a pain beyond imagining, induces one to perform acts which so violate one's sense of morality and integrity that there can be no recovery from them. Julia puts it exactly: "'Sometimes...they threaten you with something — something you can't stand up to, can't even think about. And then you say, 'Don't do it to me, do it to somebody else, do it to so-and-so'. And perhaps you might pretend, afterwards, that it was only a trick...But that isn't true...You want it to happen to the other person. You don't give a damn what they suffer. All you care about is yourself."[32] Once one has committed such an act, there is no turning back. One has become complicit in the crimes of a regime in which this kind of betrayal is a central principle; one has engaged in an act of self-contamination. A dirty secret binds one to the Party/State: the secret that the principles of one's conduct are those of the community. The Party demands the unforgivable while denying the "possible redemption from the predicament of irreversibility — of being unable to undo what one has done though one did not, and could not, have known what he was doing...the faculty of forgiveness."[33]

More correctly, the Party itself forgives, not by facilitating one's reconciliation with the consequences of an action, but by blotting them from the historical record. This act of repression occurs at both the individual and social levels. The individual engages in doublethink to conceal her/his actions her/himself, while the Party engages in political doublethink — "collective solipsism," as O'Brien calls it. In this fashion, the 'ethical' foundation of the total State is put into place, the Party functioning as a religious body, an agent of salvation. O'Brien does not lie when he refers to the Party as "the priests of power," or tells Winston that "you are in my keeping...I shall save you. I shall make you perfect."[34] Thus is a State established not on the basis of 'liberty, equality and fraternity', but their oppposites. It is a State in which it is literally true that war is peace, freedom is slavery, and ignorance is strength.[35]

II

"Freedom is the freedom to say that two plus two makes four. If that is granted, all else follows."[36] Winston Smith, and Orwell, saw in this equation the unshakable foundation of human social experience. As long as one could still see and accept it, one could retain a critical perspective on reality and a grip on sanity: "Truisms are true, hold on to that!"[37] O'Brien's ability to coerce Winston into believing that two plus two could equal whatever the Party wished it to equal is seen in *Nineteen Eighty-Four* as the crucible of Winston's defeat at the hands of Big Brother, the hallmark of the insanity of life in Oceania.

Neither Winston nor Orwell, however, considers exactly what it is that allows humans to say that two plus two equals five. Neither examines whether some positive human capacity is manifest in such an act, even if in a distorted form. Here Hannah Arendt's account of human action and freedom illuminates more fully the ontological foundations of the process of total control, the central elements of a false but functioning political universe.

The human capacity to act, the capacity of human beings to intervene through word and deed in events going on around them, is the raison d'être of a genuine politics. The political or public realm is the outcome of, and the basis of, human action: "it is the organization of the people as it arises out of acting and speaking together, and its true space lies between people living together for this purpose, no matter where they happen to be."[38] Inhabiting what Arendt calls a "common world," a domain of humanly fabricated objects — culture in its broadest sense — which simultaneously unites people while at the same time separating them, "each individual in his [sic] unique distinctness, appears and confirms himself in speech and action..."[39] The public sphere secures this "space of appearance" within which both "the reality of one's self, of one's identity...[and]...the reality of the surrounding world can be established beyond doubt."[40]

For Arendt, "worldliness" guarantees institutionally the fact of human plurality and thus renders possible the individual disclosure for which the space of appearance exists. Where a domain of stable and familiar objects is absent, or exists as a kind of pseudo-world in the form of the products of a modern consumer society, it loses its power to gather people together, to relate and separate them. This situation "resembles a spiritualistic seance where a number of people gathered around a table might suddenly, through some magic trick, see the table vanish from their midst, so that two persons sitting opposite each other were no longer separated but also would be entirely unrelated to each other by anything tangible."[41] The result is a deep uncertainty, "not only of all political matters, but of all affairs that go on between men [sic] directly, without the intermediary, stabilizing, and solidifying influence of things."[42]

This uncertainty is most acute in a totalitarian State, in which the "experience of a trembling wobbling motion of everything we rely on for our sense of direction and reality is among the most common and most vivid experiences..."[43] But it is also present in what Arendt calls "mass-society": a social order characterized by an increasingly pervasive worldlessness, or "world alienation."[44] Under the impact of this kind of "organized living," there is neither genuine autonomy nor community. People either "live in desperate lonely separation,"[45] or experience others as forces impinging on them who, because they are no longer related to them by the stable objectivity of a human artifice, are literally 'unknown quantities' and thus potentially threatening. Usually people endure both conditions simultaneously. They are thus at once crowded and alone — a bizarre parody of the difference in unity which has long been held to be the basis and purpose of a genuine politics.

Of course, when Arendt writes of worldlessness, of the loss of the objectivity of a human artifice, she does not mean that there are no 'objects' in the world, that human social relations are somehow empty of physicality. This is a clear impossibility, although it is indeed what O'-Brien tries to argue with Winston. Rather, she means that humans are increasingly unable to see themselves in the objects present to perception, and are thus increasingly blind to the nature of their sensuous presence in their relations with other humans and with physical nature. This plight is evident in Winston Smith's ambiguous encounter with his surroundings: "It was always difficult to determine the age of a London building. Anything large and impressive, if it was reasonably new in appearance, was automatically claimed as having been built since the

Revolution, while anything that was obviously of earlier date was ascribed to some dim period called the Middle Ages." The significance of this ambiguity is clear. "One could not learn history from architecture any more than one could learn it from books. Statues, inscriptions, memorial stones, the names of streets — anything that might throw light upon the past had been systematically altered."[46]

While Winston's plight seems extreme — a feature of life found only in the total State — Arendt believes that this is becoming increasingly common in modern societies. It demonstrates that it is central to both individuals and groups to perceive the impact of their activity.

Worldlessness and the loss of memory profoundly affect the possibilities for action because the reality of action can be confirmed only by and through the "stories" it "produces" as a result of its impact on the already existing "web" of human relationships. "These stories may then be recorded in documents and monuments, they may be visible in use objects or art works, they may be told and retold and worked into all kinds of material."[47] The systematic alteration of history as lived public space, or the human artifice, obliterates knowledge of the "hero" at the centre of each story, "the agent who set the whole process in motion..."[48] It denies the capacity of people autonomously to insert themselves through word and deed into the world.

As Arendt understands it, the "stories within which action is made concrete have agents but no 'authors'." The stories themselves are the outcomes of the intersections of distinct individual life trajectories within the web of relationships, and thus cannot be the willed products of anyone. This relation of agency to authorship illuminates in a distinct way the relation of the individual to the community — the core issue of politics. That human history, "a story of action and deeds rather than of trends and forces or ideas,"[49] as no author testifies to its inherently political nature. Politics as action, and history as the human significance of the relation of worldliness to action, necessarily entail each other.

Arendt's analysis helps reveal the full magnitude of the aim of the Party in Oceania. The Party seeks to become both the agent and the author of history simultaneously. It is this latter aspiration that is most lunatic and requires that the Party suppress not just alternative possibilities of agency, but also agents themselves. It is why the party must continuously alter the past, and moreover must do so nakedly and proudly.

For the Party to assume both authorship and agency is to abolish, or seek to abolish, individual disclosure. Here lies the full meaning of O'Brien's casual remark to Winston that "You do not exist," and his chilling prediction that "You will be lifted clean out of the stream of history."[50] From Arendt's perspective, the attempt to abolish disclosure is literally world-shattering: "To dispense with this disclosure, if indeed it could ever be done, would mean to transform men [sic] into something they are not..."[51]

Orwell and Winston sense this and it paralyses them. Arendt goes further. She asks in effect if there might not be some 'false' forms of disclosure, some perverted manifestations of human action which come into being when the conditions for genuine appearance have been politically suppressed. Her answer is that there are indeed such 'false' forms and they have assumed two main guises: modern science and organized lying. Because of its intrinsic significance for Orwell's account in *Nineteen Eighty-Four*, the latter will be discussed here.

There are two reasons why Orwell does not pursue the possibility that what he has described in his novel is a form of 'false' disclosure, or false action. In the first place, he wants to assert that history — that which is because it has happened — must be beyond politics. Otherwise there can be no stability in individual and social experience. In the second place, he does not address fully the implications of human freedom. This results in large measure from his tendency to blame intellectuals as a class for the horrific qualities of contemporary civilization which he satirically dissects in *Nineteen Eighty-Four*. He thus avoids an examination of the collective, historically determined foundations of those conditions, i.e. the intellectual culture as a whole.

As was suggested above, Arendt views history and politics as mutually requiring and entailing each other. They are not antagonists per se. This is not to say that historical evidence can be rewritten to conform to current political demands. "Even if we admit that every generation has the right to write its own history, we admit no more than that it has the right to rearrange the facts in accordance with its own perspective; we don't admit the right to touch the factual matter itself."[52] It is to suggest that history will be appropriated by each generation for purposes that emerge out of the interplay of human intentionality and human artifice, or activity and social structure.

It is under these circumstances that history and politics may assume an ambivalent, if necessary, relation to one another. Politics must take into account what has happened because the historical past is the unavoidable framework within which what might happen will take place. Yet in its very claims to be acknowledged as thus and so, the past weighs "like a nightmare on the brain of the living." At least some part of the past will invariably frustrate the intentions of political actors because it will testify to the apparent impossibility/undesirability of some desired state of affairs. "Seen from the viewpoint of politics, truth has a despotic character...Factual truth, like all other truth, peremptorily claims to be acknowledged and precludes debate, and debate constitutes the very essence of political life."[53] The problem is how to reconcile the necessary aspiration to initiate something new, which is at the heart of action, with the equally necessary acceptance of historical evidence.

From this perspective, the human capacity to forgive assumes added significance. It is not only the remedy for the irreversibility of action. It is also the vehicle for the reconciliation with history. The capacity to forgive allows people to 'forget' history in order that the ability to act, which would otherwise be hopelessly burdened by the weight of the past, can be exercised anew.

Reliance on the capacity to forgive seems a melancholy solution to the problem of historically bounded human activity. Thus, according to Arendt, classical political thinkers mistrusted and downplayed the realm of human affairs. The frustrating absence of an identifiable "author" of a process which was nevertheless so decisive for the fate of human community persuaded Plato, for one, that not much could truly be expected from it. For Arendt, this is the central meaning of the allegory of the cave in the Republic: the realm of human affairs is one of "darkness, confusion and deception which those aspiring to true being must turn away from and abandon if they want to discover the clear sky of eternal ideas."[54] At the same time philosophy demanded that public life be subjected to the authority of reason.

The tradition of political philosophy was thus inaugurated on the basis of a hostility to public life. The anti-political character of political philosophy has marked both politics and philosophy since. Our political tradition has bequeathed us "the opposition of thinking and acting, which, depriving thought of reality and sense, makes both meaningless."[55] In light of this opposition, the possibility of political actors scrutinizing critically the realm of human affairs is seriously impaired, and an essential element of the quest for total control is thereby put into place.

For Arendt, then, political philosophy as such, and not just the perfidy of intellectuals, is culpable in attempts to institute a tyranny of reason. Clearly this assumption has major implications for the ontological foundations of political critique. Ontological perspectives are expressed by and through those very categories which would, if 'realized', ostensibly threaten the very possibility of politics itself.

Leaving aside this issue for the moment, it is also evident that, given the relation between politics and history, frustration at the contingency of human affairs, or at least the unwillingness to be bound irrevocably by the consequences of past actions, appears fundamental to the capacity to act. It is in other words a central feature of the "human condition," of human nature. The unavoidability of action, plus the emergence of an intellectual culture which incorporates within itself an authoritarian relation between theory and action, help define for Arendt the context within which the quest for total control must be considered. In light of both the nature of human capacities and the vehicles by means of which human aspirations are expressed, it is crucial to explore what human needs might be 'satisfied' by the institutions of the total State.

Arendt's account of the politics of organized lying is her arresting attempt to confront this matter. That she discusses lying is significant: it means that the thrust toward total control is not simply an element of the totalitarian State, although it is most fully developed there. The attempt systematically to falsify the historical record is a disturbing trend in all States. But while the actual rewriting of history occurs often enough in both totalitarian and non-totalitarian States, it is not the only, or even the most common, form of historical falsification. Any effort to blur the distinction between fact and opinion can be a form of such falsification.

Hence perhaps even more important than the deliberate alteration of the historical record is the increasing prevalence of what Arendt calls "ideological" thinking. Ideologies, which Arendt defines as "isms which to the satisfaction of their adherents can explain everything and every occurrence by deducing it from a single premise,"[56] provide an effective escape from the inherent frustrations of irreversible actions. Ideology, and the propaganda with which it tends to be closely associated, allow for the recasting of history in more predictable and therefore 'logical' terms than the haphazard nature of an unbearable past can allow. And there is an awful 'truth' to this process. The escape from contingency entailed by organized lying in all its forms "has some connection with those capacities of the human mind whose structural consistency is superior to mere occurrence."[57]

Lying both echoes and parodies human creativity. The motive for this 'false' creativity is identical to that underlying genuine action. The liar "says what is not so because he wants to change the world."[58] To change the world requires that one must be able to say "no" to the prevailing reality. While as humans we "are well-equipped for the world, sensually as well as mentally, we are not fitted or embedded in it as one of its inalienable parts."[59] Our ties to the world are humanly created. Thus "the deliberate denial of factual truth — the ability to lie — and the capacity to change facts — the ability to act — are interconnected; they owe their existence to the same source: imagination."[60] Lying, the ability to say that two plus two equals five, and not truth-telling, is the hallmark of human freedom.

A disturbing question emerges from these considerations. Is the total State, in which the apparatus of organized lying is most fully developed, the ultimate testament to human freedom? Because of its apparent absurdity, this is a question which Orwell cannot address. It haunts Arendt's account of totalitarianism, however, and so at the very least forces us to move beyond certain explanations for the rise of the total State. Thus the hunger for power, which O'Brien claims to be the motive force behind the activity of the Party, cannot account for the ties that bind all Party members, much less the people as a whole. (As Arendt made brilliantly clear, it cannot account for Eichmann.) Terror alone cannot do the job either (as O'Brien well understands). Totalitarianism, and the quest for total control in general, must be seen rather as the 'solution' to a collective human 'problem'. For Arendt, this problem is human isolation and its consequent condition, human superfluousness. It is in this setting that lying, falsely creative human action, takes full root.

In a striking passage, Arendt spells out the bonds which tie people to the totalitarian order. She argues that the "masses' escape from reality" is a condemnation of their way of life. Because people require consistency as a defence against the chaos of the world they are willing to bow "before the most rigid, fantastically fictitious consistency of an ideology..." They do so not because of stupidity or wickedness but because "in the general disaster this escape grants them a minimum of self-respect." [61]

Totalitarianism can provide a surrogate polis which meets in however distorted a way the real and deeply felt needs of large numbers of people. Moreover the abandonment of common sense reality is not for Arendt an escape from freedom as such. It is an escape from historically created intolerable conditions which assumes the guise of a pursuit of 'false' freedom. It is also as much an escape for the executioners as for the executed: "The manipulators of this system believe in their own superfluousness as much as in that of all others, and the totalitarian murderers are all the more dangerous because they do not care if they themselves are alive or dead, if they ever lived or never were born."[62] (O'Brien is indeed the quintessential totalitarian figure.) Suffering, "of which there has always been too much on earth," is the main element in these intolerable conditions, and totalitarian solutions will be highly tempting "whenever it seems impossible to alleviate political, social, or economic misery in a manner worthy of man [sic]."[63] The proles and the Party are linked in a profound way that Winston Smith cannot quite comprehend. The basis of the pursuit of total control is a kind of revolt of (first) nature against a reified 'second nature', a historical creation that has turned against its creators.

The central question involves the status of this revolt. Will it express or deny the human capacity to act and provide for genuine disclosure? Will it provide not for "fear, hatred and pain," but rather for "dignity of emotion...deep or complex sorrows?"[64] Decisive here is the treatment of history. "The political attitude toward facts must, indeed, tread the very narrow path between the danger of taking them as the results of some necessary development which men could not prevent and about which they can therefore do nothing and the danger of denying them, of trying to manipulate them out of the world."[65] How is this to be done?

III

We are now in a position to appreciate more fully a key dilemma in the work of Orwell and Arendt. This dilemma concerns the status of human imagination and the relation of the imagination to human mastery over physical nature and human social relations. As such, it goes to the heart of the ironic treatment of ontology by both thinkers. It also provides clues about the fate of ontological reasoning, the relation of theory to practice, in the modern era.

Imagination is inherent in language. Conceptual reasoning is impossible without an imaginative reconstruction of the given, which incorporates such reconstruction as one of its elements. Language is by its very nature social. Even Hobbes' atomistic individuals need to agree on common definitions of words, and this is not possible without some principle of agreement which is not simply the agreements themselves.

Herein, historically, lies the connection between language and ontology. That which makes language possible itself only expressed in and through language. Language can suggest human possibilities in a fashion that challenges the congealment or reification of existing forms of human behaviour. Ontology, on the other hand, provides the ground for distinguishing meaningful from absurd speech. The limits of both language and ontology are the limits of human community. Thus both are inherently political. Because the boundaries of community are never precisely demarcated, because the limits of the political is itself a political question, the interrogation of the existing in the light of ontology, the challenge to 'what is' on behalf of 'what ought to be', can never generate apodeictic knowledge on the model of a technical science. Ontological inquiry thus must be open-ended. But it need not be arbitrary. It is limited by historical possibilities which are at the same time material ones. If this can work to limit the prospects of equality beyond drudgery, as indeed it has worked throughout most of recorded history, it can also rule out of court forms of social control which seek to 'silence' citizens by converting them into objects of administration.

The foundation of ontological inquiry, and the status of human nature itself, have been severely shaken by the modern quest for total control. For both Orwell and Arendt, this quest indeed attacks something fundamentally human. But it does so in a way that explodes our received categories of political understanding, and in fact implicates those very categories themselves. Thus while both thinkers stand in need of an ontological standard with which to grasp, reveal and condemn the effects of total control, neither is prepared to acknowledge one. More precisely, for Orwell ontology cannot interrogate the given; for Arendt it must not.[66]

Yet the question of ontology cannot so readily be disposed of, no more than human imagination can totally disappear. Ontological considerations lurk in the depth structures of each analysis. In Orwell's case, they inhere in his brilliant treatment of the process by which Winston is broken down and stripped of his will to rebel. In reproducing the institutions of the total State, this process relies upon a lingering capacity for guilt and a sense of moral betrayal. In Arendt's case, the issue of lying itself suggests ontological concerns. The distinction between worldly creation and lying, between 'true' and 'false' forms of action, requires an ontological foundation; indeed it might be thought already ontological.

Their implicit and explicit disavowal of ontology is however understandable. The fate of both thinking and acting must be uncertain in a world in which human social bonds are suffused with paranoia and despair, a world in which there seems no escape from either the unpredictability or the irreversibility of action. It may even be possible to speak of human nature at all only where and when it can truly exist as such.

Hidden within the work of Orwell and Arendt is a plea. This plea is for the creation of a human community within which human capacities reinforce, and are reinforced by, bonds of equality and mutuality that are neither the 'false' realization of philosophical categories (Orwell), nor the realization of categories which, because of their inherently authoritarian caste, are anti-political (Arendt). In this light, what must be explored are the possibilities for the establishment of communal bonds which are founded upon neither behavioural regularities which can be statistically measured and administered (a state of affairs which Arendt sees as critical for modern anti-politics[67]), nor a common physical nature (O'Brien's world of fear and pain).

Historically, it has been the left that has made these issues central to its politics. Both Orwell and Arendt knew this, and hence were hostile to the political right, whatever their reputations as a 'conservative' (Arendt) or 'disillusioned socialist' (Orwell). However, the left seems to have forgotten the need for a communal vision. Orwell and Arendt knew this, too. What they teach us is that such a vision, in whatever form, will emerge somehow; it is, so to speak, 'natural'.[68] And if it does not emerge on the left, it will emerge elsewhere.

One such alternative venue for a communal vision has been totalitarianism. More recently, and ominously, there has emerged another one: the new right in North America and Europe. This movement, with deep roots in evangelical Christianity (note again Orwell's portrayal of the Party), has stolen the left's ontological thunder by going beyond its traditional emphasis on what Robert Paul Wolff once called "productive community."[69] It focuses instead upon the need for "affective community," one bound by ties of loyalty beyond material utility.

But it is not its 'spiritualism' that gives the new right its influence. It is rather, one might say, its 'politicism': its concern for ordered relations in society as a whole within which its communal vision might be achieved.[70] To be sure, the vision is hypocritical. The new right is as ideological as Winston Smith believed the Party to be.[71] The movement and the vision could, however, crystallize into a new political universe, a political culture delimiting possible and necessary forms of political action. Such a development would bring into existence Orwell's nightmare of the transformation of 'outer' into 'inner' life and vice versa. It would also involve the most complete realization of Arendt's notion of the "social," a hybrid mixture of "private" and "public" realms which distorts and undermines both.[72]

The new right shares much in common with its totalitarian predecessor. It fans fear and hatred. It emphasizes human dispensability, to the point where some of its more zealous (honest?) adherents appear to welcome nuclear destruction as a manifestation of God's wrath, from which the truly Christian would be spared. It defends possessive individualism as community and attacks community as "secular humanism." In the name of freedom, it promotes a rigid authoritarianism, and an equally rigid conformism. In the name of universalism, it denies human status to non- believers. It confirms and affirms pain in a painful world.

The theoretical and political task facing the humanist left is clear. A true left humanism must articulate and defend an individualism that is autonomous because it is embedded in a supportive web of human relationships, and a community that is the intended and unintended product of rational individuals exercising judgment about their common affairs with a minimum of fear and terror, and thus hatred and resentment. It must promote a vision of the world worthy of those capacities which George Orwell and Hannah Arendt were fearful of acknowledging, but always hopeful of realizing.

NOTES

1. M. Horkheimer, *Eclipse of Reason* (1947) (New York: Seabury Press, 1974), pp. 122-3.
2. H. Arendt, *On Hannah Arendt*, in M. Hill (ed.), *Hannah Arendt: The Recovery of the Public World* (New York: St. Martin's Press, 1979), p.336.
3. G. Orwell, *Nineteen Eighty-Four* (Middlesex, England: Penguin Books, 1975), p.25.
4. Arendt, *Men in Dark Times* (New York: Harcourt, Brace and World, 1968), p.viii.
5. Arendt, *Between Past and Future: Eight Exercises in Political Thought* (New York: The Viking Press, 1968), pp.15, 31.
6. Arendt, *The Concept of History* in *Between Past and Future*, p. 56.
7. Ibid., p. 87.
8. Orwell, *Nineteen Eighty-Four*, pp.241-51; *Politics and the English Language*, in *In Front of Your Nose. The Collected Essays, Journalism and Letters of George Orwell* Vol.4. Orwell and I. Angus (eds.) (New York: Harcourt, Brace and World, 1968), pp.127-40.
9. I am indebted to Paul Breines for suggesting this formulation to me.
10. Orwell, *Nineteen Eighty-Four*, p. 26.
11. M. Horkheimer, *Eclipse of Reason* (1947) (New York: Seabury Press, 1974), pp.122-123.
12. H. Arendt, "On Hannah Arendt," in M. Hill (ed.), *Hannah Arendt: The Recovery of the Public World* (New York: St. Martin's Press, 1979), p.336.
13. G. Orwell, *Nineteen Eighty-Four* (Middlesex, England: Penguin Books, 1975), p.25.
14. H. Arendt, *Men in Dark Times* (New York: Harcourt, Brace and World, 1968), p.viii.
15. H. Arendt, *Between Past and Future: Eight Exercises in Political Thought* (New York: The Viking Press, 1968), pp.15, 31.
16. H. Arendt, "The Concept of History," in *Between Past and Future*, p.56.
17. Ibid., p.87.
18. G. Orwell, *Nineteen Eighty-Four*, pp.241-251; "Politics and the English Language," in *In Front of Your Nose. The Collected Essays, Journalism and Letters of George Orwell* Vol.4, S. Orwell and I. Angus (eds.) (New York: Harcourt, Brace and World, 1968), pp.127-140.
19. I am indebted to Paul Breines for suggesting this formulation to me.

20. G. Orwell, *Nineteen Eighty-Four*, p.26.
21. Ibid., p.15.
22. Ibid., p.67.
23. Ibid., p.192.
24. However, paranoia must be cultivated carefully. Winston was — wrongly — paranoid about Julia. Winston's predicament requires a paranoia that is both general and selective at the same time. Thus a dilemma: doublethink can only be challenged by doublethink itself.
25. H. Arendt, *Eichmann in Jerusalem* (New York: The Viking Press, 1965), p.150.
26. G. Orwell, *Nineteen Eighty-Four*, p.205.
27. Ibid., p.27.
28. Ibid., p.83.
29. Ibid., p.191.
30. H. Arendt, "What is Authority?," in *Between Past and Future*, pp.99-100.
31. H. Arendt, *The Origins of Totalitarianism*, Second Edition (Cleveland and New York: Meridian Books, 1958), p.445.
32. H. Arendt, *The Human Condition* (New York: Anchor Books, 1959), p.10.
33. Ibid., p.163.
34. G. Orwell, *Nineteen Eighty-Four*, p.67.
35. H. Arendt, *The Human Condition*, p.160.
36. G. Orwell, *Nineteen Eighty-Four*, p.213. O'Brien's position bears a disturbing resemblance to certain pragmatist doctrines.
37. Ibid., p.214.
38. H. Arendt, *The Origins ...*, p.139ff. In O'Brien's account of life in the total State, Orwell neatly parodies Hobbes' famous picture of the state of war from chapter 13 of Leviathan: "There will be no loyalty, except loyalty towards the Party, There will be no love, except the love of Big Brother. There will be no laughter, except the laugh of triumph over a defeated enemy. There will be no art, no literature, no science. When we are omnipotent we shall have no more need of science. There will be no distinction between beauty and ugliness. There will be no curiosity, no enjoyment of the process of life. All competing pleasures will be destroyed." (Orwell, *Nineteen Eighty-Four*, p.215.) Of course Hobbes had argued that total power would preserve people from these conditions, not institutionalize the conditions themselves. Orwell understands that the logic in each case is the same. Here lies the foundation of the destruction of traditional political language.
39. G. Orwell, *Nineteen Eighty-Four*, p.214.
40. Ibid., p.206.
41. Cf. J. Habermas, *Legitimation Crisis*, trans. T. McCarthy (Boston: Beacon Press, 1975). Habermas argues that bourgeois society requires a tradition of non-instrumental values in order successfully to legitimate itself to its members.
42. G. Orwell, *Nineteen Eighty-Four*, pp.234-235.
43. H. Arendt, *The Human Condition*, pp.212-213. Arendt notes that the performance of unconscionable acts was an element of life in Nazi concentration camps. (*The Origins...*, p.452).
44. G. Orwell, *Nineteen Eighty-Four*, pp.212, 196.
45. The process of 'reconciliation' and 'forgiveness' is complex. It involves more than the simple repression of the memory of a horrible act. For the bond between the individual and the Party/State to be fully secure, it is essential that the act be constantly remembered and 'forgiven' anew. The mockingly ironic ditty first played for Jones, Aaronson and Rutherford at the Chestnut Tree Café, and repeated for Winston after his encounter with the Ministry of Love, has a double meaning. It publicly calls to mind the victim's false betrayal of the nation, but more importantly, it privately rekindles the memory of her/his real betrayal of friends, principles, and ultimately her/himself. Like a festering sore constantly reopened and smothered with a soothing balm, the victim's past is continually brought forward to consciousness in the eternal present, to be repressed again. "'What happens to you here is forever,' O'Brien had said. That was a true word. There were things, your own acts,

from which you could not recover." (*Nineteen Eighty-Four*, p.233). Nor be allowed to recover. "The heretic, the enemy of society, will always be there, so that he can be defeated and humiliated over again." (ibid., p.215).
46. Ibid., p.68.
47. Ibid.
48. H. Arendt, *The Human Condition*, p.177.
49. Ibid., p.186.
50. Ibid., p.187.
51. Ibid., p.48.
52. Ibid., p.162.
53. H. Arendt, "Truth and Politics," in *Between Past and Future*, p.258.
54. H. Arendt discusses "mass society" throughout her work. The most detailed and politically significant discussion of the concept is in "The Crisis in Culture," in *Between Past and Future*, pp.197-226. "World alienation" is treated in *The Human Condition*, ch.VI.
55. H. Arendt, "The Concept of History," pp.89-90.
56. G. Orwell, *Nineteen Eighty-Four*, p.82.
57. H. Arendt, *The Human Condition*, p.164.
58. Ibid.
59. Ibid., p.165.
60. G. Orwell, *Nineteen Eighty-Four*, pp.208, 204.
61. H. Arendt, *The Human Condition*, p.163.
62. H. Arendt, "Truth and Politics," pp.238-239.
63. Ibid., p.241.
64. H. Arendt, "Tradition and the Modern Age," in *Between Past and Future*, p.17.
65. Ibid., p.25.
66. H. Arendt, *The Origins...*, p.468.
67. Ibid., p.352.
68. H. Arendt, "Truth and Politics," p.250.
69. H. Arendt, *Lying in Politics*, in *Crises of the Republic*, (New York: Harcourt, Bruce, Javonovich, 1972), p.5.
70. Ibid.
71. H. Arendt, *The Origins...*, p.352.
72. Ibid., p.459. The pursuit of 'false' freedom is at the core of the totalitarian attempt to establish total domination. The goal of this process, as Arendt sees it, is the conversion of humans into raw, natural beings, mere bundles of physical energies. The process of total control seeks, in other words, "to fabricate something that does not exist, namely a kind of human species resembling other animal species whose only 'freedom' would consist in 'preserving the species...'" (*The Origins...*, p.438).
73. Ibid., p.459.
74. G. Orwell, *Nineteen Eighty-Four*, p.28.
75. H. Arendt, "Truth and Politics," p.259.
76. H. Arendt's reply to Eric Voegelin's critique of *The Origins of Totalitarianism* is significant here. Voegelin had criticized Arendt for evading ontological concerns. Her response is pointed: Under conditions of totalitarian rule, "it will be hardly consoling to cling to an unchanging nature of man [sic] and conclude that either man himself is being destroyed, or that freedom does not belong to man's [sic] essential capabilities. Historically we know of man's nature only insofar as it has existence, and no realm of eternal essences will ever console us if man loses his essential capabilities." (Arendt, "A Reply," *Review of Politics*, XV (January, 1953), pp.83-84.)
77. H. Arendt, *The Human Condition*, esp. ch.II, IV.
78. H. Arendt deals with the 'naturalness' of human community throughout her work, but particularly in discussions of Kant. See, for example, "Karl Jaspers: Citizen of the World?" in *Men in Dark Times*, pp.81-94; *The Life of the Mind: Willing* (New York and London: Harcourt, Brace and Jovanovich, 1978), Appendix; *Lectures on Kant's Political Philosophy* Ronald Beiner (ed.) (Chicago: The University of Chicago Press, 1982), pp.14ff.

79. R.P. Wolff, *The Poverty of Liberalism* (Boston: Beacon Press, 1968), ch.5.
80. Cf. A. Wolfe, "Sociology, Liberalism, and the Radical Right," *New Left Review* No.128 (July-August, 1981), pp.3-28.
81. Cf. H. Chorney, M. Mendell and P. Hansen, "Les Sources de la Nouvelle Droite Americaine," en L. Jalbert et L. Beaudry (sous la direction de), *Les Metamorphoses de la Pensée Libérale* (Sillery, Québec: Presses de l'Université du Québec, 1987), pp.87-123.
82. H. Arendt, *The Human Condition*, ch.II.

8

IDEOLOGY AND BEYOND:
ADORNO, LYND AND SOME IMPLICATIONS FOR CRITICAL EDUCATION

Phillip Hansen

This essay, prepared for a conference on adult education at the University of Wyoming in 1987, attempted to relate certain ideas of Theodor Adorno, a critical theorist of the Frankfurt School, to those of Robert Lynd, an American sociologist and social theorist best known for *Middleton*, a famous study of the power structure of a midwestern American city in the 1930s. Although perhaps too brief to do full justice to any of them, the paper had three purposes. One was simply to help retrieve the ideas of two thinkers who had something relevant to say about the possibilities of democracy in American society from a kind of oblivion to which in my view they had been unjustly consigned. Another was to draw to the attention of adult educators, a group which has recently sought to apply the critical theory of Jürgen Habermas to the task of fostering a progressive and democratic adult education, to the kinds of ideas that not only influenced Habermas' own development, but which could deepen and enrich an appreciation of what a progressive and democratic education might involve. And finally, the paper sought to identify intellectual tools which could be used to grasp the power of ideology, particularly neo-conservative ideology, in the current era. The underlying assumption at work is that the dominance of neo-conservative ideas, which supposedly had been discredited by the Great Depression and the rise of the post-war welfare State, required explanation, suggesting as it did that ideological forms of social control had become both more subtle and more powerful than certain traditional left accounts of ideology had assumed.

From the vantage point of 1992, it seems that the power of neo-conservative nostrums has somewhat weakened, and may weaken further. Yet I stand by my claim in this paper that the *form* of neo-conservative "thinking" as much as the *content* of neo-conservative ideas gives us a powerful clue about its influence, and we would ignore this at our peril. Stated somewhat differently, the success of neo-conservatism should cause people on the left to rethink how to defend humanist and democratic ideas more effectively in a culture with considerable resistance and hostility to them.

One way of doing so is to unearth resources in the culture itself that can serve this process. Such an effort could yield some unexpected benefits: even as supposedly barren a cultural terrain as that of the United States can offer up the ideas of a Robert Lynd. The recent discovery of the early populists, in both the United States and Canada, is another example of what lies out there to be used in pursuit of a humane democracy and a meaningful public life. As I suggested in the paper it may be that to be radical by being conservative is one contribution a humanist left intellectual might make in the contemporary era.

These are difficult times for progressive educators. Cuts in public funding threaten the financial viability of educational institutions and the wide (although never universal) accessibility to advanced education which, at least since the Second World War, has supposedly been enshrined as a fundamental tenet of public policy. Increasing pressures from the business community and its political representatives for more 'relevant' (i.e. job-oriented) training, threaten humanistic programmes, the concerns of which have focused more on the cultivation of critical intellectual skills and less on preparation for the labour market. And educators themselves must now cope for the first time with the full impact of the television era, an era in which ever larger numbers of people exhibit a gradual erosion of historical memory and a diminution of the capacity to handle complex issues which, to be understood, require at least some measure of conceptual thinking.[1] These processes are taking place in a historical period which more and more closely resembles the nineteen thirties. Now as then, economic misery, war and the threat of war, and political authoritarianism haunt the world stage.

Not only have the "objective" conditions of the Depression period reappeared, the "subjective" conditions have returned as well, in the form of nineteen thirties-style conservative ideologies. The most notable, and certainly the most thoroughly examined, of these ideologies are the neo-conservative economic analyses — supply side theory, monetarism, rational expectations etc.[2]

But the ideological climate as a whole bears close scrutiny. This climate is one of pervasive fear. Ordinary working people, and the increasingly large body of non-working people, are told that they must 'tighten their belts,' work harder and more productively, become 'competitive' if the 'nation' is to get out of its difficulties. Once again the demands for sacrifice in the service of a 'common good' which the vast majority of people have had no role in defining are trumpeted by the heralds of public 'opinion'. There is a distinctively nineteenth century, to say nothing of Depression-era, resonance to social Darwinist claims that people should not demand or expect too much from their society, and that they must work harder if social disaster is to be averted.

What is most remarkable about the resurgence of these old canons of conservative orthodoxy is not the fact of their reappearance, but rather their capacity to shape serious policy debates and choices. It is as if fifty years of history have been forgotten, that we have experienced what Russell Jacoby has called "social amnesia."[3] This forgetting is no accident. It is the product of the process of social reproduction itself and of the mechanisms by which consciousness is formed.

And the political implications are great. While we have witnessed a return of Depression-era thinking, we have not (as yet) seen a revival of the militant opposition to the status quo which also characterized that era and laid the basis for the modern welfare State. Why and how have these notions proven so potent? Why has so little critical and political opposition emerged to challenge them? What are the implications of this state of affairs for the future development of rational consciousness and democratic citizenship? What critical tools must be developed from among the intellectual resources of the society to meet the challenge of the right? It seems that Nietzsche was correct and Marx wrong: the return of formerly discredited notions about society looks more like "eternal recurrence," and less like a "farce" which could easily be seen through. Theodor Adorno, for one, would have understood.

I

For many adult educators, the following remarks will be about something new and something old. What is new are the ideas of Adorno and the Frankfurt circle of critical theorists. What is old is the social analysis of Robert Lynd who, along with C. Wright Mills, is generally seen as a key architect of a distinctively American critical sociology.[4]

Of course Adorno's ideas are not all that "new." They were developed over a forty year period which spanned the Depression, the rise of fascism, the Second World War and the Cold War. His political position had crystallized by the early nineteen fifties, following the publication of *Dialectic of Enlightenment* (with Max Horkheimer) and *Minimamoralia*. And Lynd's analysis may not be that "old" for many educators, given that his work (and, to a surprisingly large extent, that of Mills as well) seems largely to have disappeared from the social science curricula of North American universities. All of which should alert us to a fact that neither Adorno nor Lynd would have doubted: that the terms "new" and "old" can never be treated as absolutes, divorced from a specific socio-historical context within which such terms are implicated in the social construction of meaning and the role played in this process by socially dominant interests. In other words, both thinkers were aware that novelty is not progress, nor is age obsolescence.

The structurally determined ambiguity of terms such as "new" and "old" suggests the central focus of this paper: the nature of ideology in social life and the challenge it poses for critical education. Ideology involves above all the role of language in everyday experience, the extent to which it is interwoven with processes of social reproduction and indeed provides a reflexive medium for the formulation of individual and social identities. It is of crucial importance, and no more so than in the current conservative era, for the self-understanding that people develop about their inner natures and external reality.[5] A critical account of ideology is thus vital for an understanding of political consciousness, the consciousness of what is and is not changeable, what must or must not be changed.

The vicissitudes of this consciousness, which both Adorno and Lynd assumed by its very nature to be the embodiment of critical rationality, formed a central concern in their works. Each was aware that the dominant critical accounts of ideology and its relation to political consciousness — "official" Marxism with its emphasis on "false" consciousness; the sociology of knowledge with its juxtaposition of "ideology" to "utopia" — could not deal properly with new and unforeseen barriers to the development of a broadly based critical rationality, and thus an active and progressive citizen body. They believed, in other words, that "the complex ways in which meaning is mobilized for the maintenance of relations of domination"[6] — ideology as a mask for relations of power and inequality — required the development of new critical concepts if the emancipatory promises of the era of industrial capitalism and political democracy were to be kept. This was the point at which, for both Adorno and Lynd, "the too-inner drama of Freudianism and the too-externalized drama of Marxism [could] meet and reinforce each other on the common ground of behaviour of persons-in-culture" in order that each could "make its greatest contribution to a workable theory of cultural change."[7] Psychological and cultural factors — the domain of "Mind" in the German speculative tradition from which Adorno had emerged — and not simply economic ones constituted material forces in modern society. The totality of material factors had to be explored if those elements which secured adherence to the status quo, as well as those which harboured progressive possibilities, were to be identified and made objects of a critical reason and an emancipatory political practice.

The deepening and broadening of the critique of ideology required that institutions and practices traditionally seen as immune to the distorting effects of ideological discourse be subjected to critical scrutiny. One such practice was science, the apparent epitome of apolitical objectivity and absolute truth. Science, including the rapidly expanding field of social science, was seen by its adherents as the paradigm of all knowledge, the claims of which expressed natural fate, because it stood outside the play of social interests. Both Adorno and Lynd wondered why disinterested impartiality should be seen as the hallmark of knowledge; in any event, neither accepted that science was, or could be, impartial. It was a social institution, the product of a process of historical development, and was permeated by social considerations in terms of both the questions it posed for itself and the range of possible answers it could provide.[8] Indeed for Adorno, society had even penetrated the conceptual structures of science itself.[9] The critique of science as ideology, which both Adorno and Lynd strove to formulate, sought to reclaim, in the name of science, methodically rational inquiry from its unquestioned immersion in the given state of affairs — in what Lynd called the institutional "folkways" of America — and restore to it the humanist concerns which had from its earliest origins in modernity proven decisive in its evolution.[10]

A second, equally significant, element of social life that required critical re-examination was individualism. Of course traditional Marxism and more radical strains of American pragmatism had witheringly savaged the nineteenth century image of homo economicus. But this was done in the expectation that what would emerge from any transformation of nineteenth century capitalism would be a social or co-operative individualism that would carry forward the undeniable gains in individual autonomy of the liberal era into the construction of a new, more just and equal society.

Individualism had indeed been transformed by the advent of a new form of organized capitalism. But if the individual was no longer the rational utilitarian calculator of classical liberal thought, it was also not the social individual whose communal existence was the product of free agreement (what Jürgen Habermas would later call "discursive will formation"). What had developed was a form of collective life that was reproduced by and through individuals who served as bearers of objective structural imperatives. At the same time, these same individuals were still defined as, and urged to see themselves as, free economic subjects responsible for their fate. In the United States, this potentially explosive situation was to be managed by means of the administration of consciousness: the provision of strategies of pseudo-participation involving, among other elements, consumerism and the mass media. Elsewhere, it spawned collectivist, anti-individualist ideologies and political forms, including an ostensibly Marxist one (Stalinism).[11]

For Adorno and Lynd, the fate of reason itself rested with the possibility of preserving under these new conditions at least the core of autonomous judgment, without which the notion of democratic citizenship would be rendered hollow and superfluous. But this very possibility had come to seem increasingly precarious. There loomed ominously on the social horizon the "decline" of the individual under the impact of an intensifying ideological domination facilitated by science — the force that was supposed to realize the promise of enlightenment in modern life.

The status of science (knowledge) and the qualities of the individual are obviously of fundamental importance to all educators, particularly those interested in the development of the critical intellect and the possibilities for progressive political and social change. With these concerns as a backdrop, I would like now to examine Adorno's account of ideology and Lynd's contribution to what might be called the "defrosting" of ideological categories and the fostering of critical thinking.

II

In order properly to situate Adorno's account of ideology, it is necessary to examine briefly the phenomenon of ideology itself. There are two dimensions to ideology, each significant for an understanding of the current situation confronting critical education. On the one hand, as a feature of political life, ideology has, and is intended to have, practical consequences. In this sense ideology maybe understood as a "more or less systematic set of ideas about man's [sic] place in nature, in society, and in history...which can elicit the commitment of significant numbers of people to (or against) political change."[12] But even where ideology does not directly guide the political action of large numbers of people, it nevertheless still has what might be called an 'action-theoretic' component. By entering into the intellectual and cultural realm of society, ideology can shape mass perceptions about political and social matters.

In terms of this dimension, ideology is conceived in essentially neutral terms. A body of ideas, neo-conservatism for example, may be deemed ideological without reference to either its specific content or its objective function; that is, the manner in which it determines the character of social and political conflict between various groups and classes.

On the other hand, ideology may also be understood critically. To see ideology in critical terms is to understand its historical roots and its changing social function over time. On this view it is impossible to abstract from the content of an ideology, the specific goals and purposes for which it stands, and the notion of the human essence which it ultimately attempts to illuminate. For Enlightenment thinkers such as Helvetius, Holbach or De Tracy (with whom the concept of ideology is generally said to originate), ideology — literally the science of ideas —performed the task of dissolving the inherited prejudices which blocked the realization of human progress that would necessarily ensue from unfettering both natural science and market-oriented productive forces.[13] In explicitly political terms, ideology relocated the source of authority and obligation from a transcendent, divine order to the mundane world of human affairs. It thereby conceived of these affairs as objects of rational human determination and control.

The historical shift to the dominance of capitalist market relations produced a change in the objective function of ideology. From its role as a challenger to divinely sanctioned power and authority, ideology was transformed into a mode of justification of the existing social reality. This development was implicit from the very beginning in the structure of ideology itself. The science of ideas shared with the natural sciences a technical and ultimately manipulative interest in control — over the things of nature and over people themselves. Ideology in bourgeois society thus came simultaneously to reveal and conceal. What was revealed was society as a lot of "free" individuals no longer tied to relations of immediate personal dependence. What was concealed was the actual relation of dominance and dependence entailed by the relation of wage labour to capital, and expressed as the apparently free exchange of equivalents under the conditions of market competition. Ideology as critique gave way to the critique of ideology, which sought to uncover the process of objective deception — false consciousness — at its root. This is of course central to the work of Karl Marx.

In the twentieth century, capitalism as a social system has undergone dramatic changes: centralization and concentration of capital, massive State intervention and, in many countries, formal political democratization. It was under these conditions that Adorno and the Frankfurt School sought to develop further Marxism as ideology critique. Adorno elaborated and sharpened the critique of ideology by exploring three interrelated aspects of the phenomenon. Two of these aspects clearly owed their lineage to Marx's analysis. But a third carried this analysis further, in a way that sought to demonstrate the awesome power that industrial capitalist society had come to exercise over the individuals who comprised it. As such, it called into question certain assumptions of the earlier critique.

The first two aspects of ideology had been central to Marxism. Ideology could be understood as objectively necessary but false consciousness. Such consciousness was faithful to the actual, empirical state of affairs (i.e. people were juridically free in the market; the labour theory of value was objectively true), but false because it concealed an important part of the truth, its historical roots, the constellation of interests it served to benefit, etc. Alternatively, ideology could be understood as the expression of norms and values (e.g. justice, freedom) true in themselves, but false in their claims to be actually realized.

But it is the third aspect of ideology that represented Adorno's distinctive contribution to Marxist analysis on this point. According to Adorno, ideology "in the proper sense"[14] — that is, as either false consciousness or unrealized universal claims — no longer exists. However much they were wedded to the status quo, "traditional" ideologies implicitly preserved the ancient philosophical distinction between the "is" and the "ought." Their hypocritical character was 'up front', so to speak. In contemporary society, however, ideologies, increasingly planned in terms of both their content and their effect, and intimately intertwined with the mass media, have become reduplications of existing reality. They appear where immediate relations of power and domination exist. In reduplicating reality, such ideologies do not merely copy it, but rather express irrational ideas which serve directly as instruments of social control.

In a world in which the bureaucratizing and bureaucratized power of an expanding capitalism instrumentalizes almost everything, society itself becomes, in a manner of speaking, "ideological." That is, in society ideas form part of an administered reality that forces compliance through the sheer exercise of power. Ideology and the relations of power they express create either a cynical sense of the futility of opposition to capitalism ("that's the way things are"), or — and this suggests the significance of what the Frankfurt circle called the culture industry[15] — the intense and naive celebration of what exists as the realization of the truth of human experience. As Adorno puts it, "if one were to compress within one sentence what the ideology of mass culture actually adds up to, one would have to represent this as a parody of the injunction: 'Because that which thou art'..."[16] In either case the end result is the same: "...the exaggerated duplication and justification of already existing conditions, and the deprivation of all transcendence and critique."[17]

The key point here is that the shift from the first two aspects of ideology, which imply that while ideology is false, it is also rational, to the third, charts the objective process by which the individual under the power of advanced capitalist society is gradually stripped of his/her autonomy, his/her capacity to exercise reason in a way that critically challenges existing society. The classical Marxist critique of ideology presupposed an audience of at least potentially autonomous individuals in this sense; in other words, it presupposed the possibility of a genuine public sphere. Marx felt that the rational interests of the working class were not only at odds with the reality of the market, but could be seen and understood to be so if the rationalist claims of the market were taken and applied against themselves.

Putting it another way, the institutions of the market were deemed rational in terms other than simply themselves. These terms did not of course entail a divine order but rather the immanent, universal bourgeois values of freedom and justice. Again, to quote Adorno: "For ideology in the proper sense, relationships of power are required which are not comprehensible to this power itself, which are mediated and therefore also less harsh."[18] Precisely this rational dimension of ideology, and the existing power of reason itself that such a dimension reflected, has been lost.

Adorno's argument, here presented in highly abbreviated form, was meant to account for the emergence of totalitarian mass movements, especially Nazism. But it also bears an obvious affinity to Marcuse's account of "one-dimensional" society. As such it speaks to the (re)emergence of conservative justifications of the "free market" and new forms of social Darwinism. Neo-conservatism is, in a way, ideology in the third sense of the term, as Adorno uses it. Ideas apparently discredited and consigned to the ash can of history by the Great Depression are now trumpeted as the most advanced findings of economic "science." Concepts which were already problematic under conditions of nineteenth century capitalism, and which under the vastly different circumstances of its twentieth century successor would seem even more transparently so, now have come to serve as guides to political action and expressions of what our society really "is."[19] In the ideological universe of the new right, the moment of rational representation that characterized nineteenth century free market ideology is lost. What seems to be at work is a process of social regression, or, better, *social* regression as *intellectual* regression.

In this light, the form, as opposed to the content, of neo-conservatism may well be its most important feature. Even if the impact of new right prescriptions for American (and Canadian) society were to weaken with the end of the Reagan era, the depth structural character of this kind of ideological formulation, the patterned, ritualistic nature of the cognitive cues by which people are oriented to their social world (e.g. "freedom" as "free enterprise"), could well ensure the revival of these prescriptions in the future. For Adorno, such an outcome would be almost inevitable. It would manifest — again — the descent of enlightenment into myth, the reality of the totally administered society. In this view, the mechanisms of social reproduction foster a decreasing level of citizen competence in important matters, a "falling rate of intelligence."[20]

The deeply pessimistic political conclusions of Adorno's analysis would seem to hold out little hope that a process of critical education with a political impact could be even a possibility, much less an effective force for change. To be sure, the overwhelming power of society to mould individual consciousness gives clues about the social structure of advanced capitalism: in the era of total administration, almost every detail of daily life is pregnant with ideological significance.[21] Yet the very influence of the dominant interests in society suggests the problem. Where can a serious, critical, democratic opposition gain a toehold? Where can one find at least the elements of a functioning, critical public sphere, freed from the constraining effects of ideology, within which speaking and acting individuals articulate a common good and call to account power supposedly exercised on their behalf? What are the cultural resources which might be deployed in such a task? It is my contention that work of Robert Lynd, particularly *Knowledge For What?*, is just such a resource.

III

> "...granting all due weight to the institutionalized past as it conditions present behaviour, the variables in the social scientist's equation must include not only the given set of structured institutions, but also *what the present human carriers of those institutions are groping to become.*"[22]

Robert Lynd's *Knowledge For What?*, written in 1939, sought above all to examine the increasing effect of social science on American life. But his concern was not simply to document the rise of social science; indeed for him the confusion of data with knowledge was a major failing of the new social inquiry.[23] Rather, he sought to explore the implications of social science for the pressing problems of American society, problems which social science itself was becoming increasingly important in defining, but which could only be defined properly in light of the whole of society. (Here is an important point of contact with Adorno's analysis.) He strove to explore the democratic potential of American life.

Lynd's emphasis on social science as a cultural force had a double purpose. To the extent that it represented an increasingly dominant form of knowledge as such, social science had to be examined for its social content, because knowledge was always for someone. And given that the home of social science was the university, an examination of the social role of social science was necessarily also an analysis of the role of higher education in America. In a period in which great social forces and fearfully rapid social change threatened to engulf the individual in a network of cultural forms that would increasingly deny her/him satisfaction of fundamental "cravings," Lynd believed that higher education and social science were failing in their task of structuring "new knowledge into the institutional forms that will encourage and render easy the use in daily living of the best we know."[24] He sought to define the nature of this task and the manner of its fulfilment.

Much of Lynd's book is given over to a searching examination of the fragmented condition of the social sciences within contemporary universities. I will not pursue the details of his specific criticisms here, save to note that after almost fifty years they exhibit a cogency and relevance both amazing and alarming.[25] The heart of Lynd's prescription for a critical and democratically oriented social science, which is genuinely scientific because it is critical, lies in his demand that social scientists (and by implication all critical educators and researchers) take a cue from the natural scientists and formulate "outrageous hypotheses." This involves "bringing the lagging culture not peace but a sword"[26] by the posing of testable propositions which seek not merely to describe the world as it is, but rather what it would have to look like for the most progressive cultural values especially freedom and rationality, to be realized. Science is ideological to the extent that it fails, or refuses, to do this.

Lynd advances a dozen such hypotheses which could engage all the critical and analytic skills that social scientists could possibly muster. Here are two examples with contemporary significance:

> *The problem:* Democracy is being eroded by unaccountable and irresponsible power blocs located in the economy and State.
>
> *The hypothesis:* "If democracy is to continue as the active guiding principle of our culture, it will be necessary to extend it markedly as an efficient reality in government, industry, and other areas of living; otherwise, it will be necessary to abandon it in favor of some other operating principle."[27] The task of social science in this context is to

develop strategies and resources by means of which citizen competence could be enhanced. This would include establishing new channels through which politically relevant information could be provided to people in useable form, opening up to greater scrutiny the processes through which "public opinion" is formed, and exploring more open and egalitarian alternatives to authoritarian, hierarchical modes of organization.

The problem: "Private capitalism, which operated with rough-and-ready utility to stimulate raw energy expenditure in the uncouth world of our frontier expansion, is proving a crude, recklessly wasteful, and destructive instrument for creating and diffusing welfare among a settled, highly interdependent population."

The hypothesis: "Private capitalism does not now operate, and probably cannot be made to operate, to assure the amount of general welfare to which the present stage of our technological skills and intelligence entitle us; and other ways of managing our economy need therefore to be explored."[28] The task involves specifying the possibilities of production for use as opposed to exchange and thus modifying the role of the price system in economic life; exploring the social costs of the existing mix of goods and services in terms of wasted or suppressed productive potential; and establishing more secure psychological foundations for the study of economic affairs by examining whether motives other than the quest for pecuniary gain are at work in the process of social provisioning.[29]

Of course other pressing social questions could be examined this way. Lynd wished to stimulate the "sociological imagination," not provide the tenets of a political orthodoxy. And he had good reason to believe that his hypotheses were not so "outrageous" after all, that they drew upon widely and deeply held values in the culture.

This is the issue likely to prove most controversial in any attempt to apply Lynd's analysis to the current era. Lynd wrote at a time when in spite of the attack on the democratic possibilities in American life, the strength of popular democratic values had rarely seemed greater. His own analysis was one of many critical examinations of American life. This intellectual offensive was matched by a political offensive, represented not only by the New Deal, but also by the emergence of new, democratic organizations such as the C.I.O. The contemporary situation does not seem so promising.

Yet no era is utterly without possibilities for change. Indeed two prominent inheritors of the legacy of Adorno and the Frankfurt circle have in their recent work attempted to establish the foundations of the kind of politically relevant, critical social science that Robert Lynd promoted. Jürgen Habermas, whose work has become increasingly well-known to adult educators, has sought the origins of ideology critique in the presuppositions of "communicative action": discursively redeemable validity claims that are inherent in every speech act performed by competent actors in their everyday "life world."[30] And Claus Offe practices a theoretically informed social science which strives to identify more problems of social reproduction than can be readily "solved" by the twin mechanisms of social science and administrative action. In this fashion, Offe hopes to undermine the claim of the powers that be that society is inherently rational and harmonious.[31]

To be sure, the implications of Adorno's gloomy analysis cannot easily be written off. A recent account, heavily indebted to Adorno, of social life under late capitalist conditions argues that ALL critical opposition, especially that emanating from educational institutions, functions ultimately to re-enforce the status quo by serving as a regulatory mechanism for institutions of bureaucratic power which require such mechanisms in order to maintain themselves successfully. Opposition works, in other words, to streamline domination.[32] Even Habermas's "life world," which in his view cannot successfully be invaded or "colonized" by the authoritarian forces of the State and economy without producing potentially destabilizing "pathologies," is now seen to be vulnerable to more or less successful strategies of colonization in the form of new technologies, particularly in the field of artificial intelligence.[33]

So the battle for free intellectual and political space, a working democracy, against ideology and the social forces which sustain it, and are sustained by it, is not an easy one. But then, it never has been. In spite of his pessimism, Adorno never forfeited all hope: "In America I became acquainted with a potential for real generosity that is seldom to be found in old Europe. The political form of democracy is infinitely closer to the daily life of the people themselves. There is an inherent impulse in American life toward peaceableness, good-naturedness, and generosity...America is certainly no longer the land of unlimited possibilities, yet one still has the feeling that anything would be possible."[34] Critical educators must draw upon this "inherent impulse" and begin to articulate their own "outrageous hypotheses," hypotheses which would contribute to an understanding of an outrageous reality.

And in a period which fancies itself to be conservative, this strategy has much to recommend it. For conservatism at its best has always meant the desire to preserve what is most valuable in the cultural inheritance of a people. What could be more valuable than those humanistic and democratic traditions which both Adorno and Lynd sought to defend? To be conservative by being radical — this is the responsibility of critical education and ideological criticism in the current historical epoch.[35] This is the path beyond ideology.

NOTES

1. Cf. T. Luke, "Televisual Democracy and the Politics of Charisma," *Telos*, No.70 (Winter 1986-87), pp.59-79.
2. For discussions of new right economics, see e.g. L. Thurow, *Dangerous Currents: The State of Economics* (New York: Vintage Books, 1984) and R. Kuttner, *The Economic Illusion: False Choices Between Prosperity and Social Justice* (Boston: Houghton, Mifflin, 1983). For a Canadian perspective, see C. Gonick, *The Great Economic Debate* (Toronto: Lorimer, 1987).
3. R. Jacoby, *Social Amnesia. A Critique of Contemporary Psychology from Adler to Laing* (Boston: Beacon Press, 1975).
4. In the history of American sociology, Lynd and Mills are often seen as anti-theoretical empiricists who waged a successful battle for control of the Sociology department at Columbia against defenders of theory, notably Robert MacIver and Robert Merton. I cannot comment on the debate, although the charge of anti-theoretical empiricism against Lynd and Mills strikes me as highly misleading. The Frankfurt School, which no one would call "anti-theoretical," always maintained an affinity for the critical traditions of American pragmatism, at least to the extent to which those traditions recognized historico-practical tasks as the foundation of, and outcome of, knowledge. This was in spite of a general scepticism about the political implications of pragmatism as a whole. For an example of critical theory's complex position about pragmatism, see Adorno, "Veblen's Attack on Culture," in *Prisms*, trans. S. and S. Weber (Cambridge, Mass.: M.I.T. Press, 1981), pp.73-94. The second generation of critical theorists, notably Jürgen Habermas, has been more positive about pragmatism.
5. J.B. Thompson, *Studies in the Theory of Ideology* (Berkeley: University of California, 1984). This is an excellent series of studies on contemporary accounts of the phenomenon of ideology, including the work of Castoriadis and Lefort, Giddens and Habermas.
6. Ibid., p.5.
7. R. Lynd, *Knowledge For What? The place of Social Science in American Culture (1939)*, (New York: Grove Press, 1964), p.41.
8. Cf. H. Marcuse, One-Dimensional Man (Boston: Beacon Press, 1964), ch. 6, and J. Habermas, *Toward a Rational Society*, trans. J.J. Shapiro (Boston: Beacon Press, 1970), ch.6. See also W. Leiss, *The Domination of Nature* (Boston: Beacon Press, 1974), and, for a more specifically policy-oriented focus, Leiss, "Political Aspects of Environmental Issues," in Leiss (ed.), *Ecology Versus Politics in Canada* (Toronto and Buffalo: University of Toronto Press, 1979), pp.256-279.
9. See for example Adorno et. al., *The Positivist Dispute in German Sociology*, trans. G. Adey and D. Frisby (London: Heinmann Educational Books, 1976).
10. A classic statement of these concerns is I. Kant, "What is Enlightenment?" in H. Reiss (ed.), *Kant's Political Writings*, trans. H.B. Nisbet (Cambridge: Cambridge University Press, 1977), pp.54-60. The classic critical theory statement of the historical context of science (theory) is M. Horkheimer, "Traditional and Critical Theory," in *Critical Theory*, trans. M.J. O'Connell et. al. (New York: The Seabury Press, 1972), pp.188-252.
11. The emergence of such ideologies and political forms constituted a historic turning point, according to the Frankfurt circle. For an account of the economic context and implications of these developments, see F. Pollock, "State Capitalism: Its Possibilities and Limitations," in A. Arato and E. Gebhardt (eds.), *The Essential Frankfurt School*

Reader (New York: Continuum, 1985) pp.71-94. For the political expression, see Horkheimer, "The Authoritarian State," in ibid., pp.95-117.
12. C.B. Macpherson, "Revolution and Ideology in the Late Twentieth Century," in *Democratic Theory: Essays in Retrieval*, (Oxford: Oxford University Press, 1973), p.157.
13. For an excellent treatment of the historical foundations of ideology, see A. Gouldner, *The Dialectic of Ideology and Technology* (New York: The Seabury Press, 1976).
14. Frankfurt Institute for Social Research, *Aspects of Sociology*, trans. J. Viertel (Boston: Beacon Press, 1972), p.198. Although it is nowhere expressly indicated in the body of this work, Adorno authored the article on ideology.
15. Horkheimer and Adorno, *Dialectic of Enlightenment*, (1947), trans. J. Cumming (New York: The Seabury Press, 1972), pp.120-67.
16. Ibid., p.202.
17. Ibid.
18. Ibid., p.191.
19. The title of a prominent neo-conservative tract is highly revealing: J. Wanniski, *The Way The World Works* (New York: Basic Books, 1978). A revised version of this book has recently appeared. Perhaps the world does not quite work as believed after all.
20. R. Jacoby, "A Falling Rate of Intelligence?" *Telos*, No.27 (Spring, 1976), pp.141-146. This is a witty, Adorno-esque discussion about the commodification of intellectual work in contemporary society.
21. Adorno himself brilliantly analyzed a newspaper astrology column in order to demonstrate its ideological content. See "The Stars Down To Earth: The Los Angeles Times Astrology Column" (1957), *Telos*, No.19 (Spring, 1974), pp.13-90. For a recent example of this "micrological" critique — this time involving the American television series, Columbo — see A. Heller, "The Secrets of Columbo" and M. Gonzales, "The Secrets of Heller," *Telos*, No.66 (Winter, 1985-86), pp.133-141; and J. Zaslove, "In Search of Columbo," *Telos*, No.70 (Winter, 1986-1987), pp.161-166.
22. Lynd, op.cit., p.180.
23. Ibid., p.163.
24. Ibid., p.113.
25. About political science, Lynd notes that the "technicians in public administration are tending to overreach themselves in assuming that effective administration in the public interest can be achieved by small administrative adjustments of the going system." The "students of such things as pressure politics...tend to describe it with the aloofness of a reporter covering a fire in a warehouse. They show us the blaze and the damage, but they leave largely untouched the questions: 'Is democracy workable in a world of unequal men [sic], and where, and how?" and "Can political democracy survive in a culture dominated by the power of concentrated private wealth?'" (p.140).

About economics, Lynd writes: "In economics an orthodox theoretical structure has been developed that is so imposing that it operates at many points as a deterrent to fresh realistic theorizing — as in the case of 'value theory', which, as Veblen remarked, is 'a theory of valuation with the element of valuation left out.'" (p.171)
26. Ibid., p.203.
27. Ibid., p.215. "Citizenship probably never meant as little to any generation of Americans as it tends to mean to our massed city-dwellers of today. It is becoming increasingly difficult to persuade the ablest citizens to run for municipal office. Thoughtful persons are decreasingly inclined to view Congress as an effective democratic legislative instrument. It looks as if these current tendencies are but the natural extension into an era of greater power-blocs of the democracy of America's Gilded Age..." (pp.215-216). Cf. W.D. Burnham, *The Current Crisis of American Politics* (New York: Oxford University Press, 1982).
28. Lynd, op.cit., p.220.
29. This concern about the flimsy psychological underpinnings of economic theory has been pursued in recent years by critically minded economists. See for example, W.A. Weisskopf, *Alienation and Economics* (New York: E.P. Dutton, 1971) and, especially, T. Scitovsky, *The Joyless Economy* (New York: Oxford University Press, 1975).

30. Habermas, *The Theory of Communicative Action*, trans. T. McCarthy (Boston: Beacon Press, 1984). See also Thompson, op.cit., ch.8-9.
31. P. Piccone, "The Crisis of One-Dimensionality," T. Luke, "Culture and Politics in the Age of Artificial Negativity," *Telos*, No.35, (Spring, 1978), pp.43-72; and subsequent pieces.
32. C. Offe, *Contradictions of the Welfare State*, ed. and trans. J. Keane (Cambridge, Mass.: M.I.T. Press, 1984).
33. R.D. Schwartz, "Crazy Machines," *Telos*, No.70 (Winter, 1986-1987), pp.125-137.
34. Adorno, "Scientific Experiences of a European Scholar in America," in D. Fleming and B. Bailyn (eds.), *The Intellectual Migration: Europe and America, 1930-1960* (Cambridge: Belknap Press of Harvard University, 1969), pp.367-368. Adorno gave a number of indications that he was prepared at least to entertain the possibility of a meaningful progressive political commitment — and even a politically relevant process of critical education. See for example "Resignation," *Telos*, No.35, (Spring, 1978), pp.161-168; and Adorno and H. Becker, "Education for Autonomy," *Telos*, No.56 (Summer, 1983), pp.103-110.
35. Cf. H. Arendt, "The Crisis in Education," in *Between Past and Future* (New York: The Viking Press, 1968), pp.173-196.

9

Beyond All Reason: Max Weber, Walter Benjamin and Modernity

Harold Chorney

This essay was written for a conference at York University on Max Weber in 1988. I subsequently revised it during 1990 while I was in London, England, where the year before I had finished my book, *City of Dreams*. It attempts through a examination of the work of Max Weber and Walter Benjamin to speak to a question that has troubled me for a long time — the relationship between social theory and the world of practical politics. This was a relationship to which both Weber and Benjamin were also drawn. In the case of Benjamin his utopian thought drew him to the radical Marxism of the German socialist movement of the 1920s. In the case of Weber toward the end of his life he participated in the conservative cause of German nationalism. The relationship in both of their cases was not very successful. As a policy analyst, economist, sometime political activist and social theorist I have been gradually led to the position that I articulate in this essay. Social theory is an art form whose aesthetic inevitably privileges utopian thought over pragmatic reason. Practical politics is a very different world which inevitably must be guided by different principles. The pendulum, so far to the right for so very long is now shifting back toward the values and politics of those of us who struggled in the 1960s and 1970s for social justice and political progress. The *coupure* between social theory as art and practical politics as the application of pragmatic reason in the service of human need is a lesson that I think we must to take to heart to ensure that this time we make real gains in promoting the humanist cause of justice, compassion, equity and love.

* * *

As we approach the close of the twentieth century it has become clear that the trends that were identified in the work of writers such as Max Weber and Walter Benjamin at the opening of the century will mark it at the close. The overwhelming influence of the rationalizing impulses of modernity, even in this supposedly post-modern age, have not been banished. If anything, they are stronger and more pervasive. The sense of powerlessness before the monumental scale and mass of the world system and its global technology seems greater than ever.

Part of the explanation for this is the speed and extensiveness of the modern communications system which now permits the transmission of information world wide in a matter of seconds. The media sensitive person literally can be bathed in a flood of information about coups d'état, wars, revolutions, the rise and fall of dictatorships, human hunger and ecological catastrophe around the clock. The decline in autonomy and the growth of pessimism about our prospects seems to cover sensibilities the world over. Recent events in Eastern Europe and the apparent collapse of the raison d'être for the cold war may have turned the corner temporarily on this sense of pessimism but as the joy subsides and the hard realities of both economic reconstruction in the context of world wide economic instability and right wing politics sink in this sense of euphoria is unlikely to last.

As George Simmel pointed out so perceptively in his essay on the metropolis, any prolonged exposure to intensification of nervous stimuli is likely to result in the development of a mildly depressed blase attitude as a defense mechanism in the face of such over stimulation.[1] It would seem that Simmel's insights into the metropolis apply equally well to a metropolized world.

Whereas, not very long ago one could still place ones hopes on this set of values or this political movement, now such hopes seem devalued and no longer operational. From the vantage point of North America in 1990, politics seems to some more disillusioning than ever. But this sense of disillusionment depends as we shall see very much on the objectives that one adopts from the outset.

From the pessimistic perspective then it should come as no surprise that some of the great and poetic insights of Weber and Benjamin, while preserving their lyrical beauty and literary power have all but lost their practical relevance. Each sought to diagnose and describe the forces unleashed by the inexorable march of reason. Each in his own way succeeded. Yet neither appears to have prescribed a solution that has stood the test of time in practice as opposed to theory. Benjamin's messianic Marxism while a powerful romantic utopian rallying cry must be seen for what it was — a literary masterpiece but a practical political failure.

The final desperate attempt of Max Weber to restore a creative force to politics through his notion of the charismatic personality and plebiscitary politics has to be judged from the vantage point of the ashes and destruction of the Second World War, brought on in part because of the extraordinary appeal of charismatic fanatics. In the case of either of these two great thinkers and writers it is not a sufficient defense of their work to say as some might, that after all they were theorists not political actors. This would be acceptable only if one would accept from the outset the distinction between vita activa and vita contemplativa.

But many on the left, myself included, have had a very difficult time accepting this distinction. If we are to accept their work as principally intellectual effort in the manner of the social theorist as artist then we must judge it from an aesthetic point of view. And even here there are difficulties of judgement as to what constitutes the better aesthetic.[2] The classical conception of truth as beauty may be some guide but in politics what constitutes truth is a matter of some debate. In any case we must constantly reappraise the received wisdoms of past thinkers in the context of current realities.

How then to find a way out of this cul de sac? Is there any choice beyond the utopian world of revolutionary possibilities and the dystopian one of charismatic politics that we can realistically consider? Weber seemed so much more practical than Benjamin, so much more a man of Real-Politik than the surrealist of literature and social theory. And yet, in certain respects no less than Benjamin he depended in the end on the lyrical or emotive approach to problem solving. In fact Weber was not beyond appeals to national patriotism or the glorious possibilities of German national sentiment.[3]

In Weber's case he was much more the master of political rhetoric than Benjamin. Indeed, Benjamin had little interest in the role of the politician except as the object of critical analysis as in the case of Baron Haussman, the Minister who reconstructed Paris at the behest of Napolean III. Weber, on the other hand, contemplated and then apparently rejected a role in politics.[4] Because of this, his speeches and papers sometimes reflected the politician's rhetoric.[5] But where the exercise of political power is concerned lyricism while often necessary is usually insufficient. This, of course, has always been the case, although the nature of mass politics in the pre-television age gave rhetoric far more influence than it has now. During the 1980s the anti-lyrical practical point of view has become almost a canon of religious faith.

Perhaps lyricism provides a sort of answer in an otherwise impossible and intolerable world? Or can we speak of a third way that marries the passion of lyrically inspired commitment and expression with the technocratic but humanistic power of reason? That is, where reason moves beyond philosophical speculation and analysis to embrace practical problem solving, but without losing its commitment to the service of human values. Or has reason ultimately disenchanted reason itself?

As a beginning let us grant these two Western world historical literary figures the place they deserve in any attempt to go beyond them. For each in his own way has made an extraordinary contribution to the social theory project. We must pay them their due. Let me begin with more lyrical of the two.

WALTER BENJAMIN

Walter Benjamin attempts to distil from the modern experience the essence of the forces that drive the society and the individuals who compose it. For Benjamin, of course, the source of what drives the sensual experience of urban life can be traced to the capital accumulation process. What Benjamin accomplishes in his work is the detailed, almost oriental, portrait of the senses of the experience of the individual in modern life. From the street beggar to the bourgeois gentleman, from the flaneur to the modern window shopper, from the puzzled and warm curiosity of childhood to the painful nostalgia of old age — all these sentiments and experiences are swept up in Benjamin's texts. What unites all these experiences is their situation in an increasingly impersonal and automatic environment conditioned by streams of traffic; the flashing of traffic lights and the flow of fads and fashions that make puppets of their adherents; the crossing of a street; the striking flash of a match in the night; the swirl of the crowd and the plaintive cry of the street beggar all reveal in their particularity the essence of the social system in its entirety.

Drawing upon his neo-Kantian philosophical background and his knowledge of Cabbalistic mysticism and influenced by Leibnitz, Benjamin argued that the truth of the universal could and must be gleaned from the depths of the particular.

Ideas, events and characters were like monads. Their truth was generalizable to the society from which they were drawn. Every monad contained within itself the whole of society in total.[6] Thus Benjamin set out to understand modernity through the study of the particular. He chose to focus on the minutia of Paris in the nineteenth century.

His most extraordinary application of this technique is to be found in his incomplete but posthumously published master work *The Passeng-Werk* or the arcades project...Here Benjamin attempted to comprehend the modern experience through a near encyclopedic depth survey of the monads of metropolitan experience. His list of topics under which he assembled a wide range of observations, aphorisms, citations and photographs included the following headings: Arcades, Novelty shops, salesman, Fashion, Ancient Paris, Catacombs, demolitions, Ruin of Paris, Boredom, Eternal Recurrence, Haussmanization, Barricade Fighting, Iron Construction, Methods of Display, Advertising, Grandville, The Collector, The Interior, Trace, Baudelaire, dream City and Dream House, Dreams of the Future, Anthropological Nihilism, Jung, Dream House, Museum, Fountain Hall, The Flaneur, Epistemology, Theory of Progress, Prostitution, Gambling, The Streets of Paris, Panorama, Mirror, Painting, Jugenstil, Newness, Forms of Lighting, Saint Simon, Railroads, Conspiracies, Compagnonnage, Fourier Marx, Photography, Doll, Automaton, Social Movement, Daumier, Literary History, Hugo, Stock Market, Economic History, Technologies of Reproduction, Lithography, The Commune, The Seine, oldest Paris, Idleness, Anthropological Materialism, History of Sects, École polytechnique.[7]

Theodor Adorno in assessing the part of the Passeng-werk that was dealing with Baudelaire, called Benjamin's approach "too much mechanical thinking that mistakenly applied Marxist categories in an unmediated way in order to pay tribute to Marxism."[8] But Benjamin, as Adorno knew, was not an orthodox German Marxist. In fact, in his youth, he leaned towards anarcho-socialism. Later under the influence of Asja Lacis his lover and Bertolt Brecht, Benjamin flirted with the communist party but he never was comfortable with this position. At the same time he was critical of the German Social Democrats from the left.

In reality Benjamin's politics were largely romantic and he himself was opposed to party participation. His Marxism was his own brand of extraordinary synthesis. He approached his subject from the perspective of Jewish mysticism and artistic surrealism filtered through a philosophical heritage that went well beyond conventional Marxism integrated, as it were, in a cloud of hashish. Has orthodoxy ever had such a heterogeneous heritage?

For Benjamin, the modern world was increasingly a world of minute experiences integrated by the rapid pacing of the accumulation process. The proletariat as the motive force of history had been converted into the shopper of the mass metropolis. And yet, Benjamin refused to give up on his utopian dream of proletarian revolution.

Of course, this dream was in keeping with his appreciation for the redemptive possibilities of religious mythical messianism, Benjamin's fascination with this aspect of Judaism and his close friendship with Gershom Scholem made it logical that he would attempt to reshape Marxism in a mystical direction. His closeness to the surrealists and to Brecht also figured strongly in his literary method. His use of radical juxtaposition in the literary sense and his belief in the doctrine of particularistic essence are derived from these influences.

The notion of radical juxtaposition which Benjamin derived from surrealism and the device of cinematic montage, and from a consideration of the work of Brecht was designed to shock the reader into insights into the nature of modern society. Shocking juxtaposition was in fact the very essence of the modern factory production system. As such Benjamin believed that social knowledge would come about by the placing side by side of seemingly unrelated images which together revealed something of the modern experience. Just as the dramatic gesture and didactic declaration in Brechtian theatre or the movement from the riflemen on the Odessa steps to the shattered eyeglasses of the screaming woman in Eisenstein's film or the outrageous images of surrealistic art were designed to inform and shock the audience into social knowledge, Benjamin hoped to capture these qualities in his own writing.[9]

Thus no matter how powerful the forces of rationalization and mechanical control, Benjamin still believed in the explosive possibilities of the modern condition. It was as if all the canalized energy that was exposed by the steel, glass and concrete of the city and all of the repressed longing that was trapped by the conditioned reflexes of bourgeois society could one day explode and smash the bourgeois world that imprisoned people. Writing about the Paris Commune and surrealism Benjamin noted:

> (The surrealists) bring the immense forces of "atmosphere" concealed in these (urban) things to the point of explosion...

> But only revolt completely exposes (Paris's) surrealist face...And no face is surrealistic to the same degree as the true face of a city.[10]

Benjamin's vision was, in a word, messianic. As a messianic vision, then, it cannot be refuted. But as a matter of political insight it must be subjected to critical scrutiny. There is no doubt that Benjamin accurately and acutely captured many of the forces that have shaped the modern metropolitan world. His discussion of the arcades and the role of the flaneur in pointing the way to the twentieth century cult of window shopping and the role of galleries and interiors is unequalled for its brilliance and explanatory power.

The flaneur in Benjamin is the urban dweller who points the way from the pre-industrial culture of which he is a residual artefact to the culture of modern commodity capitalism. The art of idle strolling through the earliest arcades of central Paris, "glass covered, marble floored passages...(in which) are arrayed the most elegant shops" is converted into the frenzied shopping in the department stores of the modern metropolis. The interior space symbolic at first of privacy, and intimacy is converted over time into the shrine for the commodity.

His analysis of the commodity and the painful way that people, in particular the poor, relate to the commodity in a society that enshrines the commodity to the point of fetishism offers powerful insights into the social psychology of the modern era. In this respect Benjamin had no equal. But his vision of the political future in terms of the victory of a Marxist-inspired socialism in the West is clearly a failure and must be seen as essentially nothing more than a grand utopian dream. In this, of course, Benjamin was not alone.

But what goes beyond pure lyricism and does stand the test of time is Benjamin's attempt to capture the impact of rationalizing impulses in the full range of everyday experience and built environment. It is quite simply impossible to understand the way it feels to a modern metropolitan person to be alive and a creature of the city on an everyday basis, without attempting to do what Benjamin pointed the way towards. While the original objectives of Benjamin's massive unfinished arcades project was his attempt to document the coming of age of capitalist modernity in Paris, his method points us in the right direction in seeking to make sense of the modern experience.

For to be modern has meant to be subject to the constant bombardment of events, encounters and images that shape our consciousness of the human experience. Indeed, much of our behaviour is shaped in this way at the subconsciousness level. For most urban dwellers the modern experience with its rush of sensations does not leave time for contemplation. Objects, sensual impressions, movements, colours, even glances, fragments of daily life that impact upon our consciousness and our subconscious mind help determine how the modern person relates to her/his world.

We are simultaneously duressed by a number of sources that are linked together more often than not by centrally controlled media. Traditions that may have lasted for centuries including the social organization of community upon which so many socialist aspirations have been built are simply washed away and dissolve under the steady pressure of such experience. While there are still centres of community-based opposition to the march of technology and the agenda of corporate capitalism, their power is greatly weakened by the pressure of the speed of change and the nature of the modern urban environment. Where dissenting groups and individuals seek to influence the political process in a different direction they are forced to communicate with a body politic that has been largely reconstructed under the pressure of this flow of stimulation. The result is a body politic with which it is difficult to communicate except through the electronic media. It has a low concentration span, tends to passivity, finds it difficult to empathize and all too often considers fellow citizens as competitors or even worse as distant and threatening strangers.

Thus Benjamin's resort to a kind of mystical messianism is not surprising in a world that increasingly seems to have escaped from the control of society embedded tradition. It represents a logical response for a marginal man with powerful insights into the human condition and in particular the foundations of modern mass society. It is this mass that surrounds him, threatens him and indeed ultimately kills him.

It is no secret that fundamentalism has developed as a reaction to the threat of traditional disintegration that modernism has posed in many developing societies. In a not dissimilar fashion, messianic Marxism is an understandably conservative reaction to the pressure of modernism. In an increasingly hostile and unjust world in which barbaric impulses appear dressed in fashionable clothing, it is no wonder that sensitive intellectuals would resort to romantic solutions as a possible bulwark against disintegration.

Europe in the 1920s and 1930s is clearly a society on the brink of disaster. In such experiences it is always the artistic individual who can divine from the surroundings what lies in store. Often this occurs without the individual being totally conscious of the implications of her/his own sensibilities. In Benjamin's case he did so by exploring the architechtronics of the society he lived in. Like many writers he seemed unaware of the ultimate contemporary implications of his own work. For in a world that could be driven by impersonal forces like the commodity, in which humans could be reduced to members of the crowd and even at times mimic the behaviour of puppets it was not such a great step to go beyond toward the nightmare years of Hitler.

There is a tragic irony then to Benjamin's personal fate. Realizing too late what had befallen him, partially blinded as it were by the power and intensity of his own microscopic vision, he stumbles and is caught in the flood of humanity that seeks to flee from the Nazis. In this, of course, he was no different from millions of others. His fate was that of much of European humanity in this period. But what is particularly poignant and quite in keeping with the religious and mystical overtones to Benjamin's work is the fact that he dies like the biblical prophet of old with his manuscript in his hands outside the gates of the promised land where his sanctuary might have been found. And like the prophet that he was he dies by his own hand as a protest against the barbarism of his time.

MAX WEBER

The case of Max Weber is rather different. Yet he too is marked by a special poignancy. Like Benjamin, Weber's life project is a great and unfinished attempt to document the impact of capitalist rationalization upon the modern world and see his theories applied to action. But because Weber was neither a Marxist nor a religious messianist, his project looks very different from that of Benjamin. Despite these differences, I would argue that there are definite and striking parallels in what Weber attempted.

As Brian Caterino has shown[11] there are also definite precursors to Benjamin's thinking in the work of Weber that are transmitted in the Frankfurt School's concern with the project of enlightenment.

Weber traces the roots of modernity and the overwhelming tendency toward rationalization back beyond the modern capitalist epoch. Indeed, he traces them back to the Romans and the introduction of rational functionalism into Roman religious practice. In general, in the Weberian schema religion plays a very critical role in transmitting rational impulses that become the essence of modern life. His vast tracts that compare Christianity, Judaism, Confucianism and pagan values form the backdrop to the famous essays that suggest that Protestantism is the well-spring from which modern capitalist society springs.

Unlike Marx who views capitalism as the product of fundamental changes in the material accumulation process that move forward with an inexorable and pervasive logic to dominate all of social life, Weber sees its origins in the inner world of ascetic religion. In this sense Weber seeks a deeper and innermost source for the mysterious world that we moderns find ourselves in. Yet, Weber's insistence that the roots of capitalist transformation lay in the world of religious asceticism is not an attempt to substitute a one sided spiritualism for an equally one sided materialism.[12]

In a footnote to his text Weber added that attempts to reduce social reality to monocausal explanations were appropriate for a certain "type of dilettante who believes in the unity of the group mind and its reducibility to a single formula."[13] According to Wolfgang Schlucter, Weber conceded that material interests could not be totally banished from the analysis. Indeed, any careful reading of Weber shows him to be minutely concerned with the material content of life. As Schlucter puts it:

> This dual position of an economic ethic points to the existence of two classes of causes, interest constellations and idea constellations. We can attribute a priori primacy to either class of causes. We must assume that both originated at the same time.[14]

Religious faith and devotion to spiritual values were, of course, not strangers to Marx either. For after all, he began his intellectual career as a devout, if radical, Christian.[15] In his later intellectual development his own break with religion was the basis of his conversion to communism. But in Weber religious faith and practice represent the well-spring of modern rationality, of which capitalism is but an expression.

How does such a strange transformation come about? Just as with Benjamin, the inspiration for his unorthodox analysis of modern capitalism is ultimately religious in origin, so too in Weber. But Benjamin, the assimilated Jew, finds in his consciousness the roots of mystical messianism. Weber, not surprisingly because of his Protestant background and in particular the influence of his mother, turns toward Protestantism as the answer.[16] In keeping, however, with Weber's apparently more scientific bent, he distances himself from his own religious heritage. In doing so he describes the role of Protestantism in disenchanting the world of faith and ultimately of the very notion of brotherhood (and sisterhood) and therefore community itself.

The roots of disenchantment begin as far back as the Judaic and Hellenic religions where religious precepts became the equivalent of functional legal codes for the conduct of everyday life. Weber's scholarly tracts on the history of the world's religions are thus intended to explore the foundations of Western rationality in contrast to the prevailing integrative belief systems in non-Western cultures. Weber's project in terms of its scholarly sweep and ambition is every bit as daunting as that of Marx. Yet, despite his own commitment to reason, Weber, like Benjamin and Marx in his struggle to find a political voice, cannot escape from his personal roots in a redemptive belief system.

The importance of early character development in the shaping Weber's thought is explored in an intriguing work by Arthur Mitzman. Whether or not Mitzman is completely correct in suggesting that Weber's depression and subsequent concentration upon the secular significance of religion is the result of the break with his father prior to his father's death and the religious influence of his mother, such an analysis points to the importance of personal psychological factors in shaping a writer's consciousness. I suspect that we can learn much about the origins of social theory by paying more attention to such influences. Psychoanalytic and psychologistic theory have much to offer us here. Political behaviour and theory, like most human activity, is at root deeply personal and sometimes better understood by seeking its inner meaning and significance in relation to the person or persons involved. This does not mean that the resulting body of theory ought to be dismissed as the acting out of personal conflict. Rather it enables us to put the theory in better perspective and sort out its emotional origins.[17] Whatever its psychoanalytic origins Weber's conception of disenchantment, is one of his most fruitful notions. For it, like Benjamin's notion of the sensual microscopic particularism of modern urban life, still continues to ring true at the close of the century.

According to Weber, the spirit of capitalism is more than simply the spirit of unlimited greed. Indeed, in the days of Wall Street, the 1987 crash, Ivan Boesky and Mike Milkin, and the rebirth of social darwinism sponsored by Reagan, Thatcher and now Bush and Mulroney, greed would seem to be enough to characterize the phenomenon.[18]

But Weber's point is that this is nothing new or quintessentially capitalistic. Rather it is part of the instinct for power, understood as the desire for domination over others of which the ostentatious display of wealth is merely a symbol. This greed for wealth can be found as far back as antiquity. As Weber points out it has nothing to do with capitalism, per se. Rather it has existed among all sorts of people drawn from all social classes — "among waiters, physicians, coachmen, artists, prostitutes, dishonest officials, soldiers, nobles, crusaders, gamblers and beggars." He dismisses the notion that pure greed is the essence of capitalism as a "kindergarten" idea. Instead the root of capitalism is found in restraint in consumption to permit the accumulation of capital and its continuous reinvestment by rationalistic corporations that seek ever-increasing domain.

Weber goes on to define capitalism in terms of a highly rationalized free labour market that is linked to the production for profit system through the wages system. In this sense he defines the system in terms that are quite consistent with those of Marx. He emphasizes the separation of the household from the corporate business, rational bookkeeping, the development of stock exchanges and the general rationalization of speculation. But for Weber the key characteristic is "the rational capitalistic organization of labour…Exact calculation — the basis of everything else — is only possible on a basis of free labour."[19]

He then asks how this rational calculating technical utilization of scientific knowledge and the creation of a labour force subject to its dictates arose. He poses the question of why, unlike in other cultures, did not religion "inhibit the development of these rational demystifying tendencies."[20]

Now frankly from the perspective of the orgy of wealth accumulation and personal aggrandizement that characterizes contemporary American capitalism, as well as the manifestly irrational qualities such as mass unemployment, ecological catastrophe and the enormous gaps that exist between the wealthy and the impoverished in the major metropolitan centres of America, Weber's definition of capitalism seems out of step with the realities of the system. Indeed, the notion of restraint seems particularly absent from the picture. But perhaps it is because American capitalism is in the process of decay in comparison with Japanese capitalism, for example. Of course, from the Weberian perspective, Japanese capitalism is a fascinating hybrid of Confucianist influences and imported occidental ones, presumably of the Protestant variety.[21]

In any case, let us leave aside for the moment the question of whether or not Weber's vision continues to be completely accurate. Instead, I would like to concentrate on how this notion of the rationalization process helps us to understand certain tendencies in modern society. Just as Benjamin is indispensable for making sense of the consumer driven world of modern society, Weber is indispensable for understanding the pervasiveness of cold, impersonal and calculating circumstances that govern most aspects of daily life in our industrial metropolises.

There are very few life situations (including those that lie within the relatively sheltered circumstances of the family and home) that are immune from these influences. Just as Marx so perceptively divined the outlines of the alienated circumstances of daily life even in the homes of workers in *The Economic and Philosophical Manuscripts*, Weber points to the invasion of cold calculating reason as the organizing principle of modern times.

The fact that this impulse has its origins in the religious asceticism of Protestantism comes as little comfort. The iron cage of calculation and reason that the rationalizing process constructs cannot easily be escaped from. Once ascetic Protestantism released the genie of rationalization out of the bottle it was impossible to put him back in.[22] Weber thus had considerable influence over the Frankfurt School's conception of instrumental reason and its notion of its pervasive destructive grip on modern society. The approach of critical theory to the notion of the enlightenment and its notion of capitalism's march toward a "bureaucratically rationalized society" is clearly borrowed from Weber.[23]

While Benjamin clung to messianic Marxism for deliverance, Weber had no such faith. Instead he reverted to his conservative familial influences, his nationalist sentiments and, despite his own critique of the will to power, to the influence of Nietzsche when he proposed the charismatic political leader as the only way out of the iron cage that rationalization had created.[24]

Both Wolfgang Mommsen and David Beetham have documented Weber's peculiar brand of conservative nationalist politics that he polemicized on behalf of, during, and at the close of the First World War. His essays on the labour situation of the East Elbe workers and on the issue of Germany as a national industrial power are clear in their commitment to an elitist German nationalism.[25] It is also intriguing to note that at the Versailles Peace talks when that other great polemicist of the period John Maynard Keynes, advised the British, Weber was his opposite number on the German side.[26]

Weber's own brand of politics emphasized the importance of shoring up German nationalism against the threat from the East and ensuring the fuller participation of the working class in an elite directed democratic system that would be able to move out from under the autocracy of Whilhelmine Germany. However, Beetham's explanation of Weber's vision of the greater working class participation in political life was a far cry from any kind of socialist conception of mass society. Indeed, Weber made it quite clear that as far as the working class was concerned, their political immaturity prevented them from assuming the leadership role in modern German society. [27] Instead, he regarded them as "politically uneducated philistines" and therefore untrustworthy.[28]

Nevertheless, despite this view of the proletariat, Weber believed that without greater working class participation the political life of Germany was doomed to become that of a polarized society along class lines. In this respect it is again intriguing to note certain similarities in his thinking with that of Maynard Keynes. In many ways he shared both Keynes' liberal corporatist vision of modern capitalism as a preferred policy option and his distrust of working class politics. Weber, like Keynes, stated his loyalties clearly. "I have been brought up to share bourgeois views and ideas." [29]

Speaking of the necessity of an improved way of life for working people as part of his strategy of building the German nation Weber spoke in terms of long-term political education in order to create a "labour aristocracy" that could provide political leadership once it matured.

Weber thus sought greater working class participation in order to increase the degree of social stability and solidarity. His political model emphasized the importance of the charismatic leader who drawing upon the support of the masses could rescue Germany from its plight. In articulating this vision, Weber used language that seems hauntingly prophetic. He described the "shameless longing" of the "haute bourgeoisie" for a new Caeser.

Weber's belief in the charismatic political leader was premised on his assessment of the requirements of mass society and the nature of political behaviour in such a society. A strong individual, personally capable of arousing the masses to the cause, while able to act independently of the masses, could provide the leadership necessary in this case.[30]

Mass democracy of the plebiscitary kind called for precisely this kind of individual who would rise above narrow sectional, class or party interests in order to serve the nation as a whole. There is some evidence to suggest that Weber saw himself as precisely this kind of leader. Certainly his premature death robbed Germany of an important political influence. The coming to power of Hitler only a decade later, however, would demonstrate the tragic error in Weber's analysis.

For this reason and on account of his "idealist interpretation of history," George Lukacs associated him with the irrationalist movement that swept Europe in the early part of this century.[31] Herbert Marcuse in one of his essays described Weber as having confused "technical reason with bourgeois capitalist reason.[32]

Perhaps Marcuse was correct in thinking that Weber had confused the two forms of reason. On the basis of present evidence however, I remain sceptical. Mass society does appear to have certain internal tendencies that go beyond which social class dominates it. Furthermore the will to power, and by this I mean the deeply psychologically rooted desire to dominate among humans, to control and to exercise authority over others, appears to be more deeply rooted than most socialists have been prepared to admit.

Of course, Reichian and Freudian socialists have always understood this problem and its critical importance but unfortunately this tendency has made very little headway in practical politics. The fate of the New Left in the 1970s and 1980s and the apparent authoritarian tendencies in the Green movement exemplify this failure. Nevertheless, there is something in Marcuse's hope that technical reason might be appropriated for the cause of human liberation as much as for the cause of human domination. There remains an irrepressible utopian aspiration that has the capacity to motivate people in critical circumstances courageously to support social justice and social reform even when the risks are great. The disillusionment that often follows close on the heels of such great acts of courage must seem bitter indeed.

But it is here that we leave the realm of the artist and social theorist and make our way to the much more plebian realm of the practical political actor. For in the end, neither Marcuse's powerful utopian vision, nor Benjamin's messianic mysticism, nor Weber's hope for a charismatic political leader can measure up to the political task. The smashing of the goddess of democracy by the tanks and fire of the State's troops in Tiananmen Square revealed, at least for the moment, the critical weakness of the reform movement in China, as well as the dangers of overblown rhetoric in the face of autocratic State power. The demands of practical politics in the democracies of the West force us to confront the reality that gradual but nevertheless progressive economic and political reform are more likely to succeed. As imperfect as they may be, and as unromantic as they may seem, they are in fact the only realistic option.

Such social democratic reforms involve increasing social justice by widening access to the fruits of industrial society to the many, restoring full employment, encouraging industrial democracy and wide ownership of the stocks of public companies and a decent level and quality of public services that ensure that people live in dignity and relative comfort, as well as respecting the environment that supports such a society. The methods of accomplishing these objectives may vary but they are certain to include a level of community and public involvement in the general direction of society that reverses most of the selfish laissez-faire inspired public policy of today.

Whether such reforms can ever be enough to overcome the pervasive attraction of mass consumption, the sensuality of desire that is the essence of modern metropolitan experience, or the powerful forces of bureaucratic and social control that are the outgrowth of the cold calculating impersonal forces of the rationalizing process, we cannot foresee in advance. Whether the corrupting will to dominate can ever be therapeutically purged from the body politic is equally unclear.

Social democratic and liberal reforms may fail on the aesthetic barometer of utopian and artistic thought. But then at the very mundane level of social improvement and reform, these approaches may just offer human beings meaningful improvements in their lot and the opportunity to focus their attention on what really counts in the life of the everyday as opposed to the life of the mind: to live in good health, to have the opportunity to love and be loved, to create, to raise a family or live in harmony with ones partner and friends, to have a say in the organization and governance of one's society on the principles of social justice and greater equality of the human condition, and to work with dignity and respect in the limited years that nature has chosen to call a man or woman's life.

In the lyrical language of the artist as social theorist that may not seem enough. But in the lives of the multitudes that inhabit our globe it is a very great deal indeed.

NOTES

1. See my discussion of Simmel and his essay "The Metropolis and Mental Life" in Harold Chorney, *City of Dreams: Social Theory and the Urban Question*. (Toronto: Nelson Canada, 1990)
2. Herbert Marcuse, *The Aesthetic Dimension* Boston: Beacon Press, 1978.
3. See Max Weber, "The National State and Economic Policy," in Keith Tribe ed. *Reading Weber* (London: Routledge, 1989.) pp.207-208.
4. See Wolfgang J. Mommsen, *Max Weber and German Politics 1890-1920* Chicago: University of Chicago Press, 1984; K. Tribe,Ibid.; David Beetham, Max Weber and the Theory of Modern Politics, (London: Polity Press, 1985).
5. See, for example, his essay *The National State and Economic Policy*. Translated in K.Tribe ed. *Reading Weber*. W. Mommsen also discusses this aspect of Weber's work in his *Max Weber und Die Deutsche Politik*.
6. See "Walter Benjamin: The Culture of Technical Reproduction and the Metropolis" in H.Chorney, *City of Dreams*, p.123.
7. W.Benjamin, Gessamelte Schriften, Vol.5, Parts 1&2 eds. R. Tiedemann and H. Schweppenhauser, (Frankfurt am Main: Suhrkamp Verlag, 1972-); S.Buck-Morss, Walter Benjamin, *The Dialectics of Seeing: Walter Benjamin and the Arcades Project*, (Cambridge: MIT Press,1989) p.50-51 and H.Chorney, *City of Dreams: Social Theory and the Urban Experience*, p.128.
8. S.Buck-Morss, p.205-206 & note 3, p.437; Chorney, p.147-8.
9. Walter Benjamin, "What is Epic Theatre?" in *Understanding Brecht*, (London:Verso,1984) H.Chorney, "Walter Benjamin: The Culture of Technical Production and the Modern Metropolis" in *City of Dreams*, pp.141 ff.

10. W. Benjamin, "Surrealism" in *Reflections: Walter Benjamin, Essays, Aphorisms, Autobiographical Writing (New York: Harcourt, Brace, Jovanovitch, 1978.)*, ed. P.Demetz p.17.
11. Brian Caterino,"Rationality and Societal Rationalization: Max Weber and the Frankfurt School." Ph.D. thesis, University of Toronto, 1986.
12. Max Weber,*The Protestant Ethic and the Spirit of Capitalism*(P.E) (New York: Charles Scribner & Sons, 1958)
13. P.E., note 118, p.284
14. Wolfgang Schlucter, *The Rise of Western Rationalism: Max Weber's Developmental History* (Berkeley: University of California Press,1981) p.141.
15. See my discussion of Zvi Rosen, *Bruno Bauer and Karl Marx* (The Hague: Martinus Nijhoff,1977) in *City of Dreams*.
16. Arthur Mitzman, *The Iron Cage*. (New York:Knopf, 1974)
17. This is an approach that is pursued in the work of writers like Wilhelm Reich. Contemporary practitioners include among others G. Horowitz, *Repression*, Toronto: University of Toronto Press, 1977; R. Jacoby, *Social Amnesia: A Critique of Contemporary Psychology*, Boston:Beacon Press, A. Mitzman, *Max Weber and the Iron Cage of Reason*, New York: Knop, 1974.
18. In a recent visit to the thirtieth floor of one of the towers of Babel in Montréal to interview a stockbroker about the 1987 crash I was struck by the lavish opulence of the furnishings right down to the oriental rugs and solid teak, mahogany and black Chinese lacquer furniture and the display of trendy art on the walls. This pattern of decor was repeated in a number of other interviews I conducted with stockbrokers in Montréal and Toronto. I should not imagine that New York is any different. Conspicuous displays of the fruits of greed as testament to the successful accumulation of wealth would seem to be characteristic of contemporary capitalism — at least the financial branch.
19. *Protestant Ethic*, p. 22.
20. Ibid.
21. See M. Morishima, *Why Has Japan Succeeded?* (London:1985)
22. See PE, p. 182.
23. See Caterino.
24. Caterino, ch.2.
25. Wolfgang Mommsen, Max Weber and German Politics; David Beetham, Max Weber and the Theory of Modern Politics; K. Tribe, Reading Weber.
26. It is intriguing to speculate as to what may have transpired had they met and discussed their alternative liberal visions of the post-war world. In any case both Keynes and Weber were strongly opposed to the terms of the peace settlement on the grounds that Versailles would lead to major instability and eventually another war. In this prognosis, they were correct.
27. Max Weber, "The national state and economic policy" in Tribe, p.206.
28. This statement resembles one made by Keynes some years later when he called the labour movement "an immense and dangerous force of destruction, led by sentimentalists and pseudo-intellectuals who have 'feelings in the place of ideas'." (Keynes, *Collected Works*, 1X:318-319)
29. p.204 *Weber in Tribe*
30. W. Mommsen; David Beetham, p.230ff; and Weber in K. Tribe, "The national state and economic policy" pp.205-208; Friedrich Tenbruck in Tribe pp.69-70, "The problem of thematic unity in the works of Max Weber."
31. See G. Lukacs, The Destruction of Reason (Atlantic,N.J.:Humanities Press, 1981).
32. "Industrialization and Capitalism in Max Weber" in Herbert Marcuse, *Negations*, (Boston: Beacon Press, 1974) p. 223.

Also published by
BLACK ROSE BOOKS

YEAR 501
The Conquest Continues
Noam Chomsky

In Noam Chomsky's characteristic style, *Year 501* offers a succinctly written, logical analysis, firmly grounded in the documentary record. Noting that the current period has much in common with the Colombian age of imperialism, during which western Europe conquered most of the world, Chomsky focuses on various historical moments in this march of imperial power, up to an including the current axis where the United States, Germany, and Japan share world economic control with the United States, revelling in a virtual monopoly of military might.

250 pages
ISBN: 1-895431-62-X
ISBN: 1-895431-63-8

URBANIZATION WITHOUT CITIES
The Rise and Decline of Citizenship
revised edition
Murray Bookchin

In this original work, Murray Bookchin introduces provocative ideas about the nature of community, and what it means to be a fully empowered citizen. He believes that the tension that exists between rural and urban society can be a vital source of human creativity, thereby defining a new, richly imaginative politics which can help us recover the power of the individual, restore the positive values and quality of urban life, and reclaim the ideal of the city as a major creative force in our civilization.

340 pages
Paperback ISBN: 1-895431-00-X
Hardcover ISBN: 1-895431-01-8

GREEN POLITICS
Agenda For a Free Society
Dimitrios Roussopoulos

An international survey of various Green political parties is presented, featuring their programmes and progress. The result is a stimulating book that challenges accepted ideas about how the world should be organized and suggests the possibility of a safe and more satisfying future for all of us.

200 pages
Paperback ISBN: 0-921689-74-8
Hardcover ISBN: 0-921689-75-6

BLACK ROSE BOOKS
has published the following books of related interests

Dissidence: Essays Against the Mainstream, *by Dimitrios Rousspoulos*
Shock Waves: Eastern Europe After the Revolutions, *by John Feffer*
Ethics, *by Peter Kropotkin*
Mutual Aid, *by Peter Kropotkin*
Political Arrangements: Power and the City, *edited by Henri Lustiger-Thaler*
Bringing the Economy Home From the Market, *by Ross Dobson*
People, Potholes and City Politics, *by Karen Herland*
Remaking Society, *by Murray Bookchin*
The Myth of the Market: Promises and Illusions, *by Jeremy Seabrook*
Race, Gender and Work: A Multi-Cultural Economic History of Women in the United States, *by Teresa Amott and Julie Matthaei*
Behind the Silicon Curtain: The Seduction of Work in a Lonely Era, *Dennis Hayes*
The Canadian City, *edited by Kent Gerecke*
Dominion of Debt: Centre, Periphery and the International Economic Order, *by Jeremy Brecher and Tim Costello*
Bankers, Bagmen and Bandits: Business and Politics in the Age of Greed, *by R.T. Naylor*
The Economy of Canada: A Study of Ownership and Control, *by Jorge Niosi*
Essays on Marx's Theory of Value, *by Issak Illich Rubin*
Closing the Iron Cage: The Scientific Management of Work and Leisure, *by Ed Andrew*
Trade Unions and the State, *Walter Johnson*
The History of the Labour Movement in Québec, *the Education Committees of the CSN and the CEQ*
The Radical Papers, *edited by Dimitrios Roussopoulos*
The Radical Papers 2, *edited by Dimitrios Roussopoulos*

send for a free catalogue of all our titles
BLACK ROSE BOOKS
P.O. Box 1258
Succ. Place du Parc
Montréal, Québec
H3W 2R3

Printed by
the workers of
Editions Marquis, Montmagny, Québec
for
Black Rose Books Ltd.